Lecture Notes in Artificial Intelligence 8625

Subseries of Lecture Notes in Computer Science

LNAI Series Editors

Randy Goebel
University of Alberta, Edmonton, Canada
Yuzuru Tanaka
Hokkaido University, Sapporo, Japan
Wolfgang Wahlster
DFKI and Saarland University, Saarbrücken, Germany

LNAI Founding Series Editor

Joerg Siekmann
DFKI and Saarland University, Saarbrücken, Germany

T0213846

Brian Davis   Kaarel Kaljurand
Tobias Kuhn (Eds.)

Controlled
Natural Language

4th International Workshop, CNL 2014
Galway, Ireland, August 20-22, 2014
Proceedings

 Springer

Volume Editors

Brian Davis
National University of Ireland
Galway, Ireland
E-mail: brian.davis@deri.org

Kaarel Kaljurand
University of Zurich, Switzerland
E-mail: kaljurand@gmail.com

Tobias Kuhn
ETH Zurich, Switzerland
E-mail: tokuhn@ethz.ch

ISSN 0302-9743   e-ISSN 1611-3349
ISBN 978-3-319-10222-1   e-ISBN 978-3-319-10223-8
DOI 10.1007/978-3-319-10223-8
Springer Cham Heidelberg New York Dordrecht London

Library of Congress Control Number: 2014945825

LNCS Sublibrary: SL 7 – Artificial Intelligence

Typesetting: Camera-ready by author, data conversion by Scientific Publishing Services, Chennai, India

Printed on acid-free paper

Springer is part of Springer Science+Business Media (www.springer.com)

Preface

CNL 2014 was the fourth workshop on controlled natural language, which has been established within the last years as a series of biennial events bringing together a diverse and multi-disciplinary community. This year's event was hosted by Insight (formerly DERI) at the National University of Ireland in Galway.

We emphasize the workshop's inclusive and broad scope embracing all approaches that are based on natural language but apply restrictions on vocabulary, grammar, and/or semantics. We explicitly invited contributions from different branches and communities, including what has been called simplified language, plain language, formalized language, processable language, fragments of language, phraseologies, conceptual authoring, language generation, and guided natural language interfaces.

We received 26 submissions, each of which was evaluated by at least two reviewers — if both turned out to be positive — or at least three reviewers otherwise. Submissions with a positive average score were accepted; those with a negative one were rejected. For papers with both positive and negative reviews, we made sure to only accept papers after they had received at least two positive reviews and to only reject papers that had at least two negative reviews. This procedure led to the acceptance of 17 submissions, i.e., the acceptance rate was 65%. In addition, these proceedings include an invited paper by Aarne Ranta on "Embedded Controlled Languages."

We would like to thank the authors for their submissions, the Program Committee members for their reviews and discussions, and the invited speakers for agreeing to present their work at the workshop. We also thank our host and sponsor Insight[1] at the National University of Ireland, and our sponsors Digital Grammars[2] and Eurosentiment[3].

June 2014

Brian Davis
Kaarel Kaljurand
Tobias Kuhn

---

[1] http://insight-centre.org/
[2] http://www.digitalgrammars.com/
[3] http://eurosentiment.eu/

Organization

Program Committee

Krasimir Angelov	Chalmers University, Sweden
Johan Bos	University of Groningen, The Netherlands
Paul Buitelaar	National University of Ireland
Olga Caprotti	University of Helsinki, Sweden
Eugene Creswick	Galois, USA
Danica Damljanovic	University of Sheffield, UK
Brian Davis	National University of Ireland
Ronald Denaux	iSOCO, Spain
Vania Dimitrova	University of Leeds, UK
Ramona Enache	Charlmers University, Sweden
Esra Erdem	Sabanci University, Turkey
Sébastien Ferré	Université de Rennes 1, France
Norbert E. Fuchs	University of Zurich, Switzerland
Normunds Gruzitis	University of Latvia
Siegfried Handschuh	National University of Ireland
Stefan Höfler	University of Zurich, Switzerland
Kaarel Kaljurand	University of Zurich, Switzerland
Peter Koepke	University of Bonn, Germany
Tobias Kuhn	ETH Zurich, Switzerland
Hans Leiß	University of Munich, Germany
Reinhard Muskens	Tilburg University, The Netherlands
Adegboyega Ojo	National University of Ireland
Gordon Pace	University of Malta
Richard Power	Open University
Laurette Pretorius	University of South Africa
Stephen Pulman	Oxford University, UK
Allan Ramsay	University of Manchester, UK
Aarne Ranta	University of Gothenburg, Sweden
Mike Rosner	University of Malta
Uta Schwertel	IMC Information Multimedia Communication AG
Rolf Schwitter	Macquarie University, Australia
Silvie Spreeuwenberg	LibRT, Netherlands
Geoff Sutcliffe	University of Miami, USA
Irina Temnikova	Qatar Computing Research Institute
Allan Third	The Open University, UK
Camilo Thorne	Free University of Bozen-Bolzano, Italy

Jeroen Van Grondelle	HU University of Applied Sciences Utrecht, The Netherlands
Yorick Wilks	University of Sheffield, UK
Adam Wyner	University of Aberdeen, UK

Additional Reviewers

Abdelaal, Hazem
Arcan, Mihael   Unger, Christina

Table of Contents

Embedded Controlled Languages

Aarne Ranta

Department of Computer Science and Engineering
Chalmers University of Technology and University of Gothenburg

Abstract. Inspired by embedded programming languages, an embedded CNL (controlled natural language) is a proper fragment of an entire natural language (its host language), but it has a parser that recognizes the entire host language. This makes it possible to process out-of-CNL input and give useful feedback to users, instead of just reporting syntax errors. This extended abstract explains the main concepts of embedded CNL implementation in GF (Grammatical Framework), with examples from machine translation and some other ongoing work.

Keywords: controlled language, domain-specific language, embedded language, Grammatical Framework, machine translation.

1 Introduction

A controlled natural language (CNL) is a strictly defined fragment of a natural language [1]. As fragments of natural languages, CNLs are analogous to **embedded domain-specific languages**, which are fragments of general purpose programming languages [2]. Such languages have been introduced as an alternative to traditional **domain-specific languages** (DSL), which have their own syntax and semantics, and require therefore a specific learning effort. An embedded DSL is a part of a general-purpose programming language, the **host language**, and is therefore readily usable by programmers who already know the host language. At its simplest, an embedded DSL is little more than a **library** in the host language. Using the library helps programmers to write compact, efficient, and correct code in the intended domain. But whenever the library does not provide all functionalities wanted, the programmer can leave its straight-jacket and use the host language directly, of course at her own risk.

Embedding a language fragment in the full language presupposes that a grammar of the full language is available. In the case of natural languages, this is by no means a trivial matter. On the contrary, it is widely acknowledged that "all grammars leak", which means that any formal grammar defining a natural language is bound to be either incomplete or overgenerating. As a consequence, defining CNLs *formally* as subsets of natural languages looks problematic.

However, *if* a grammar of the host language exists, then it is useful to define the CNL as an embedded language. It enables us to build systems that provide, at the same time, the rigour of controlled languages and the comfort of graceful degradation. The user of the system can be guided to stay inside the controlled language, but she will also be understood, at least some extent, if she goes outside it.

In this extended abstract, we will outline some recent work on building controlled languages in the embedded fashion. Our focus will be on multilingual systems,

B. Davis et al. (Eds.): CNL 2014, LNAI 8625, pp. 1–7, 2014.

where the CNL yields high-quality translation and the host language yields browsing quality. But the same structure should be useful for other applications of CNLs as well, such as query languages.

In Section 2, we will summarize how CNLs are traditionally defined by using GF, Grammatical Framework. In Section 3, we will show how they can be converted to embedded CNLs. In Section 4, we summarize some on-going work and suggest some more applications.

2   Defining Controlled Languages in GF

GF [3] is a grammar formalism based on a distinction between **abstract syntax** and **concrete syntax**. The abstract syntax is a system of **trees**. The concrete syntax is a reversible mapping from trees to **strings** and **records**, reminiscent of **feature structures** in unification-based grammar formalisms. The separation between abstract and concrete syntax makes GF grammars **multilingual**, since one and the same abstract syntax can be equipped with many concrete syntaxes. The abstract syntax is then usable as an **interlingua**, which enables **translation** via **parsing** the source language string into a tree followed by the **linearization** of the tree into the target language.

As an example, consider a predicate expressing the age of a person. The abstract syntax rule is

```
fun aged : Person -> Numeral -> Fact
```

defining a **function** with the name aged, whose **type** is a function type of two arguments, of types Person and Numeral, yielding a value of type Fact. A simple concrete syntax rule for English is

```
lin aged p n = p ++ "is" ++ n ++ "years old"
```

stating that a function application (aged p n) is **linearized** to the string where the linearization of p is concatenated (++) with the string "is", the linearization of n, and the string "years old". The corresponding rule for French is

```
lin aged p n = p ++ "a" ++ n ++ "ans"
```

producing sentences literally equivalent to *p has n years*. Thus the concrete syntax allows the production of different syntactic structures in different languages, while the abstract syntax form (aged p n) remains the same, and stands in a compositional relation to the linearizations.

GF is widely used for defining CNLs; [4,5,6,7,8] are some examples. Much of its power comes from the **resource grammar libraries** (RGL), which are general purpose grammars enabling GF grammar writers to delegate the "low-level" linguistic details to generic library code [9,10]. If we dig deeper into the concrete syntax of the aged predicate, we will find lots of such details to cope with: number agreement (*one year* vs. *five years*), subject-verb agreement: (*I am, you are, she is*), word order (*you are* in declaratives vs. *are you* in questions), etc; French generally poses harder problems than English. The use of feature structures instead of plain strings does make it possible to express all this compositionally in GF. But these details can make the grammar prohibitively difficult to write, especially since controlled language designers are not always theoretical linguists but experts in the various domains of application of CNLs. The RGL addresses this problem by providing general-purpose functions such as

```
mkCl : NP -> VP -> Cl
```

which builds a clause (Cl) from a noun phrase (NP) and a verb phrase (VP) and takes care of all details of agreement and word order. The CNL linearization rules can be written as combinations of such functions. The English rule, in full generality, comes out as compact as

```
lin aged p n = mkCl p (mkVP (mkAP (mkNP n year_N) old_A))
```

and the French,

```
lin aged p n = mkCl p (mkVP avoir_V2 (mkNP n an_N))
```

If a function quest is added to turn facts into questions, the linearization is in both languages just a simple RGL function call:

```
lin quest fact = mkQS fact
```

The API (application programmer's interface) is the same for all languages in the RGL (currently 29), but the low-level details that it hides are language-dependent.

3   Embedding a Controlled Language in the Host Language

The standard practice in GF is to define CNLs by using the RGL rather than low-level hand-crafted linearization rules. In addition to saving effort, this practice guarantees that the CNL is a valid fragment of a natural language. The reason is that the RGL is designed only to allow grammatically correct constructions.

But what is missing in a CNL built in this way is the rest of the host language—the part that is not covered by the RGL rule combinations actually used in the CNL. In general, a random sentence has a probability close to zero to be recognized by the parser. The standard solution is to guide the user by a predictive editor [11,4,12]. But there are many situations in which this does not work so well: for instance, with speech input, or when processing text in batch mode. Then it can be more appropriate to include not only the CNL but also the host language in the system. The system as a whole will then be similar to an embedded DSL with its general-purpose host language.

The easiest way to combine a CNL with a host language is to introduce a new start category S with two productions: one using the CNL start category as its argument type, the other using the host language start category:

```
fun UseCNL : S_CNL  -> S
fun UseHost : S_Host -> S
```

The CNL trees can be given priority by biasing the weights of these functions in prob-abilistic GF parsing [13]. The CNL parse tree will then appear as the first alternative, whenever it can be found. Since the system sees where the tree comes from, it can give feedback to the user, for instance by using colours: green colour for CNL trees, yellow for host language trees, and red for unanalysed input, as shown (in greyscale in the printed version) in Figure 1.

Since the RGL is designed to guarantee grammaticality, and since all grammars leak, the RGL does not cover any language entirely. But if the purpose is wide-coverage parsing, we can relax this strictness. An easy way to do this is to extend the grammar with **chunking**. A chunk can be built from almost any RGL category: sentences, noun phrases, nouns, adjectives, etc:

```
fun ChunkS   : S_Host -> Chunk
fun ChunkNP : NP      -> Chunk
fun ChunkN  : N       -> Chunk
```

The top-level grammar has a production that recognizes lists of chunks ([Chunk]):

```
fun UseChunks : [Chunk] -> S
```

It is relatively easy to make the chunking grammar **robust**, in the sense that it re-turns some analysis for any combination of words. If the input has out-of-dictionary words, they can be dealt with by named entity recognition and morphological guessing. Weights can be set in such a way that longer chunks are favoured. For instance, *this old city* should be analyzed as one NP chunk rather than a determiner chunk followed by an adjective chunk and a noun chunk. The user can be given feedback, not only by a red colour indicating that chunks are used, but also by showing the chunk boundaries.

A further step of integration between CNL and the host language is obtained if CNL sentences are treated as chunks:

```
fun ChunkCNL : S_CNL -> Chunk
```

In the resulting trees, one can use different colours for different chunks inside one and the same sentence.

But since both the CNL and the host language are defined in terms of the same RGL structures, one can take the integration much further, by *intertwining* the CNL and host language rules. Consider again the CNL predicate

```
fun aged : Person -> Numeral -> Fact
```

where Person and Fact are CNL categories and Numeral is an RGL category. One can generalize the use of this predicate and other ones by introducing coercions from RGL categories to CNL categories used as arguments, and from CNL categories used as values to RGL categories (making sure that no cycles are created):

```
fun np2person : NP -> Person
fun fact2cl   : Fact -> Cl
```

The effect of this is seen when we analyse the English sentence

John does not believe that the queen is sixty-five years old

The resulting tree is

```
mkS negativePol (mkCl John believe_VS (fact2Cl
        (aged (np2person (mkNP the_Det queen_N)) (mkNumeral "65"))))
```

where those parts that belong to the CNL are boldfaced. Thus the predicate aged is from the CNL, but uses as argument *the queen*, which is not in the CNL. The resulting Fact is used as a complement to the verb *believe*, which requires an RGL clause. The resulting French translation is

John ne croit pas que la reine **ait soixante-cinq ans**

which correctly renders the aged idiom defined by the CNL, even though its subject is not in the CNL, and even though the negated main verb puts it into the subjunctive mood, which might never occur in the CNL itself.

Fig. 1. From left: CNL embedded in general purpose RGL embedded in a chunk grammar; the corresponding levels in the Vauquois triangle; a mobile translation application showing the level of confidence in colours (from top: semantic translation from CNL, syntactic translation from RGL, chunk-based translation)

4   Work in Progress

The translation example with the aged predicate shows that embedded CNL functions introduce semantic structures in translation. This has been exploited in the wide-coverage GF-based translation system [14] [1] where three levels are distinguished by colours: green for the CNL (the MOLTO phrasebook [6]), yellow for the RGL syntax, and red for chunks (Figure 1). These levels correspond to levels in the **Vauquois triangle**, where translation systems are divided on the basis of whether they use a semantic interlingua, syntactic transfer, or word-to-word transfer [15]. The effect of the

---

[1] "The Human Language Compiler",
http://grammaticalframework.org/demos/app.html

layered structure with an embedded CNL is that these levels coexist in one and the same system. The system is currently implemented for 11 languages. Its architecture permits easily changing the CNL to some other one and also including several CNLs in a single system. At least two experiments are in progress: one with a mathematical grammar library [5], another with the multilingual version of Attempto Controlled English [8].

In addition to translation, embedded CNLs could be used in query systems, where "green" parse trees are semantically well-formed queries and other colours are interpreted as key phrases and key words. It can also be interesting to match out-of-CNL trees with CNL trees and try to find the closest semantically complete interpretations. Yet another application of embedded CNLs would be to implement languages of the "Simplified English" type, which are not defined by formal grammars but by restrictions posed on the full language [1]. Such a language could be parsed by using the host language grammar together with a procedure that checks on the tree level how the restrictions are followed.

Acknowledgement. Thanks to Krasimir Angelov and Normunds Gruzitis for useful comments. Swedish Research Council (Vetenskapsrådet) has supported this work under grant nr. 2012-5746 (Reliable Multilingual Digital Communication).

References

1. Kuhn, T.: A Survey and Classification of Controlled Natural Languages. Computational Linguistics 40, 121–170 (2014)
2. Hudak, P.: Building domain-specific embedded languages. ACM Computing Surveys (CSUR) 28, 196 (1996)
3. Ranta, A.: Grammatical Framework: Programming with Multilingual Grammars. CSLI Publications, Stanford (2011)
4. Angelov, K., Ranta, A.: Implementing Controlled Languages in GF. In: Fuchs, N.E. (ed.) CNL 2009. LNCS, vol. 5972, pp. 82–101. Springer, Heidelberg (2010)
5. Saludes, J., Xambo, S.: The GF mathematics library. In: THedu 2011 (2011)
6. Ranta, A., Enache, R., Détrez, G.: Controlled language for everyday use: the molto phrasebook. In: Rosner, M., Fuchs, N.E. (eds.) CNL 2010. LNCS (LNAI), vol. 7175, pp. 115–136. Springer, Heidelberg (2012)
7. Davis, B., Enache, R., van Grondelle, J., Pretorius, L.: Multilingual Verbalisation of Modular Ontologies using GF and lemon. In: Kuhn, T., Fuchs, N.E. (eds.) CNL 2012. LNCS, vol. 7427, pp. 167–184. Springer, Heidelberg (2012)
8. Kaljurand, K., Kuhn, T.: A multilingual semantic wiki based on Attempto Controlled English and Grammatical Framework. In: Cimiano, P., Corcho, O., Presutti, V., Hollink, L., Rudolph, S. (eds.) ESWC 2013. LNCS, vol. 7882, pp. 427–441. Springer, Heidelberg (2013)
9. Ranta, A.: The GF Resource Grammar Library. Linguistics in Language Technology 2 (2009)
10. Ranta, A.: Grammars as Software Libraries. In: Bertot, Y., Huet, G., Lévy, J.J., Plotkin, G. (eds.) From Semantics to Computer Science. Essays in Honour of Gilles Kahn, pp. 281–308. Cambridge University Press (2009)
11. Khegai, J., Nordström, B., Ranta, A.: Multilingual Syntax Editing in GF. In: Gelbukh, A. (ed.) CICLing 2003. LNCS, vol. 2588, pp. 453–464. Springer, Heidelberg (2003)
12. Kuhn, T.: Codeco: A Practical Notation for Controlled English Grammars in Predictive Editors. In: Rosner, M., Fuchs, N.E. (eds.) CNL 2010. LNCS, vol. 7175, pp. 95–114. Springer, Heidelberg (2012)

13. Angelov, K., Ljunglöf, P.: Fast statistical parsing with parallel multiple context-free grammars. In: Proceedings of the 14th Conference of the European Chapter of the Association for Computational Linguistics, pp. 368–376. Association for Computational Linguistics, Gothenburg (2014)
14. Angelov, K., Bringert, B., Ranta, A.: Speech-enabled hybrid multilingual translation for mobile devices. In: Proceedings of the Demonstrations at the 14th Conference of the European Chapter of the Association for Computational Linguistics, pp. 41–44. Association for Computational Linguistics, Gothenburg (2014)
15. Vauquois, B.: A survey of formal grammars and algorithms for recognition and transformation in mechanical translation. In: IFIP Congress (2), pp. 1114–1122 (1968)

Controlled Natural Language Processing as Answer Set Programming: An Experiment

Rolf Schwitter

Department of Computing
Macquarie University
Sydney NSW 2109, Australia
Rolf.Schwitter@mq.edu.au

Abstract. Most controlled natural languages (CNLs) are processed with the help of a pipeline architecture that relies on different software components. We investigate in this paper in an experimental way how well answer set programming (ASP) is suited as a unifying framework for parsing a CNL, deriving a formal representation for the resulting syntax trees, and for reasoning with that representation. We start from a list of input tokens in ASP notation and show how this input can be transformed into a syntax tree using an ASP grammar and then into reified ASP rules in form of a set of facts. These facts are then processed by an ASP meta-interpreter that allows us to infer new knowledge.

Keywords: Answer Set Programming, Controlled Natural Language Processing, Meta-programming.

1 Introduction

Controlled natural languages (CNLs) are subsets of natural languages whose grammars and vocabularies have been restricted in order to eliminate ambiguity and complexity of natural languages for automated reasoning [11,17]. These CNLs are engineered for a specific purpose and look seemingly informal like natural languages, but they have by design the same properties as their formal target languages. Typically, the writing process of a CNL is supported by an authoring tool that guides the writing of a text or a question by a feedback mechanism [4,10,14,16].

Most existing CNLs are processed with the help of a pipeline architecture that relies on different software components for parsing and translating the CNL input into a formal representation before this representation can be processed by an automated reasoning service [2,5]. In this paper, we investigate in an experimental way whether answer set programming (ASP) can be used as a unifying framework for CNL processing, knowledge representation and automated reasoning. After a brief introduction to the ASP paradigm in Section 2, we show in Section 3 how grammar rules for a CNL can be written in ASP and how CNL sentences can be parsed into a syntax tree. In Section 4, we discuss how a formal representation can be generated for these syntax trees. In Section 5, we

B. Davis et al. (Eds.): CNL 2014, LNAI 8625, pp. 8–19, 2014.

illustrate how this representation can be used for reasoning in ASP with the help of a meta-interpreter. In Section 6, we summarise our findings and conclude.

2   Answer Set Programming (ASP)

ASP is a form of declarative programming that has its roots in logic programming, disjunctive databases and non-monotonic reasoning [1,13]. ASP provides an expressive formal language for knowledge representation and automated reasoning and is based on the answer set semantics for logic programs [7,8]. In ASP, problems are represented in terms of finite logic theories and these problems are solved by reducing them to finding answer sets which declaratively describe the solutions to these problems. An ASP program consists of a set of rules of the form:

1. h_1 ; ... ; h_m :- b_1, ..., b_n, not b_{n+1}, ..., not b_o.

where h_i and b_i are classical literals (l_i). A classical literal l is either an atom a or a negated atom -a. A literal of the form not l is a negation as failure literal. The disjunction (;) is interpreted as epistemic disjunction [9]. The part on the left of the implication (:-) is the head of the rule and the part on the right is the body of the rule. If the body is empty ($o{=}0$), then we omit the symbol for the implication and end up with a *fact*. If the head is empty ($m{=}0$), then we keep the symbol for the implication and end up with an *integrity constraint*. Note that ASP distinguishes between strong negation (-) and weak negation (not); these two forms of negation build the prerequisites for non-monotonic reasoning [9]. For example, the ASP program in (2) consists of two rules, six facts and one integrity constraint:

2.  ```
    successful(X) :- student(X), work(X), not absent(X).
    -work(X) :- student(X), not work(X).
    student(john). work(john). student(sue). work(sue).
    student(mary_ann). absent(mary_ann).
    :- student(X), cheat(X), successful(X).
    ```

This program can be processed by an ASP tool such as *clingo* [6] that computes the following answer set:

3.  ```
    { student(john) work(john) student(sue) work(sue) student(mary_ann)
        absent(mary_ann) successful(sue) successful(john) -work(mary_ann) }
    ```

We call an ASP program *satisfiable*, if it has at least one answer set. Through inspection of the above answer set, we can immediately see that John and Sue are successful and that Mary Ann does not work. Note that the second rule in (2) specifies the closed world assumption [15] for the literal work/1. If we add the following facts to our program:

4.  ```
    student(ray). work(ray). cheat(ray).
    ```

then we end up with an *unsatisfiable* program since the situation in (4) is excluded by the constraint in (2).
    ```

3   Writing a CNL Grammar in ASP

The CNL that we will use in the following discussion is similar to Processable English (PENG) [18] and to Attempto Controlled English (ACE) [5], but the language is less expressive since ASP does not support full first-order logic (FOL). However, ASP is still expressive enough to represent function-free FOL formulas of the $\exists^*\forall^*$ prefix class in form of a logic program [12]. The following text (5) is written in CNL and expresses the same information as the ASP program in (2):

5. Every student who works and who is not provably absent is successful.
   If a student does not provably work then the student does not work.
   John is a student who works.
   Sue is a student and works.
   Mary Ann who is a student is absent.
   Exclude that a student who cheats is successful.

In order to process this text in ASP, we split it into a sequence of sentences and each sentence into a sequence of tokens. Each token is represented in ASP as a fact (token/4) with four arguments: the first argument holds the string, the second argument holds the sentence number, and the third and fourth argument represent the start and the end position of the string, for example:

6. `token("Every", 1, 1, 2). token("student", 1, 2, 3).   ...`

Each string is stored as a fact (lexicon/5) in the ASP lexicon that distinguishes between function words and content words. Function words (e.g., *and, every, who*) define the structure of the CNL and content words (e.g., *student, works, successful*) are used to express the domain knowledge. These lexical entries contain information about the category, the string, the base form, as well as syntactic and semantic constraints (n stands for nil):

7. ```
lexicon(cnj, "and", n, n, n).
lexicon(det, "Every", n, sg, forall).
lexicon(rp, "who", n, n, n).
lexicon(noun, "student", student, sg, n).
lexicon(iv, "works", work, sg, n).
lexicon(adj, "successful", successful, n, n).
```

We can write the grammar for the CNL directly as a set of ASP rules that generate a syntax tree bottom-up, starting from the tokens up to the root. Let us have a look at the grammar rules that process the first sentence in (5). This sentence is interesting, since it contains a coordinated relative clause that is embedded in the main sentence. The first relative clause *who works* is positive, and the second relative clause *who is not provably absent* contains a weak negation. It is important to note that this form of negation can only occur in a universally quantified CNL sentence or in a CNL sentence that results in an integrity constraint.

The grammar rule (rule/7) specifies in a declarative way that a sentence (s) starts at position P1 and ends at position P4, if there is a noun phrase (np) that starts at P1 and ends at P2, followed by a verb phrase (vp) that starts at P2 and ends at P3, followed by a punctuation mark (pm) between position P3 and P4:
```

```
8. rule(s, s(T1, T2, T3), n, n, N, P1, P4)   :-
     rule(np, T1, Y, n, N, P1, P2),
     rule(vp, T2, Y, n, N, P2, P3),
     rule(pm, T3, n, n, N, P3, P4).
```

The second argument position of this rule is used to build up a syntax tree, the third argument position is used for syntactic constraints, the fourth for semantic constraints, and the fifth for the sentence number. The variable Y in (8) is used to enforce number agreement between the np and the vp.

The following grammar rule in (9) further describes the noun phrase of our example sentence. This noun phrase (np) consists of a determiner (det), followed by a nominal expression (n1). The variable M holds a quantifier that controls – as we will see later – the use of weak negation in our example sentence:

```
9. rule(np, np(T1, T2), Y, n, N, P1, P3) :-
     rule(det, T1, Y, M, N, P1, P2),
     rule(n1, T2, Y, M, N, P2, P3).
```

The nominal expression (n1) expands in our case into a noun (noun) and a relative clause (rcl):

```
10. rule(n1, n1(T1, T2), Y, M, N, P1, P3) :-
      rule(noun, T1, Y, n,  N, P1, P2),
      rule(rcl, T2, Y, M, N, P2, P3).
```

The noun (noun) is a preterminal category and processes the input token (token/4) with the help of the lexical information (lexicon/5):

```
11. rule(noun, noun(S), Y, n, N, P1, P2) :-
      token(S, N, P1, P2),
      lexicon(noun, S, B, Y, n).
```

Note that the relative clause in our example sentence is coordinated and consists of a positive and a negative part. The grammar rule in (12) for relative clauses (rcl) deals with this coordinated structure. In contrast to the positive part, we use the variable M in the negative part of the coordinated structure to enforce that this form of negation occurs under universal quantification (additional grammar rules exist that deal with relative clauses where the order of the positive and negative part is different):

```
12. rule(rcl, rcl(T1, T2, T3), Y, M, N, P1, P4) :-
      rule(rcl, T1, Y, n, N, P1, P2),
      rule(cnj, T2, n, n, N, P2, P3),
      rule(rcl, T3, Y, M, N, P3, P4).
```

As the following two grammar rules in (13) illustrate, the relative clause expands in both cases into a relative pronoun (rp) followed by a verb phrase (vp): the first vp occurs without a variable (n) at the fourth argument position and the second vp occurs with a variable (M) that holds the quantifier:

```
13. rule(rcl, rcl(T1, T2), Y, n, N, P1, P3) :-
      rule(rp, T1, n, n, N, P1, P2),
      rule(vp, T2, Y, n, N, P2, P3).
```

```
rule(rcl, rcl(T1, T2), Y, M, N, P1, P3) :-
    rule(rp, T1, n, n, N, P1, P2),
    rule(vp, T2, Y, M, N, P2, P3).
```

The first verb phrase (vp) in (13) expands into an intransitive verb (iv):

```
14. rule(vp, vp(T1), Y, n, N, P1, P2) :-
        rule(iv, T1, Y, n, N, P1, P2).
```

and the second verb phrase (vp) expands into a copula (cop), followed by a weak negation (naf) and an adjective (adj):

```
15. rule(vp, vp(T1, T2, T3), Y, M, N, P1, P4) :-
        rule(cop, T1, Y, n, N, P1, P2),
        rule(naf, T2, n, M, N, P2, P3),
        rule(adj, T3, n, n, N, P3, P4).
```

As we have seen, weak negation is expressed on the surface level of the CNL with the help of the key phrase *not provably*. The rule (naf) in (16) processes this key phrase if it occurs in the scope of a universal quantifier (forall):

```
16. rule(naf, naf(T1, adv("provably")), n, forall, N, P1, P3) :-
        rule(neg, T1, n, n, N, P1, P2),
        rule(adv, adv("provably"), n, n, N, P2, P3).
```

We still have to deal with the verb phrase (vp) on the sentence level that is part of rule (8). This verb phrase expands into a copula (cop), followed by an adjective (adj):

```
17. rule(vp, vp(T1, T2), Y, n, N, P1, P3) :-
        rule(cop, T1, Y, n, N, P1, P2),
        rule(adj, T2, n, n, N, P2, P3).
```

In ASP, these grammar rules are processed bottom-up and during this model generation process the following syntax tree is produced for our example sentence:

```
18. s(np(det("Every"),
        n1(noun("student"),
        rcl(rcl(rp("who"),
                vp(iv("works"))),
            cnj("and"),
            rcl(rp("who"),
                vp(cop("is"),
                    naf(neg("not"),
                        adv("provably")),
                    adj("absent")))))),
        vp(cop("is"),
            adj("successful")),
        pm("."))
```

This syntax tree needs to be translated into a suitable ASP representation for automated reasoning as we will see in Section 4.

Before we do this, please note that it is relatively straightforward to generate look-ahead information that informs the author about the admissible input. To generate look-ahead information, we add one or more dummy tokens that contain a special string (lah) to the last input token, for example:

```
19. token("Every", 1, 1, 2).
    token("student", 1, 2, 3).
    token("$lah$", 1, 3, 4).
```

Additionally, we add for each category a lexical entry that contains this special string, for example:

```
20. lexicon(iv, "$lah$", n, sg, n).
```

The following ASP rules in (21) are then used to collect those syntax tree fragments that span the input string and contain look-ahead information. The last rule in (21) is a constraint and makes sure that the entire input string is considered:

```
21. lah(C, T, Y, M, N, 1, P2) :-
      rule(C, T, Y, M, N, 1, P2),
      end_pos(P2, N).

    lah :-
      lah(C, T, Y, M, N, 1, P2),
      end_pos(P2, N).

    -end_pos(P2, N1) :-
      token("$lah$", N1, P1, P2),
      token("$lah$", N2, P3, P4),
      N1 <= N2, P2 < P4.

    end_pos(P2, N) :-
      token("$lah$", N, P1, P2),
      not -end_pos(P2, N).

    :- not lah.
```

In our example, the addition of the first token (token("lah", 1, 3, 4)) in (19) results in an unsatisfiable program. The addition of a further token (token("lah", 1, 4, 5)) results in two tree fragments that span the input string. From these trees, we can extract the relevant look-ahead information.

4   From Syntax Trees to Reified ASP Rules

We choose an indirect encoding for ASP rules where rules are reified as facts. This kind of encoding is necessary since there exists no mechanism within ASP that would allow us to assert new rules. The reified rules are then further processed by an ASP meta-interpreter as we will see in Section 5. A reified rule consists of up to four different fact types: a fact type (`rule/1`) for the identification of the rule, a fact type (`head/2`) for the head of the rule, a fact type (`pbl/2`) for positive body literals (if any), and a fact type (`nbl/2`) for negative body literals (if any). For example, the translation of the syntax tree in (18) will result in the following encoding:

22. ```
    rule(1).
       head(1, lit(func(successful), arg(sk(1)))).
       pbl(1, lit(func(work), arg(sk(1)))).
       pbl(1, lit(func(student), arg(sk(1)))).
       nbl(1, lit(func(absent), arg(sk(1)))).
    ```

The fact type (`rule/1`) stores the rule number (`1`). This rule number occurs as first argument in the other fact types and specifies rule membership. The actual literals that belong to a rule are encoded with the help of the term `lit/2` where the first argument (e.g., `func(successful)`) is the functor name of the literal and the second argument (`arg(sk(1))`) represents a Skolem constant[1] that replaces the variable in the literal. Note that all facts that have been derived from rules need to be grounded and cannot contain any variables.

In the following, we will show in detail how the syntax tree in (18) is translated into the proposed ASP notation for rules in (22). The syntax tree is first split into three main parts: a part (`to_qnt/3`) to be translated into a quantifier, a part (`to_body/3`) to be translated into a rule body, and a part (`to_head/3`) to be translated into a rule head. In our case, these parts correspond to the determiner (`det`), the nominal expression (`n1`), and the verb phrase (`vp`) of the first sentence in (5):

23. ```
    to_qnt(N, det("Every"), M) :-
        rule(det, det("Every"), Y, M, N, P1, P2),
        rule(n1, T2, Y, M, N, P2, P3),
        rule(vp, T3, Y, n, N, P3, P4).

    to_body(N, T2, M) :-
        rule(det, det("Every"), Y, M, N, P1, P2),
        rule(n1, T2, Y, M, N, P2, P3),
        rule(vp, T3, Y, n, N, P3, P4).

    to_head(N, T3, M) :-
        rule(det, det("Every"), Y, M, N, P1, P2),
        rule(n1, T2, Y, M, N, P2, P3),
        rule(vp, T3, Y, n, N, P3, P4).
    ```

In the next step, the determiner (`"Every"`) is processed and this results in a new predicate (`qnt/4`) that stores a rule number (`R`), the universal quantifier (`M`), the sentence number (`N`), and a Skolem constant (`K`) for the universal quantifier. Note that the rule number and the number for the Skolem constant are generated with the help of Lua[2] and assigned (`:=`) to the variables (`R`) and (`K`):

---

[1] The number i in $sk(i)$, represents the ith Skolem constant.

[2] Lua (http://www.lua.org) is available as integrated scripting language in *clingo*.

```
24. qnt(R, M, N, sk(K)) :-
      to_qnt(N, det("Every"), M),
      R := @rule_num(),
      K := @sk_num().
```

Given the new predicate (qnt/4) for the universal quantifier, the syntax tree fragments for constructing the head of a rule and the body of a rule can be further split up:

```
25. to_head(R, adj(S2), K)  :-
      to_head(N, vp(cop(S1), adj(S2)), M),
      qnt(R, forall, N, K).

    to_body(R, noun(S), K)  :-
      to_body(N, n1(noun(S), RCL), M),
      qnt(R, forall, N, K).

    to_body(R, RCL, K)  :-
      to_body(N, n1(noun(S), RCL), M),
      qnt(R, forall, N, K).
```

In the case of the head (to_head/3), this process results in a preterminal category (adj(S2)) that can be used to generate the head literal of the rule. In the case of the body (to_body/3), only the first rule generates a preterminal category (noun(S)) that can directly be used to generate a positive body literal. The second rule is used to split the relative clause (RCL) into its basic constituents in order to extract the relevant preterminal categories:

```
26. to_body(R, RCL1, K)  :-
      to_body(R, rcl(RCL1, cnj(and), RCL2), K).

    to_body(R, RCL2, K) :-
      to_body(R, rcl(RCL1, cnj(and), RCL2), K).

    to_body(R, iv(S2), K) :-
      to_body(R, rcl(rp(S1), vp(iv(S2))), K).

    to_body(R, naf(adj(S3)), K)  :-
      to_body(R, rcl(rp(S1), vp(cop(S2), naf(T1, T2), adj(S3))), K).
```

The preterminal categories for content words together with the Skolem constant (K) and the rule number (R) are then used to generate the head literal, the positive and negative body literals. During this process the string (S) of these preterminal categories is replaced by the base form (B) via a lexicon lookup. The rule identifier (rule/1) is generated with the help of the head literal (head/2):

```
27. rule(R) :- head(R, L).

    head(R, lit(func(B), arg(K))) :-
      to_head(R, adj(B), K),
      lexicon(adj, S, B, _, _).
```

```
pbl(R, lit(func(B), arg(K))) :-
   to_body(R, noun(S), K),
   lexicon(noun, S, B, _, _).

pbl(R, lit(func(B), arg(K))) :-
   to_body(R, iv(S), K),
   lexicon(iv, S, B, _, _).

nbl(R, lit(func(B), arg(K))) :-
   to_body(R, naf(adj(S)), K),
   lexicon(adj, S, B, _, _).
```

Note that checking for anaphoric references can be done over the existing model during the translation process of the syntax tree into rules. For example, the second sentence of (5) contains a definite noun phrase (*the student*) that is anaphorically linked to an indefinite noun phrase (*a student*). Depending on the context in which an anaphoric expression occurs, we either check the body of the current rule for an antecedent or the heads of all existing rules that don't have a body and give preference to the closest match in terms of rule numbers.

5 Reasoning with Reified ASP Rules

In order to process these reified ASP rules, we use a meta-interpreter that is based on the work of Eiter et al. [3]. We substantially extended this meta-interpreter so that it can deal with variables that occur as Skolem constants in the reified notation. On the meta-level we represent answer sets with the help of the predicate in_AS/1 and use the following two rules to add literals to an answer set:

```
28. in_AS(lit(F, A2)) :-
       head(R, lit(F, A1)),
       pos_body_true(R, A1, A2),
       not neg_body_false(R, A1, A2).

    in_AS(lit(F, A)) :-
       head(R, lit(F, A)),
       rule(R),
       not pos_body_exists(R).
```

The first rule specifies that a literal (lit/2) is in an answer set (in_AS/1), if it occurs in the head (head/2) of a rule with number R whose positive body (pos_body_true/3) is true and whose negative body (neg_body_false/3) is not false and if the Skolem constant that occurs as argument (A1) of that literal can be replaced by other constants that occur as argument (A2) of a corresponding literal in the answer set. The second rule specifies that if no positive body literal (pbl/3) for a rule exists, then we can directly process the head (head/2) of a rule.

The positive body (pos_body_true/3) of the first rule in (28) is true up to some positive body literal with respect to a built-in order. If the positive body is true up to the last positive body literal then the whole positive body is true. The first rule in (29) deals with this case; the second rule takes care of the first positive body literal, and the third rule makes sure that the positive body literals follow the specified order:

```
29. pos_body_true(R, A1, A2) :-
       pos_body_true_up_to(R, F, A1, A2),
       not pbl_not_last(R, F).

    pos_body_true_up_to(R, F, A1, A2) :-
       pbl_in_AS(R, F, A1, A2),
       not pbl_not_first(R, F).

    pos_body_true_up_to(R, F1, A1, A2) :-
       pbl_in_AS(R, F1, A1, A2),
       F2 < F1,
       not pbl_in_between(R, F2, F1),
       pos_body_true_up_to(R, F2, A1, A2).
```

The rule (pbl_in_AS/4) in (30) checks if a positive body literal (pbl/2) for a rule (R) exists, looks in the current answer set (in_AS/1) for a literal that has the same functor name (F) as the body literal but shows a different argument (A2) and returns that argument:

```
30. pbl_in_AS(R, F, A1, A2) :-
       pbl(R, lit(F, A1)),
       in_AS(lit(F, A2)),
       A1 != A2.
```

There exist similar rules that deal with cases where the positive body literal has more than one argument. The successor relation on positive body literals of each rule is defined with the help of the following auxiliary rules:

```
31. pbl_in_between(R, F1, F3) :-
       pbl(R, lit(F1, A1)),
       pbl(R, lit(F2, A2)),
       pbl(R, lit(F3, A3)),
       F1 < F2, F2 < F3.

    pbl_not_last(R, F1) :-
       pbl(R, lit(F1, A1)),
       pbl(R, lit(F2, A2)),
       F1 < F2.

    pbl_not_first(R, F1) :-
       pbl(R, lit(F1, A1)),
       pbl(R, lit(F2, A2)),
       F2 < F1.
```

The negative part of the body (neg_body_false/3) in the first rule of (28) is false, if it can be shown that one of its literals is in the answer set (in_AS/1). The rule in (32) checks this condition for literals with one argument (other rules deal with literals that have more than one argument):

```
32. neg_body_false(R, A1, A2) :-
       nbl(R, lit(F, A1)),
         in_AS(lit(F, A2)).
```

Finally, the rule pos_body_exists/1 in (33) is used as part of the second rule in (28) and simply checks if a positive body literal (pbl/2) exists:

```
33. pos_body_exists(R) :- pbl(R, L).
```

After parsing and translating the CNL text in (5) into reified rules represented as a set of facts, the ASP meta-interpreter will generate the following answer set as solution:

```
34. { in_AS(lit(func(student), arg(john)))
       in_AS(lit(func(work), arg(john)))
       in_AS(lit(func(student), arg(sue)))
       in_AS(lit(func(work), arg(sue)))
       in_AS(lit(func(student), arg(mary_ann)))
       in_AS(lit(func(absent), arg(mary_ann)))
       in_AS(lit(func(successful), arg(sue)))
       in_AS(lit(func(successful), arg(john)))
       in_AS(lit(func(neg(work)), arg(mary_ann))) }
```

This answer set contains the same information as the answer set in (3) and can be used for question answering.

6   Conclusion

In this paper, we investigated in an experimental way if it is possible to process a controlled natural language entirely in ASP and if ASP can serve as a unified framework for parsing, knowledge representation and automated reasoning. ASP is a powerful declarative knowledge representation language that provides support for non-monotonic reasoning and this makes the language particularly attractive for controlled natural language processing. We showed in detail how a grammar for a controlled natural language can be written as an ASP program. This grammar is processed bottom-up and the syntax trees are constructed starting from the leaves up to the root. The resulting syntax trees are translated into reified rules that consist of a set of facts. These facts are then used by a meta-interpreter written in ASP for automated reasoning. The translation into reified rules is necessary because ASP does not provide a mechanism that would allow us to generate and assert normal ASP rules in the same program. Alternatively, we could take the resulting syntax trees and translate them outside of the ASP program into normal ASP rules and then generate a new ASP program that executes these rules. With the help of the presented ASP grammar it is possible to generate look-ahead information to guide the writing process of the author. It is also possible in ASP to perform anaphora resolution over the reified rules during the translation process using the standard constraints on anaphoric accessibility. We believe that ASP is an interesting paradigm for controlled natural language processing and plan to extend the presented approach or aspects of it and integrate them into a controlled language authoring system.

References

1. Brewka, G., Eiter, T., Truszczyński, M.: Answer Set Programming at a Glance. Communications of the ACM 54(12) (December 2011)
2. Clark, P., Harrison, P., Jenkins, T., Thompson, J., Wojcik, R.H.: Acquiring and using world knowledge using a restricted subset of English. In: Proceedings of FLAIRS 2005, pp. 506–511. AAAI Press (2005)
3. Eiter, T., Faber, W., Leone, N., Pfeifer, G.: Computing Preferred Answer Sets by Meta-Interpretation in Answer Set Programming. INFSYS Research Report 1843-02-01, Technische Universität Wien (January 2002)
4. Franconi, E., Guagliardo, P., Trevisan, M., Tessaris, S.: Quelo: an ontology-driven query interface. In: Proceedings of the 24th International Workshop on Description Logics (DL 2011) (2011)
5. Fuchs, N.E., Kaljurand, K., Kuhn, T.: Attempto Controlled English for knowledge representation. In: Baroglio, C., Bonatti, P.A., Małuszyński, J., Marchiori, M., Polleres, A., Schaffert, S. (eds.) Reasoning Web. LNCS, vol. 5224, pp. 104–124. Springer, Heidelberg (2008)
6. Gebser, M., Kaminski, R., Kaufmann, B., Ostrowski, M., Schaub, T., Schneider, M.: Potassco: The Potsdam Answer Set Solving Collection. AI Communications 24(2), 105–124 (2011)
7. Gelfond, M., Lifschitz, V.: The stable model semantics for logic programming. In: Proceedings of ICLP 1988, pp. 1070–1080 (1988)
8. Gelfond, M., Lifschitz, V.: Classical negation in logic programs and disjunctive databases. New Generation Computing 9(3-4), 365–386 (1991)
9. Gelfond, M., Kahl, Y.: Knowledge Representation, Reasoning, and the Design of Intelligent Agents. Cambridge University Press (2014)
10. Kuhn, T.: Controlled English for Knowledge Representation. Doctoral thesis, Faculty of Economics, Business Administration and Information Technology of the University of Zurich (2010)
11. Kuhn, T.: A Survey and Classification of Controlled Natural Languages. Computational Linguistics 40(1), 121–170 (2014)
12. Lierler, Y., Lifschitz, V.: Logic Programs vs. First-Order Formulas in Textual Inference. In: Proceedings of the 10th International Conference on Computational Semantics (IWCS 2013), Potsdam, Germany, pp. 340–346 (2013)
13. Lifschitz, V.: What is Answer Set Programming? In: Proceedings of AAAI 2008, pp. 1594–1597 (2008)
14. Power, R.: OWL Simplified English: a finite-state language for ontology editing. In: Kuhn, T., Fuchs, N.E. (eds.) CNL 2012. LNCS, vol. 7427, pp. 44–60. Springer, Heidelberg (2012)
15. Reiter, R.: On closed world data bases. In: Gallaire, H., Minker, J.,, J. (eds.) Logic and Data Bases, pp. 119–140. Plenum Publ. Co., New York (1978)
16. Schwitter, R., Ljungberg, A., Hood, D.: ECOLE – A Look-ahead Editor for a Controlled Language. In: Proceedings of EAMT-CLAW 2003, Dublin City University, Ireland, May 15-17, pp. 141–150 (2003)
17. Schwitter, R.: Controlled Natural Languages for Knowledge Representation. In: Proceedings of COLING 2010, Beijing, China, pp. 1113–1121 (2010)
18. White, C., Schwitter, R.: An Update on PENG Light. In: Pizzato, L., Schwitter, R. (eds.) Proceedings of ALTA 2009, Sydney, Australia, pp. 80–88 (2009)

How Easy Is It to Learn a Controlled Natural Language for Building a Knowledge Base?

Sandra Williams, Richard Power, and Allan Third

The Open University, Walton Hall, Milton Keynes, MK7 6AA, U.K.
sandra.williams@open.ac.uk

Abstract. Recent developments in controlled natural language editors for knowledge engineering (KE) have given rise to expectations that they will make KE tasks more accessible and perhaps even enable non-engineers to build knowledge bases. This exploratory research focussed on novices and experts in knowledge engineering during their attempts to learn a controlled natural language (CNL) known as OWL Simplified English and use it to build a small knowledge base. Participants' behaviours during the task were observed through eye-tracking and screen recordings.

This was an attempt at a more ambitious user study than in previous research because we used a naturally occurring text as the source of domain knowledge, and left them without guidance on which information to select, or how to encode it. We have identified a number of skills (competencies) required for this difficult task and key problems that authors face.

1 Introduction

Controlled Natural Language (CNL) has been proposed as a convenient and accessible medium for building knowledge bases such as semantic web ontologies, e.g., ACE [3], Sidney OWL syntax [1], OSE [15], CLOnE [4], Rabbit [2] or software requirements specifications [20]. CNLs for these tasks are designed to be unambiguously interpreted, usually by machine, into formal languages; consequently, they have been proposed as an alternative to formal representation languages such as the Web Ontology Language (OWL).[1] It has been assumed that since a CNL closely resembles a natural language (NL) it will be easy to learn, especially if the editor has a predictive interface [18], and thus the task of constructing a knowledge base will be reduced to the task of constructing syntactically correct and semantically plausible CNL sentences. CNLs have been proposed as particularly useful for non-experts in knowledge representation (KR) languages, enabling them to encode their own domain knowledge into a formal representation, perhaps without any help from a knowledge engineer.

However, these underlying assumptions have undergone little previous evaluation (see section 2). Thus, the study described here investigated: (i) Is a CNL easy to learn? and (ii) Would a CNL interface enable someone who is unfamiliar with KR or KR languages to build a knowledge base without help?

---

[1] www.w3.org/TR/owl-features/

B. Davis et al. (Eds.): CNL 2014, LNAI 8625, pp. 20–32, 2014.

This paper presents empirical observations on a Controlled Natural Language (CNL) authoring task for two OWL experts and four OWL novice participants who were learning the CNL known as OWL Simplified English, or OSE [15]. Participants were shown three video tutorials on OSE, each followed by a 10-minute exercise during which they used the SWAT Editing Tool[2] to construct OSE sentences from domain knowledge in the form of a paragraph of text taken from a Simple Wikipedia article. In a sense, they were performing a translation exercise to convert natural language (English text) into OSE and thus directly into OWL (through typing OSE into the editor interface).

This task was particularly difficult because the knowledge to be encoded in CNL was not *artificially prepared* by the experimenters but a *naturally-occurring* text written by wikipedia authors. It was thus a radical departure from the kinds of data supplied in other evaluations (see section 2). Our motivation to use such data was that it more closely represents the kind of knowledge that a domain expert might carry in his/her head, i.e., a genuine example of domain data 'from the wild'. Consequently, it presented an additional burden on participants because some parts of the source text could *not* be expressed in OWL (or OSE) and some parts were not in a convenient form, therefore participants had to select and organise information as well as encoding it in CNL.

Knowledge engineering in CNL is a complex task requiring such a large number of skills (or competencies) that it seems unlikely that someone who knows nothing of the underlying formal semantics could be expected to perform well. We break down the requisite skills into three areas (knowledge representation, sentence construction, and identifier name construction). In observing participants' actions from screen recordings with eye-tracking, our aim was to find out how exactly they modelled the domain knowledge from the text, how they went about constructing ontology axioms and identifier names, and whether they encountered problems whilst doing so. From our analysis of the screen recordings, we present some insights about their attempts to learn the CNL and construct a knowledge base. From these, we make predictions about the difficulties that novices, in particular, face and hence the feasibility of CNL as an interface for novices and experts.

2   Related Studies

Our exploratory study differed radically from other evaluations of CNL knowledge editors in that the material it provided for participants as 'knowledge to be encoded' was *not* artificial. We provided a naturally-occurring, human-authored text; other evaluations provided participants with artificial 'knowledge', e.g., schematic diagrams [9–11], or NL sentences contrived with different phrasing and wording from that of the CNL. For example, Funk et al.'s evaluation of the CLOnE language for semantic web ontology editing [4] gave participants sentences such as, 'Create a subclass *Journal* of *Periodical*.' Hallett, Power and Scott [6] gave their participants artificial texts for the task of constructing SQL queries, e.g., 'How many patients who received surgical treatment for malignant neoplasm of the central portion of the breast had no curative radiotherapy?' García-Barriocanal et al. [5] provided what we assume was an artificially-contrived text for the task of constructing a small ontology. An exception is the study of Laing et al.

---

[2] http://mcs.open.ac.uk/nlg/SWAT/editor.html

[12] which used short texts written by ontology engineers describing a few OWL statements. The major differences between all of these texts and our text is that with the artificial texts and Laing et al.'s texts, participants were provided with convenient terms and, more importantly, only with data that *could be* successfully encoded; whereas, some of our naturally-occurring text *could not be* encoded, nor were identifier names provided in a convenient form.

These are important differences because they made more realistic domain experts of our participants, assuming that knowledge inside a domain expert's head is not conveniently organised in a form that would lend itself to CNL encoding. Thus we forced our participants to *select and reorganise knowledge* before encoding it. On the other hand, the studies above were focussed on particular competencies (e.g., one aspect of Funk et al.'s study tested whether users had learnt the CNL sentence pattern for expressing a subclass relationship), whereas the purpose of our study was to explore which competencies are important for the task of encoding knowledge in CNL.

An exception was a study in which participants were encouraged to find encyclopedia articles from which to encode geographical knowledge [8]. Because of the constraints of the system used, several hundred domain vocabulary names had to be prepared in advance. Using the vocabulary provided, participants were able to choose to encode any geographical information they wanted. Unsurprisingly, this produced differing contents that were hard to compare. However, as in our study, participants used different modelling styles to represent similar information according to their different views of the world and had difficulties producing syntactically acceptable formulations.

Studies exist that compare new ontology editors to popular alternatives like Protégé, e.g., [7]. This was not the aim of our study, which is concerned with the details of learning a CNL for knowledge editing, not with the broader issue of which approach is best.

3   Tools, Materials and Method

3.1   OWL Simplified English

OWL Simplified English (OSE), [15], is a relatively free-form language in which each sentence expresses an OWL statement, and entity names (for individuals, classes and properties) are recognised by their relationship to a handful of common English keywords such as 'the', 'is', 'has', and 'a', with minimal classification of content words. It is left to the writer to decide whether to create text that would be recognisable or understandable as natural English. For instance, in the sentence 'A dog is an animal.', text between 'A' and 'is' is interpreted as a class name. Likewise, 'animal' is a class name because it is delimited by 'an and '.'. Thus 'A because because is an of of of.' would also be a valid OSE sentence, meaning that the class 'because because' is a subclass of the class 'of of of'.[3]

OSE is relatively unconstrained when contrasted with other CNLs which require predefined vocabularies. Because the grammar is finite-state, sentences can quickly be

---

[3] A tutorial is available at
mcs.open.ac.uk/nlg/SWAT/EditingToolApril2012/tutorial.pdf

verified as correct, and interpreted in OWL. The language disallows sentence patterns using connectives like 'and', 'or', 'that', which people would interpret as structurally ambiguous.

3.2 SWAT Editing Tool

The editing tool[4] used in this study was developed for the SWAT project[5] as described in Power [16]. It implements OSE [15], building OWL statements dynamically as the user types OSE sentences. Its predictive interface provides sentence patterns (as full or partial sentences) and feedback on the OWL statement being built. As it is typed, text is parsed character-by-character and automatically coloured brown for class names, purple for individuals, blue for properties, and green for literals. Figure 1 shows a screenshot of the editor set up for the study with the source text inserted as a comment at the top of the editing pane (which was larger than shown here), a context-sensitive list of allowed sentence or continuation patterns (RHS), and a context-sensitive message area for dynamic feedback.

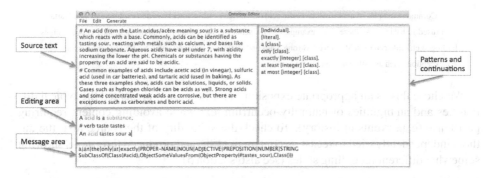

Fig. 1. SWAT Editing Tool

In the editing area, a sentence, 'A acid is a substance.', containing an English grammatical error has been, nonetheless, accepted by the OSE finite-state parser. Another sentence is being typed, 'An acid tastes sour a . . .', the message area shows the partially-constructed OWL statement in which 'tastes sour' is recognised as a property name (possibly the author intended 'sour' as a literal, denoted by double quotes in OSE).

3.3 Materials

Instructional Videos. To ensure that all participants received identical tuition, we recorded three 5- to 8-minute instructional videos with screen recordings and spoken commentaries demonstrating how to construct OSE sentences and identifier names[6].

---

[4] Downloadable from http://mcs.open.ac.uk/nlg/SWAT/editor.html

[5] Semantic Web Authoring Tool (SWAT) project funded by EPSRC grant G033579/1. Dr Third was funded by VPH share (European Commission ICT-FP7-269978).

[6] Videos may be viewed at http://mcs.open.ac.uk/nlg/SWAT/editor.html

Additionally, participants were given 'crib' sheets summarising all sentence patterns taught in the videos. In video 1, participants were taught to construct three types of OSE sentences (class subsumption, class membership, and disjoint classes) using class (concept) names and individual (class member) names. In video 2, participants were taught to construct multi-word property and individual names, literals in quotes for previously-taught sentences, and new sentence patterns for existential property restrictions. In video 3, participants were taught to construct sentence patterns for equivalent classes, property restrictions 'only', 'exactly, 'at least', 'at most', and property domains and ranges.

Text to be 'translated'. The source text containing the domain knowledge was from a Simple Wikipedia[7] article about acid:

> An acid (from the Latin acidus/acēre meaning sour) is a substance which reacts with a base. Commonly, acids can be identified as tasting sour, reacting with metals such as calcium, and bases like sodium carbonate. Aqueous acids have a pH under 7, with acidity increasing the lower the pH. Chemicals or substances having the property of an acid are said to be acidic.
>
> Common examples of acids include acetic acid (in vinegar), sulfuric acid (used in car batteries), and tartaric acid (used in baking). As these three examples show, acids can be solutions, liquids, or solids. Gases such as hydrogen chloride can be acids as well. Strong acids and some concentrated weak acids are corrosive, but there are exceptions such as carboranes and boric acid.

We chose this as an appropriate expository text because it presented the typical difficulties and ambiguities of naturally-occurring text while avoiding content requiring past tense (e.g., events in history). To check the suitability of the source text, the authors independently tried to recast its content in OSE, and produced three texts showing somewhat different modelling styles (see also section 5).

Task Instructions. Participants were given written instructions as follows:

> Your task is to enter information about classes and individuals from the text that you have been given using the sentence patterns shown in the tutorial. Try to use only information that you find in the text but you may use alternative phrases if you wish. There will be information in the text that you do not know how to express yet; do not worry, just leave it out for now. You will be adding more after the next tutorial.

3.4   Method

Six participants, two OWL experts and four novices, completed the study individually in a small room in the Open University human interaction laboratory supervised by the first author who calibrated the eye-tracker, started the videos, controlled the timings of each 10-minute CNL authoring session, and saved participants' OSE text files.

---

[7] Downloaded from `http://simple.wikipedia.org/wiki/Acid` on 29th November 2012

4 Results

OSE texts written and edited by participants range from 3 to 30 sentences.[8] Overall, it is surprising how much text they managed to write. Even though the resulting knowledge modelling in OWL is sometimes not ideal,[9] nevertheless, all participants except one managed to construct a simple ontology about acids.

4.1 Learning OSE

Analysis of screen recordings of participants' authoring sessions revealed that all quickly learnt the patterns 'A [class] is a [class].' and '[Individual] is a [class].' Experts seemed to pick up the controlled language with remarkable ease.

Some novices attempted to write in natural English rather than OSE, e.g., 'A is B, so is C.' and a conjunction in the subject NP 'A and B are ...'. A novice had problems with verb tenses (s/he tried to use the past tense form) and with plural nouns when the singular is required. Further problems are noted in the following subsections.

4.2 Knowledge Modelling

Building Class Hierarchies. A major difference between experts and novices was that *experts had one more level of depth in their hierarchies*. Experts identified more sub-classes than novices who would typically fail to state, e.g., that strong, and concentrated weak acids are types of acid. An expert would include these and also 'base' and 'metal' as subclasses of 'substance', and 'aqueous acid' as a subclass of 'acid'.

Defining Class Members. Regarding class membership, everyone constructed 'Acetic acid is an acid', 'Tartaric acid is an acid', and so on from the original sentence where these are clearly stated: 'Common examples of acids include acetic acid (in vinegar), sulfuric acid (used in car batteries), and tartaric acid (used in baking).'

Explicit vs. Implicit Information. In general, where class subordination and class membership information is *explicit* in the source text, all participants managed to model it; however, where information is *implicit*, only experts modelled it.

Constructing Relationships (Properties) between Individuals. All participants managed to construct at least one property; however, nearly everyone had problems constructing property names (see section 4.4). Some novices had problems attempting to construct relationships in the text that are difficult, or impossible, to model in OWL, e.g., the vague 'can be' in 'Gases such as hydrogen chloride can be acids'.

Translating Source Text Information. There is evidence that everyone tried to translate directly from the source text. All participants started constructing their ontologies with some variation of the sentence 'An acid is a substance.' This corresponds with part of the first sentence in the original text, *'An acid (from the Latin acidus/acēre meaning*

---

[8] Available from
   mcs.open.ac.uk/nlg/SWAT/WilliamsEtAl2014-ParticipantTexts.pdf
[9] We chose *not* to view any particular modelling style as being 'correct'.

sour) is a substance which reacts with a base.' One person even copied the sentence from the original text, pasted it into the editor and deleted redundant parts of it. Often, they wrote many OSE sentences for a single source text sentence; indeed, expert E7 wrote six for the first source text sentence, perhaps exploring the range within OSE.

Table 1. Modelling the sentence *'Aqueous acids have a pH under 7, with acidity increasing the lower the pH. Chemicals or substances having the property of an acid are said to be acidic.'*

OSE Sentence	N4	N5	N6	N2	E3	E7
Aqueous acids are under 7.				✓		
Aqueous acids has ph under 7.			✓			
An aqueous acid is defined as a liquid that has pH below 7.						✓
An acid has as pH "7 or less".					✓	
Acid has ph under 4.			✓			
Acid is definied as a substance that has ph under 7.			✓			
An acidic is defined as a subtance that has as property of an acid.					✓	
Acidity is inverted proportion to a ph.			✓			

Participants demonstrated surprising consensus in modelling the second source text sentence (apart from class-individual differences). The screen recordings revealed that most struggled to interpret the vague term 'commonly' in 'commonly, acids can be identified as tasting sour', encoding the meaning as *'all* acids taste sour'.

Again, screen recordings revealed difficulties with constructing a property for 'pH' (all participants that attempted it had difficulties). See also table 1 for a comparison of their attempts.

In modelling usages of acids and whether they are solids, liquids or gases, only novice N2 and expert E7 attempted to model usages of common acids but N2 seemingly misunderstood the universal restriction by writing 'Tartaric acid is used only in baking'. Expert E3 provided a plausible disjoint union for solution, liquid, solid, and gas classes.

As a final example, consider how participants modelled the knowledge that acids can be weak or strong, or corrosive or non-corrosive. E7 was inventive in writing 'Boric acid corrodes exactly 0 substances.' N2 specified 'non-corrosive' and 'corrosive' classes with the latter equivalent to 'acid'. If, as indicated by their names, s/he had made 'corrosive' and 'non-corrosive' disjoint, a non-corrosive acid could not logically exist.

4.3   Sentence Construction

Sentence Pattern Usage. Table 2 shows a breakdown of sentence pattern usage by participant. It is clear that the OWL experts, E3 and E7, produced more sentences than OWL novices (N4, N5, N6 and N2). The mean number is 26 for experts and 15 for novices not including N4. *Experts attempted a greater variety and more complex patterns than novices.* Eleven of the patterns taught in the videos were used, six were taught but not used, and a further seven patterns were used that were not taught.

Table 2. Sentence pattern frequencies in participants' final texts (*error in editor)

Pattern	N4	N5	N6	N2	E3	E7	Total
[Individual] is a [class].	1	7	6	10	7	9	40
A [class] is a [class].	1	2	1	3	6	7	20
No [class] is a [class].		3			3	1	7
A [class] [has-property] a [class].				1	3	2	6
[Individual] [has-property] [Individual].	1		1			2	4
[Individual] [has-property] a [class].			3			1	4
[Individual] [has-data-property] [literal].				2	1		3
A [class] [has-property] [Individual].						3	3
*[Individual] is defined as a [class].					3		3
A [class] is defined as a [class] that [has-property] a [class].		1			1	1	3
[Individual] [has-property] a [class] that [has-data-property] [literal].			1				1
[Individual] [has-property] only [class].				1			1
[Individual] [has-property] exactly [integer] [class].						1	1
A [class] is defined as a [class] that [has-data-property] [literal].						1	1
A [class] is a [class] or a [class] or a [class] or a [class].					1		1
A [class] [has-data-property] [literal].					1		1
A [class] [has-property] at least [integer] [class].						1	1
Anything that [has-property] something is a [class].						1	1
Total Sentences	3	13	14	19	22	30	101
Total Unique patterns	3	4	6	6	7	12	18

Understanding That OSE Sentences Must Conform to Syntactic Rules and Ability to Correct Errors. There is evidence in the screen recordings that participants noticed when sentences were incorrect and tried to correct them. Eye tracks and gaze duration circles over sentences being written before and after adding a full stop seem to indicate sentence checking. Sometimes a sentence pattern was selected in what looked like an attempt to correct a half-written sentence. On the other hand, there was often little attempt to conform to English grammar rules ('a acid' was not corrected to 'an acid' by three participants); indeed OSE does not recognise (or colour-code) them as errors.

Some participants failed to correct sentences with syntactic flaws that could not be parsed by the finite state automaton in the editor. 'An acid tastes Sour and reacts with metals.' was produced by N4 who had successfully declared 'tastes' and 'reacts' as verbs but failed to remember that if it were a class, 'metal' should be singular with a determiner, or if an individual, it should be capitalised. Consequently, the entire phrase 'reacts with metals' was treated as a property name by the editor so the sentence was incomplete. Similar errors were produced by other novices.

Eye-Tracking during Sentence Construction. Table 3 shows the proportion of total visit duration times, i.e., total times that the eye tracker recorded the participant looking at the source text, editing area, patterns and continuations area and message area (see figure 1). Data for E7 are missing; the eye tracker did not work for this participant. The table shows times for the first exercise only, because most participants had written enough material by the second exercise to start scrolling the editing pane and thus the source text and editing area were no longer fixed inside the relevant areas marked for automatic calculation of visit duration. From the videos, we observed that *most participants spent a long time re-reading text that they had already written* (especially E3), perhaps checking consistency or for missing information. This observation only accounts for part of the total visit durations, however, since time was also spent composing and editing text. Some people looked at messages and OWL statements in the message pane, but these did not receive much attention overall (zero or 1% of total visit duration).

Table 3. Total visit durations (1st exercise only)

Part of Editor	N4	N5	N6	N2	E3
Source text	17%	25%	54%	45%	27%
Editing area	54%	47%	30%	48%	72%
Sentence Patterns	28%	28%	16%	6%	1%
Message Pane	1%	1%	0%	1%	1%

4.4 Identifier Name Construction

Table 4 shows a breakdown of identifier names in the final CNL texts by type (class names, individual names, or property names) and participant. All participants successfully produced at least one of the three types, and all produced 19 to 25 different names except N4. There was considerable variety in the identifiers constructed with 58 unique names amongst 119 total, where type is treated as a difference (e.g., 'acid' the class name is counted as different from 'acid' the named individual).

Modifications to Names from the Source Text. Table 4 shows frequencies of class, individual and property names and a breakdown whether these are identical to, or modified from, the source text, or were not present in the source text. It is immediately apparent that most identifier names were derived from words and phrases in the source texts (94%). Surprisingly, although most identifiers were similar to terms in the source text, only around half had exactly the same morphological forms. Creation of entirely new terms, such as synonyms of source text terms ('below' from 'under') or antonyms ('non-corrosive' from 'corrosive') was rare, only 6% used other English phrases; this could be because participants thought that using alternative words would change the meaning, or because it requires greater mental effort.

With *class names*, almost all modifications to source text terms consisted of changing plural nouns into singular nouns (32 of 33 modifications, or 97%), e.g., 'gases' to 'gas' and 'car batteries' to 'car battery'. This evidence indicates that plural-to-singular noun modification presented no difficulties. Other modifications were construction of a new term, 'non-corrosive', not in the source, and conversion of the progressive verb 'tasting' into the noun 'taste'. Fewer than half, or 24 of the total 59 class names, (41%) were identical to strings in the source text.

Conversely, *named individual identifiers* are almost all identical to strings in the source text (35 out of 39, 90%); this was expected since most were names of chemical compounds. Of those that were not, one was a plural noun made singular, two were separated adjectives and nouns, and the other, 's-acid', did not exist in the source text.

As for *property names*, all except one were different from strings in the source text; 16 out of 21, 76%, were different. The majority of modifications were the insertion of 'is' or 'has' before a noun and optional preposition (83% of modifications), e.g., 'is used in', 'has common taste' (14, including those containing nouns that were not in the source text). This type of name is commonly used by ontology authors (Power, 2010; Power and Third, 2012, Williams, 2013) and, indeed, it was taught in our tutorials. Other modifications were varied, including changing the progressive verb 'tasting' to the noun 'taste' or to the verb 'tastes' and the adjective 'corrosive' to the 3rd person present singular verb 'corrodes', and the verb 'reacts' to the noun 'reactant'.

Table 4. Frequencies and origins of identifier names by type

Type	N4	N5	N6	N2	E3	E7	Total	Identical to source text	Modified source text	Other
Class	2	13	6	13	15	10	59	24 (41%)	33 (56%)	2 (3%)
Indiv	2	7	9	7	6	8	39	35 (90%)	3 (8%)	1 (2%)
Prop	1	2	4	3	4	7	21	5 (24%)	12 (57%)	4 (19%)
Total	5	22	19	23	25	25	119	64 (54%)	48 (40%)	7 (6%)

Difficulties. Three OWL novices had difficulty understanding the difference between classes and individuals. They constructed 'acid' as both a class and an identifier (even though the editor colours them differently and shows their different OWL expressions).

Constructing multi-word names and understanding how quotes are used was another difficulty. OSE uses quotes for two different purposes: (i) class names containing keywords such as 'and', and (ii) literals. Some participants had initial difficulties, however, everyone except N4 managed to create multi-word names, e.g., Boric acid, Hydrogen chloride. N4 seemed to have the idea that multi-word names could not be used, hence his/her attempts to use quotes and camel case 'reactsWith'.

A third difficulty was constructing property names; evidence from failed attempts in the screen recordings showed that all participants experienced some difficulty. All except N4 managed to use the OSE syntax for declaring a verb, e.g., '#verb react reacts'.

Participants' Comments. Regarding the task itself, participants did not mention their difficulties constructing syntactically correct sentences. One commented that it is hard to build an ontology without a particular application in mind. Regarding OSE, some participants were interested in how exactly each sentence is parsed. A participant who is a computer programmer noted that the syntax of OSE seemed more complex than a programming language. Other comments tended to be about the user interface: it should give more help; provide better handling of placeholders in generic sentence patterns; and display new verbs immediately in the options list. One expert Protégé user requested a display of the complete OWL ontology and class hierarchy rather than just the statement under construction.

5 General Discussion

Is a CNL Easy to Learn? Nearly everyone in the study was able to quickly learn to: construct simple sentence patterns; make use of words and phrases (suitably modified) from the source text to create identifier names; declare verbs for use in property names; and correct at least some syntactic errors. All participants made strikingly similar modifications to source text phrases, converting plural nouns to singular for class names and inserting 'is' or 'has' before nouns to form property names.

Compared with novices, OWL experts produced a larger number of well-formed OSE sentences, utilising a wider range of patterns. We assume that this was not because they were better at learning the syntax of the language, but because they were more familiar with the KR task.

All participants had difficulty constructing sentences with properties. Some novices, in particular, tended to *avoid* properties by introducing more classes, e.g., rather than 'An acid corrodes a metal.', they would write 'An acid is a corrosive substance.'

Participants spent a lot of time reading previously-written text. Perhaps they were looking to see what worked before, in the same way that programmers search for code examples. If so, it suggests that providing many examples of well-formed sentences might benefit OSE learners.

Regarding differences in modelling, we are aware that styles differ; it is unclear whether, for instance, 'tartaric acid' should be modelled as an instance or as a subclass of 'acid'. We therefore decided *not* to treat any particular model as 'correct'. Likewise, we choose a naturally occurring source text expecting that it would elicit different models (since we tried the exercise ourselves before the experiment). In an ideal world, domain experts would collaborate with knowledge engineers to build ontologies; CNLs such as OSE could provide a useful communication medium between the two.

Although our focus was on learning OSE, user interface issues emerged, particularly lack of attention to the message pane suggesting that it should be re-positioned.

Would a CNL Enable Someone Unfamiliar with KR to Build a KB? All participants largely agreed on class subsumption and membership *explicitly* present in the source text, demonstrating that certain aspects of building a KB are accessible to everyone. However, a marked difference between OWL experts and novices was the greater organisation and depth of experts' class hierarchies. Experience with knowledge engineering enabled the experts to model knowledge that was not *explicit* in the source text but *implied*. OWL novices did not model implict knowledge, perhaps indicating that they did not realise that the implied subclass relationship between, say, strong acid and acid, so obvious to a human reader, must be specified. See also Third [19].

OWL novice errors noted by Rector et al. [17] were: (i) failure to make 'hidden information' in identifier names explicit, (ii) misunderstanding the universal restriction, (iii) misuse of logical 'and' and 'or', (iv) ignorance of the open-world assumption (and consequent failure to specify disjoint classes), and (v) incorrect placement of logical 'not'. *OWL novices* in our study made errors (i) and (iv). Features in (ii), (iii), and (v) were little used.

Novices in our study made the error of modelling the same thing as a class *and* an individual; therefore, to Rector et al.'s list we would add (vi) confusion of *general* concepts (classes) with *specific* instances of the classes ('individuals' in OWL).

6   Conclusion and Future Work

While OWL experts seemed to master OSE quickly and produced small ontologies with ease. Clearly, novices experienced difficulties and require more guidance such as examples of syntactically correct sentences.

Alternative interfaces such as WYSIWYM [14] have achieved some success with novices at the expense of freedom to type text as in a conventional editor. Dialogue systems currently under development, e.g., in the WhatIf! project [13], might provide a way forward. If a system were to have the ability to respond with intelligent and appropriate questions and remarks about possibly unintended entailments present in knowledge entered, it might enable even novices to gain some insight into the formal semantics and hence construct KBs that are logically consistent.

Acknowledgements. Dr Third was supported by VPH Share (European Commission ICT-FP7-269978). Dr Williams and Dr Power were supported by The Open University (OU). We are grateful to the anonymous reviewers and to members of the OU NLG group for their help in preparing this paper.

References

1. Cregan, A., Schwitter, R., Meyer, T.: Sydney OWL Syntax - towards a Controlled Natural Language Syntax for OWL 1.1. In: Golbreich, C., Kalyanpur, A., Parsia, B. (eds.) OWLED Workshop on OWL: Experiences and Directions. CEUR Workshop, vol. 258 (2007)
2. Dolbear, C., Hart, G., Kovacs, K., Goodwin, J., Zhou, S.: The RABBIT language: description, syntax and conversion to OWL. Tech. rep., Ordnance Survey Research (2007)
3. Fuchs, N.E., Kaljurand, K., Schneider, G.: Attempto Controlled English Meets the Challenges of Knowledge Representation, Reasoning, Interoperability and User Interfaces. In: Florida Artificial Intelligence Research Society (FLAIRS) Conference, pp. 664–669 (2006)
4. Funk, A., Tablan, V., Bontcheva, K., Cunningham, H., Davis, B., Handschuh, S.: CLOnE: Controlled Language for Ontology Editing. In: Aberer, K., et al. (eds.) ASWC 2007 and ISWC 2007. LNCS, vol. 4825, pp. 142–155. Springer, Heidelberg (2007)
5. García-Barriocanal, E., Sicilia, M.A., Sánchez-Alonso, S.: Usability evaluation of ontology editors. Knowledge Organization 32(1), 1–9 (2006)
6. Hallett, C., Scott, D., Power, R.: Composing Questions through Conceptual Authoring. Computational Linguistics 33(1), 105–133 (2007)
7. Hermann, A., Ferré, S., Ducassé, M.: An interactive guidance process supporting consistent updates of RDFS graphs. In: ten Teije, A., Völker, J., Handschuh, S., Stuckenschmidt, H., d'Acquin, M., Nikolov, A., Aussenac-Gilles, N., Hernandez, N. (eds.) EKAW 2012. LNCS, vol. 7603, pp. 185–199. Springer, Heidelberg (2012)
8. Kaljurand, K., Kuhn, T., Canedo, L.: Collaborative multilingual knowledge management based on controlled natural language. Semantic Web Journal, 1–18 (under review)
9. Kuhn, T.: How to Evaluate Controlled Natural Languages. In: Fuchs, N.E. (ed.) Pre-Proceedings of the Workshop on Controlled Natural Language (CNL 2009). vol. 448 (2009)
10. Kuhn, T.: Controlled English for Knowledge Representation. Ph.D. thesis, Faculty of Economics, Business Administration and IT, University of Zurich (2010)
11. Kuhn, T.: The Understandability of OWL Statements in Controlled English. Semantic Web 4(1), 101–115 (2013)
12. Liang, S.F., Stevens, R., Scott, D., Rector, A.: OntoVerbal: a Generic Tool and Practical Application to SNOMED CT. International Journal of Advanced Computer Science and Applications 4(6), 227–239 (2013)
13. Parvizi, A., Jay, C., Mellish, C., Pan, J., Ren, Y., Stevens, R., van Deemter, K.: A Pilot Experiment in Knowledge Authoring as Dialogue. In: 10th International Conference on Computational Semantics (IWCS), pp. 376–382. Association for Computational Linguistics (2013)
14. Power, R., Scott, D., Evans, R.: What You See Is What You Meant: direct knowledge editing with natural language feedback. In: ECAI 1998, pp. 677–681 (1998)
15. Power, R.: OWL Simplified English: a finite-state language for ontology editing. In: Kuhn, T., Fuchs, N.E. (eds.) CNL 2012. LNCS, vol. 7427, pp. 44–60. Springer, Heidelberg (2012)

16. Power, R.: SWAT Editing Tool: a tutorial. Tech. Rep. Unpublished, Department of Computing and Communication, The Open University (2013)
17. Rector, A.L., Drummond, N., Horridge, M., Rogers, J.D., Knublauch, H., Stevens, R., Wang, H., Wroe, C.: OWL pizzas: Practical experience of teaching OWL-DL: Common errors & common patterns. In: Motta, E., Shadbolt, N.R., Stutt, A., Gibbins, N. (eds.) EKAW 2004. LNCS (LNAI), vol. 3257, pp. 63–81. Springer, Heidelberg (2004)
18. Schwitter, R.: Creating and Querying Formal Ontologies via Controlled Natural Language. Applied Artificial Intelligence 24(1&2), 149–174 (2010)
19. Third, A.: Hidden semantics: what can we learn from the names in an ontology? In: 7th International Natural Language Generation Conference (INLG), pp. 67–75 (2012)
20. Zapata, C., Losada, B.: Transforming Natural Language into Controlled Language for Requirements Elicitation: A Knowledge Representation Approach, chap. 5, pp. 117–134 (2012)

Linguistic Analysis of Requirements of a Space Project and Their Conformity with the Recommendations Proposed by a Controlled Natural Language

Anne Condamines* and Maxime Warnier*

CLLE-ERSS, CNRS and Université Toulouse 2 – Le Mirail / CNES
{anne.condamines,maxime.warnier}@univ-tlse2.fr

Abstract. The long term aim of the project carried out by the French National Space Agency (CNES) is to design a writing guide based on the real and regular writing of requirements. As a first step in the project, this paper proposes a linguistic analysis of requirements written in French by CNES engineers. The aim is to determine to what extent they conform to two rules laid down in INCOSE, a recent guide for writing requirements. Although CNES engineers are not obliged to follow any Controlled Natural Language in their writing of requirements, we believe that language regularities are likely to emerge from this task, mainly due to the writers' experience. The issue is approached using natural language processing tools to identify sentences that do not comply with INCOSE rules. We further review these sentences to understand why the recommendations cannot (or should not) always be applied when specifying large-scale projects.

Keywords: requirements, specifications, technical writing, corpus linguistics, controlled natural language.

1 Introduction

The study presented in this paper was conducted with a view to improving the writing of requirements at CNES (Centre National d'Études Spatiales).

The CNES and our laboratory have been collaborating for several years on questions concerning terminology, text management and the study of risks related to the use of language [1]. As linguists, we propose methods and results based on a corpus linguistics approach, assisted by tools such as parsers, statistical tools, terminology extractors, concordancers or scripting languages. More recently, we were approached on the specific problem of writing requirements.

The CNES is the French space agency and, as such, is responsible for designing space systems. Therefore, it has to draft specifications (that must clearly and precisely describe its needs) which are intended for companies that respond to the bids; and, in

---

* Study carried out as part of a PhD thesis granted by the CNES and the Regional Council Midi-Pyrénées.

B. Davis et al. (Eds.): CNL 2014, LNAI 8625, pp. 33–43, 2014.

turn, it also responds to bids from other scientific, commercial or military partners. The Quality Department of the CNES, however, is aware that these specifications are not always clear, and that as a result there may be divergent interpretations, leading to additional costs, delays or even litigation (since requirements are part of the contract clauses).

In order to improve the quality of requirements, many projects have been developed by computational researchers to check the consistency of the requirements after they were written (see [2–4], among others). Still, we believe that the writing itself can be improved by proposing a guide closer to the actual way in which engineers write requirements.

In the present study, two kinds of documents were used: the Guide for Writing Requirements recommendations proposed by INCOSE (International Council on Systems Engineering) [5] (a controlled natural language, see below); and a subset of the specifications of a project: Pleiades (see below).

We propose a linguistic diagnosis of the way requirements are written in the project by comparing these requirements with the recommendations of the INCOSE guide.

The point of view underlying our approach is that guides for writing specifications are not fully adapted to the real writing process: they are sometimes too constraining, and sometimes insufficiently so. They are not written by linguists but by domain experts with a prescriptive point of view based on their experience. This is the case for example in the field of air-traffic control where the ICAO (International Civil Aviation Organization) phraseology is written by controllers [6]. Even if these guides are not always adapted to the reality of language use, we consider that they constitute a good starting point because of the experience of the domain experts. Our other starting point is constituted by specifications that are not written following the recommendations of a guide: this is the case at CNES.

Indeed, CNES engineers do not use a controlled natural language in order to write better specifications, only requirement management tools (such as IBM Rational DOORS). Nevertheless, they are all experienced in this type of writing. Thus, even if the writers do not consciously follow a controlled natural language, we assume the existence of regularities in the way they write requirements. Writers are indeed influenced both by existing specifications and by certain spontaneous regularities which tend to occur in each recurrent writing situation, two characteristics attributed to textual genres. According to Bhatia [7], a *textual genre* may be defined as "a recognizable communicative event characterized by a set of communicative purpose(s) identified and mutually understood by the members of the professional or academic community in which it regularly occurs".

It can be noted that the notion of textual genre is not always properly distinguished from that of *sublanguage*. See for instance the definition given by Somers: "A sublanguage is an identifiable genre or text-type in a given subject field, with a relatively or even absolutely closed set of syntactic structures and vocabulary" [8]. Other authors such as Kurzon [9], Temnikova [10] or Kuhn [11] have highlighted this point. Historically, the most important difference is that the notion of sublanguage was proposed by Harris from a mathematical and distributional perspective [12], while that of textual genre comes from a more sociolinguistic approach [7, 13] or even a corpus linguistic one [14]. In both cases, one of the most important characteristics is that linguistic regularities are associated with speakers of the same community. This feature of spontaneous linguistic regularities has been characterized as *normaison* ("norming') by the French Linguistic School of Rouen [15] as opposed to *normalisation* ("normalization") that concerns the case where linguistic norms are imposed by an organism. In short, we could say that our aim is to propose a normalisation based on the identification of normaison, or, in other words, to improve the writing of specifications without imposing a standard that is too far removed from the engineers' natural practice.

The paper comprises two main parts. In the first one (see section 2), we present the tool-assisted method used for making the diagnosis. In the second one (see section 3), we describe and discuss our preliminary results.

2   Methodology

Several guides for writing requirements exist, and most of them were designed to avoid undesirable properties of natural language ("unrestricted natural language brings with it a host of well-known problems" [16]), such as ambiguity, polysemy, vagueness, and so on [1, 17].

To ensure that these guidelines are close enough to actual practices, and thus really usable, we decided to carry out a diagnosis of the way the specifications are drafted at CNES and then to compare this process with the recommendations made by one of those guides. The aim is to evaluate the conformity of the requirements to the recommendations, and see if the latter can be brought closer to reality.

We will first briefly describe our corpus of requirements and the tools we used, and then the linguistic phenomena selected for study in the controlled natural language that we used as a reference.

2.1   Description of the Corpus

A subset of the specifications of an Earth observation satellite called Pleiades, launched in 2011, was obtained from the CNES. From these specifications, we extracted the requirements, that is to say only those parts that play the role of contractual obligations between the CNES and its subcontractors. Requirements should not contain unnecessary information, such as examples or comments.

Requirements are intended to be autonomous; they are therefore supposed to have no link with the textual segments which precede or follow them. In the specifications we were given, the requirements were easily identifiable because they were framed by specific tags.

The requirements were all written in natural language, but some also contained tables or diagrams (which were removed, since they cannot be analyzed automatically). In theory, they should be fully understandable even without those figures – but in practice, this is not always the case.

The resulting corpus is composed of 1,142 requirements (nearly 53,000 words) in French.

2.2   Tools and Resources

We used several tools to perform the tasks described in section 3. The syntactic analysis was done using Talismane [18], an open-source parser developed in our laboratory, while the open-source corpus processor Unitex [19] was used for sentence chunking. Short handmade Perl scripts were written for other needs (extraction of the requirements, detection of long sentences, and so on).

We also compared our corpus to two other corpora (reduced to the exact same size): (1) a handbook written by experts from the CNES about techniques and technologies used for building and operating spacecraft, intended for semi-experts, and (2) some articles from the French national newspaper *Le Monde*.

2.3   INCOSE Recommendations

In order to compare the requirements corpus with a controlled natural language, we used the Guide for Writing Requirements recommendations proposed by INCOSE. The aim of this guide is presented as follows: "to draw together advice from a variety of existing standards into a single, comprehensive set of rules and objectives" (p. 10). It is quite general since it "is intended to cover the expression of requirements from across disciplines" (p. 12). INCOSE is therefore intended for engineers who write or review requirements. It can be clearly considered a "naturalist" controlled language (as opposed to the "formalist" approach) [20], whose goal is to facilitate human-to-human communication [21].

Like many other controlled natural languages (CNL) aimed at improving communication among humans, the main purpose of INCOSE is to ensure that the message written in natural language has only one possible interpretation. It is worth noting that this point of view about natural language is far from the one adopted by linguistics.[1] It can be reasonably assumed, however, that by establishing guidelines in narrowly-defined situations, it may be possible to limit (if not to remove completely) the inherent difficulties linked to natural language such as ambiguity.

INCOSE has the four characteristics of controlled natural languages proposed by Kuhn [11], since it has one base language (English), it is a constructed language, it sets constraints on the vocabulary, the syntax and the semantics, and the resulting textual requirements are still understandable by English speakers.

It is not a mere style guide, because the recommendations are real rules, not hints – even if the authors admit that "rules have to constantly be adapted to particular situations". All of them are followed by objectives that explain why the rules are useful.

The main "objectives for writing requirement statements" are: singularity, completeness, necessity, comprehensibility, concision, precision and non-ambiguity. These recommendations are translated into linguistic instructions. We selected several of these instructions and analyzed our corpus to see how often they appear.

Because the phenomena we chose to observe are quite general (i.e. not highly language-dependent), we assume that most of the conclusions we propose for French are

---

[1]   According to Jakobson, for example, the referential function, which is the closest to the one consisting in transmitting information, is only one among the six functions of language [22].

valid for English as well. In fact, INCOSE, while written in English and mainly based on older English guides, sometimes gives examples in French.

Since it was not possible to check the conformity of the requirements to all the recommendations proposed by INCOSE (partly because the study is still in its initial stage, and partly because several of the recommendations cannot be verified in an automated manner), we decided to focus on a selection, all related to what could be called "comprehensibility"; that is, the fact that every (sentence composing a) requirement should be easily understandable by the reader, and that it cannot be misinterpreted, i.e. given a different meaning from the one originally intended by the writer. This notion is closely connected to that of complexity: the more complex a sentence is, the less easy it is to understand.

The first rule from INCOSE that we chose to examine is called "Singularity/Propositionals" and states that "combinators" must be avoided: *"Combinators are words that join clauses together, such as 'and', 'or', 'then', 'unless'. Their presence in a requirement usually indicates that multiple requirements should be written."* Nevertheless, some of them are still present in the examples of "acceptable" specifications; this paradox suggests that the "combinators" cannot always be avoided.

The second rule is called "Completeness/Pronouns" and states that it is better to repeat nouns in full, rather than using pronouns to refer to nouns in other statements: *"Pronouns are words such as 'it', 'this', 'that', 'he', 'she', 'they', 'them'. When writing stories, they are a useful device for avoiding the repetition of words; but when writing requirements, pronouns should be avoided, and the proper nouns repeated where necessary."* However, there is no indication about the conditions required for this repetition to be "necessary"; we can merely infer that the aim is to avoid problems due to anaphora resolution. Besides, in the only example given by INCOSE[2], the ambiguity lies in a determiner, not in a pronoun.

We can already point out that these two rules are very general and seem way too restrictive, and that their justifications are evasive.

3   First Results

In subsection 3.1, we present our results concerning the frequency of conjunctions, pronouns and long sentences in our corpus. In subsection 3.2, we propose a selection of examples that break the two rules from INCOSE and try to classify them according to their necessity (mandatory, useful or undesirable).

3.1   Quantitative Analysis

Thanks to the syntactic analysis, we were able to retrieve all the occurrences of the so-called combinators (since no exhaustive list was given, we looked for all coordinating and subordinating conjunctions) and all the pronouns in the corpus. As can be

---

[2] "The controller shall send the driver's itinary (sic) for the day to the driver" must be preferred to "The controller shall send the driver his itinary (sic) for the day".

seen from table 1, both are numerous, suggesting that they are common in unrestricted natural language.

Still, they are much less frequent in requirements than in the other two corpora, handbooks and newspapers. This is particularly clear in the case of pronouns, which are nearly three times more frequent in newspapers (where repetition is seen as an error of style in French) than in requirements (which are usually much shorter). We believe that such a marked difference is an argument in favor of our initial hypothesis that regularities spontaneously arise in daily practice, and that requirement writing can be considered a textual genre, even when not taught as such.

Table 1. Number of conjunctions and pronouns in the three corpora

		Conjunctions		Pronouns
	Coordinators	Subordinators	(total)	
Requirements	882	365	1247	986
	(1.66%[3])	(0.69%)	(2.35%)	(1.86%)
Handbook	1455	442	1897	1554
	(2.75%)	(0.83%)	(3.58%)	(2.93%)
Newspaper	1274	579	1853	2710
	(2.40%)	(1.09%)	(3.50%)	(5.11%)

Finally, we also considered the length of the sentences composing the requirements. Although INCOSE simply recommends "concise" requirements, several guides for technical writing (such as ASD Simplified Technical English [23]) impose a word limit for each sentence[4], because it is believed that longer sentences are harder to process. The results of our measures are shown in table 2.

Table 2. Length of sentences in the three corpora

	# sentences	# sentences with > 25 words	Average sentence length (# words)
Requirements	4859	350 (7.2%)	11
Handbook	3456	591 (17.1%)	15
Newspaper	2201	839 (38.1%)	24

Once again, significant differences exist between the three types of documents: sentences tend to be shorter in requirements, and much longer in newspaper articles. However, long sentences are not rare in the requirements corpus; there is even one unusually long sentence containing over 70 words:

"Si la différence (en valeur absolue) entre les dates de fin de lecture de deux fichiers, lus sur tranche de COME M - canal TMI i et sur tranche de COME N - canal TMI j, est inférieure à OPS_DELAI_INTER_FIN_LEC secondes, alors il est interdit

---

[3]   Percentages indicate the number of occurrences in relation to the total number of words.

[4]   Usually around 20 words for English. We arbitrarily decided that long sentences (in French) are composed of more than 25 words, and that a new sentence begins after each line break.

d'enchaîner (lecture enchaînée) par la lecture de la tranche de COME N sur le canal
i et de la tranche de COME M sur le canal j."

3.2   Qualitative Analysis (Analysis of Examples)

As a first step in the diagnosis, we focus on the description of some examples of sentences that do not follow the INCOSE recommendations and try to understand why.

Combinators
Some combinators are mandatory:
   (1) *"Le générateur de TCH vérifiera **que** la valeur du champ PHASE est comprise*
       *entre 0 **et** FREQ_DIV -1." ["The generator of TCH will check **that** the value of*
       *the field PHASE is between 0 **and** FREQ_DIV-1"]*
In example 1, the subordinating conjunction "que" cannot be avoided, since it introduces the dependent clause[5], and the coordinating conjunction "et" is necessary to set the lower and higher limits of the interval.

Some combinators are not mandatory, but prevent repetitions and multiple sentences:
   (2) *"Les champs SM_ID **et** FM_ID seront extraits à partir de la BDS" ["Fields*
       *SM_ID **and** FM_ID will be extracted from the BDS"]*
If the use of "et" were not allowed in example 2, two distinct sentences would be necessary ("Le champ SM_ID sera extrait à partir de la BDS." and "Le champ FM_ID sera extrait à partir de la BDS."). This would lead to longer and probably more confusing requirements: since the two sentences differ by only a single character, the reader may not notice the difference and think it is a duplicated sentence.
    However, longer sentences may become less readable:
   (3) *"Cette TC permet de passer contrôle thermique plate-forme en mode*
       REDUCED, c'est-à-dire de sélectionner des seuils de régulation "larges" pour
       *le contrôle thermique grossier (pour limiter la puissance consommée), **et** de*
       modifier la valeur d'écrêtage de la puissance injectée pour le contrôle ther-
       mique fin." ["This TC makes it possible to switch the heat control of the plat-
       form to REDUCED mode, i.e. to select "broad" regulation thresholds for a
       *coarse heat control (to limit the power consumed), **and** to change the cut-off*
       value of the injected power for precise heat control."]
In example 3, it would have been better to clearly distinguish the two actions permitted by the TC – for example, with a bullet list.

Some combinators provide logical information that may help the reader to better
understand the requirements:
   (4) *"pour n=2 la loi de la taille est respectée de fait **mais** le test 'FIFO vide' reste*
       *nécessaire" ["for n=2 the size rule is always respected, **but** the 'empty FIFO'*
       test is still required"]

---

[5]   In French, the complementizer 'que' must always be used.

In example 4, the reader is certain that the test is necessary in all cases. Without the first main clause and the logical connector "mais", he could have doubted it.

Nonetheless, in several cases, the use of a coordinator does not seem justified; in particular when two sentences are coordinated by "and":

(5) *"Le format des données de mesure angulaire et Doppler est conforme au standard CCSDS décrit dans le document DA9 **et** le schéma XML respecte le standard décrit dans DA11."* [*"The data format of the angular and Doppler measurement is in accordance with the CCSDS standard described in document DA9 **and** the XML schema complies with the standard described in DA11."*]

(6) *"Les demandes sont saisies sur le FOS **et** le logiciel ARPE gère les conflits entre les demandes Spot, Hélios et Pléïades."* [*"The requests are to be entered on the FOS **and** the ARPE software manages conflicts between the requests from Spot, Hélios and Pléïades"*]

In examples 5 and 6, there is no apparent reason why separate sentences should not be used (parataxis).

In some cases, problems arise because of the (absence of proper) coordinators:

(7) *"Pour cela, on utilisera les données BDS (LENGTH et LOCATION_UNIT) de la table des OBCD (globaux) **ou** la description (LONGUEUR) des paramètres diagnostic déjà crées."* [*"For this, we will use the BDS data (LENGTH and LOCATION_UNIT) from the (global) OBCD table **or** the description (LONGUEUR) of the already created diagnostic parameters"*]

In example 7 above, there are two possible solutions (alternative), but no explanation is given to the reader to tell him in which case(s) one of them should be preferred (or whether they are in fact identical).

(8) *"Sur réception de cette TC, le LVC met à jour la table des surveillances standards de l'application destinataire **et** ré-initialise le compteur d'erreur (remise à 0) associé à cette surveillance."* [*"Upon reception of this TC, the LVC updates the table of standard surveillances of the destination application **and** resets the error counter associated to this surveillance"*]

In example 8, we know that the LVC has to do two distinct operations, but it is not clear whether they are supposed to be done at the same time or one after the other.

(9) *"(eg : 2 **et** 10 **ou** 3 **et** 11)"* [*"e.g. : 2 **and** 10 **or** 3 **and** 11)"*]

In example 9, the priorities of the logical operators "et" and "ou" are not clear.

(10) *"Cet ordre est rejeté **si** :* [*"This order is rejected **if:**"*]
- *le mode NORM automatique est actif*
- *le satellite est en mode MAN*
- *le satellite n'est pas en mode convergé (GAP ou SUP)*
- *un ordre MAN/CAP est déjà en attente d'exécution"*

In example 10, the absence of coordinators between the items in the list is the source of uncertainty: is the order rejected if any of the following conditions is met ("or"), or only if they are all met ("and")? Lists of this kind are very common in our corpus.

Pronouns

Some pronouns must be avoided, because otherwise the requirement is no longer autonomous:

(11) *"Il calculera aussi, a une fréquence paramétrable (ordre de grandeur 1 mois), la moyenne de mise en œuvre et la comparera à la moyenne maximum afin d'anticiper un problème éventuel."* [*"It will also calculate, at a frequency that can be parameterized (at monthly intervals), the average time for commissioning and will compare it to the maximum average in order to anticipate any problems."*]

The requirement given in example 11 cannot be understood by itself, because the pronoun "il" ("it") refers to the subject defined in the previous requirement. (And in another requirement, a reference is made to a "previously stated rule", but there is no indication as to which rule is meant.)

Some pronouns are mandatory:

(12) *"Sur réception de cette TC, le LVC met à jour le paramètre **qui** donne la taille maximum d'un paquet TM de type dump"* [*"Upon reception of this TC, the LCV updates the parameter **that** gives the maximum size of a TM dump packet"*]

Without the relative pronoun "that", it would not be possible to specify which parameter is referred to in example 12.

(13) *"Il ne sera pas utile de vérifier ce paquet " vide ""* [*"**It** won't be necessary to check that "empty" packet"*]

Impersonal pronouns like the one given in example 13 are widespread in our corpus and can hardly be avoided. They do not refer to another noun.

Some pronouns are not mandatory, but prevent unnecessary repetitions of words:

(14) *"La liste des TCD est définie en BDS. **Elle** est donnée ici à titre informatif:"* [*"The list of TCD is defined in BDS. **It** is given here for information:"*]

Compare example 14 with the same sentences without a pronoun: "La liste des TCD est définie en BDS. La liste des TCD est donnée ici à titre informatif:". [*"The list of TCD is defined in BDS. The list of TCD is given here for information:"*]

(15) *"Le paquet ne sera généré que s'**il** est activé par le LVC."* [*"The packet will be generated only if **it** is activated by the LVC"*]

Example 15 seems even less natural if rewritten without a pronoun: "Le paquet ne sera généré que si le paquet est activé par le LVC." [*"The packet will be generated only if the packet is activated by the LVC"*]

Moreover, French demonstrative pronouns make it possible to avoid ambiguity between the subject and the object of a sentence:

(16) *"Le générateur de TC ne rejettera pas la création du PARAM_ID diagnostic si **celui-ci** est déjà défini à bord."* [*"The TC generator will not reject the creation of the PARAM_ID diagnostic if **the latter** is already defined on board"*]

In example 16, "celui-ci" refers to the closest noun and is therefore unambiguous, whereas "il" could have been ambiguous.

4   Conclusions and Future Work

We analyzed a corpus composed of genuine requirements that had been written and used by engineers of the CNES to design a space system. We showed that, even if they did not explicitly follow guidelines, their texts have some interesting particularities, such as shorter sentences than in other textual genres.

We also examined two rules (concerning conjunctions and pronouns) from INCOSE, a guide for writing requirements. Using several examples from our corpus, we considered cases where those rules were justified and others where they were inapplicable (at least if literally applied) and should be refined. In fact, we believe that INCOSE, like the guides it is based on, lacks proper linguistic foundations and is not close enough to engineers' real practices. For instance, the recommended absence of pronouns from the requirements – which implies sometimes cumbersome repetitions – seems hardly compatible with its ideal of "concision" (itself seen as "an aid to Comprehensibility, and therefore subsumed by it", p. 16).

In the future, we intend to conduct a deeper linguistic analysis of our results and to focus on terminology so as to study the use and evolution of terms between comparable corpora. We also want to test the rules of INCOSE on another corpus of requirements. More generally, our intention is to inventory all existing rules in French CNL and to try to automatically test them with our corpora. The final step will be to propose a set of rules that is more consistent and closer to established practice in requirements writing.

Acknowledgments. We would like to thank the CNES for their active cooperation as well as for providing us with the requirements corpus. We are also grateful to the four reviewers for their relevant suggestions and references.

References

1. Condamines, A.: Variations in Terminology. Application to the Management of Risks Related to Language Use in the Workplace. Terminology 16, 30–50 (2010)
2. Nair, D.K., Somé, S.S.: A Formal Approach to Requirement Verification. In: SEDE, pp. 148–153 (2006)
3. Barcellini, F., Albert, C., Grosse, C., Saint-Dizier, P.: Risk Analysis and Prevention: LELIE, a Tool dedicated to Procedure and Requirement Authoring. In: LREC, pp. 698–705 (2012)
4. Sateli, B., Angius, E., Rajivelu, S.S., Witte, R.: Can Text Mining Assistants Help to Improve Requirements Specifications? In: Proceedings of the Mining Unstructured Data (MUD 2012) (2012),
   http://sailhome.cs.queensu.ca/mud/res/sateli-mud2012.pdf
5. International Council on Systems Engineering: Guide for Writing Requirements (2011)
6. Lopez, S., Condamines, A., Josselin-Leray, A., O'Donoghue, M., Salmon, R.: Linguistic Analysis of English Phraseology and plain Language in Air-Ground Communication. Journal of Air Transport Studies 4, 44–60 (2013)
7. Bhatia, V.K.: Analysing genre: Language use in professional settings. Longman, London (1993)

8. Somers, H.: An Attempt to Use Weighted Cusums to Identify Sublanguages. In: Powers, D.M.W. (ed.) NeMLaP3/CoNLL 1998: New Methods in Language Processing and Computational Natural Language Learning, pp. 131–139. ACL (1998)
9. Kurzon, D.: "Legal Language": Varieties, Genres, Registers, Discourses. International Journal of Applied Linguistics 7, 119–139 (1997)
10. Temnikova, I.: Text Complexity and Text Simplification in the Crisis Management domain, PhD thesis (2012)
11. Kuhn, T.: A Survey and Classification of Controlled Natural Languages. Computational Linguistics 40, 121–170 (2014)
12. Kittredge, R., Lehrberger, J.: Sublanguage: Studies of Language in Restricted Semantic Domains. Walter de Gruyter, Berlin (1982)
13. Swales, J.: Research Genres: Explorations and Applications. Cambridge University Press, Cambridge (2004)
14. Biber, D.: Variation Across Speech and Writing. Cambridge University Press (1988)
15. Guespin, L.: Socioterminology Facing Problems in Standardization. In: Proceedings of TLK 1990, pp. 642–647 (1990)
16. Pace, G.J., Rosner, M.: A Controlled Language for the Specification of Contracts. In: Fuchs, N.E. (ed.) CNL 2009. LNCS, vol. 5972, pp. 226–245. Springer, Heidelberg (2010)
17. Condamines, A., Rebeyrolle, J.: Searching for and Identifying Conceptual Relationships via a corpus-based approach to a Terminological Knowledge Base (CTKB): method and results. In: Bourigault, D., L'Homme, M.-C., Jacquemin, C. (eds.) Recent Advances in Computational Terminology, pp. 127–148. John Benjamins, Amsterdam/Philadelphia (2001)
18. Urieli, A.: Robust French syntax analysis: reconciling statistical methods and linguistic knowledge in the Talismane toolkit, PhD thesis (2013)
19. Paumier, S.: Unitex, http://www-igm.univ-mlv.fr/~unitex/
20. Clark, P., Murray, W.R., Harrison, P., Thompson, J.: Naturalness vs. Predictability: A Key Debate in Controlled Languages. In: Fuchs, N.E. (ed.) CNL 2009 Workshop. LNCS, vol. 5972, pp. 65–81. Springer, Heidelberg (2010)
21. Wyner, A., et al.: On Controlled Natural Languages: Properties and Prospects. In: Fuchs, N.E. (ed.) CNL 2009. LNCS, vol. 5972, pp. 281–289. Springer, Heidelberg (2010)
22. Jakobson, R.: Linguistics and Poetics. In: Sebeok, T. (ed.) Style in Language, Cambridge, pp. 350–353 (1960)
23. ASD: Simplified Technical English. International specification for the preparation of maintenance documentation in a controlled language (Issue 4) (2007)
24. Bünzli, A., Höfler, S.: Controlling Ambiguities in Legislative Language. In: Rosner, M., Fuchs, N.E. (eds.) CNL 2010. LNCS, vol. 7175, pp. 21–42. Springer, Heidelberg (2012)
25. Fuchs, N., Schwitter, R.: Controlled English for Requirements Specifications. IEEE Computer Special Issue on Interactive Natural Language Processing (1996), http://citeseerx.ist.psu.edu/viewdoc/summary?doi=10.1.1.52.8814
26. Höfler, S.: Legislative Drafting Guidelines: How Different Are They from Controlled Language Rules for Technical Writing? In: Kuhn, T., Fuchs, N.E. (eds.) CNL 2012. LNCS, vol. 7427, pp. 138–151. Springer, Heidelberg (2012)
27. O'Brien, S.: Controlling Controlled English. An Analysis of Several Controlled Language Rule Sets. In: Proceedings of EAMT-CLAW, pp. 105–114 (2003)
28. Vogel, C.: Law matters, syntax matters and semantics matters. Formal linguistics and Law, Trends in Linguistics. Studies and Monographs. 212, 25–54 (2009)

Evaluating the Fully Automatic Multi-language Translation of the Swiss Avalanche Bulletin

Kurt Winkler[1], Tobias Kuhn[2], and Martin Volk[3]

[1] WSL Institute for Snow and Avalanche Research SLF, 7260 Davos Dorf, Switzerland
[2] Department of Humanities, Social and Political Sciences, ETH Zurich, Switzerland
[3] Universität Zürich, Institut für Computerlinguistik, Binzmühlestrasse 14, CH-8050 Zürich

Abstract. The Swiss avalanche bulletin is produced twice a day in four languages. Due to the lack of time available for manual translation, a fully automated translation system is employed, based on a catalogue of predefined phrases and predetermined rules of how these phrases can be combined to produce sentences. The system is able to automatically translate such sentences from German into the target languages French, Italian and English without subsequent proofreading or correction. Our catalogue of phrases is limited to a small sublanguage. The reduction of daily translation costs is expected to offset the initial development costs within a few years. After being operational for two winter seasons, we assess here the quality of the produced texts based on an evaluation where participants rate real danger descriptions from both origins, the catalogue of phrases versus the manually written and translated texts. With a mean recognition rate of 55%, users can hardly distinguish between the two types of texts, and give similar ratings with respect to their language quality. Overall, the output from the catalogue system can be considered virtually equivalent to a text written by avalanche forecasters and then manually translated by professional translators. Furthermore, forecasters declared that all relevant situations were captured by the system with sufficient accuracy and within the limited time available.

Keywords: machine translation, catalogue of phrases, controlled natural language, text quality, avalanche warning.

1 Introduction

Apart from the requirements of being accurate and easy to understand, avalanche bulletins are highly time-critical. The delivery of up-to-date information is particularly challenging in the morning, when there is little time between incoming field observations and the deadline for publishing the bulletin – not enough time for manual translations or manual post-editing. For that reason, the new Swiss avalanche bulletin (Fig. 1) is generated by a fully automated translation system, which we have described in a previous publication [17]. Here we present evaluation results of this system after two winter seasons of operational use.

B. Davis et al. (Eds.): CNL 2014, LNAI 8625, pp. 44–54, 2014.

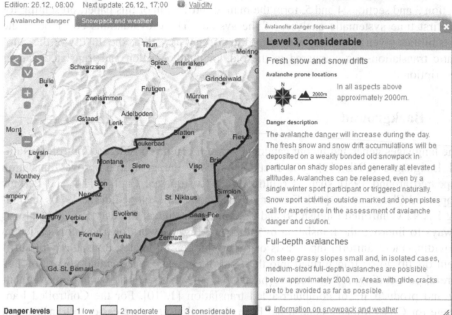

Fig. 1. Swiss avalanche bulletin. The danger descriptions originate from the catalogue of phrases (here in English). More examples and other languages are available at www.slf.ch (in summertime only as .pdf in the archive: www.slf.ch/schneeinfo/Archiv).

Despite the large effort on machine translation approaches and despite their promising results, the quality of fully automatic translations is still poor when compared to manual translations. For the publication of life-critical warnings when there is no time for proofreading or manual corrections, the reliability of existing translation systems is clearly insufficient.

For many years, the daily Swiss national avalanche bulletin was manually translated from German into French, Italian and English. A translation memory system, containing the translations of the avalanche bulletins of the last 15 years, helped to reduce the translation time. A comparison of this text corpus with the Canadian TAUM-Météo translation model [8] showed that the sentences collected over all those years cannot be expected to be comprehensive enough to directly extract a catalogue of phrases, or to be used for statistical machine translation (let alone for a system that does not require proofreading or manual corrections). For these reasons, a custom-made and fully automated translation system was built, which implements an approach based on a catalogue of standard phrases and has been in productive use since November 2012.

This kind of catalogue-based translation system has been used before, e.g. for severe weather warnings [15], but to our knowledge only for simpler domains and less complex sentence types. Our approach to create the catalogue was already described in [17], from where we summarize some content at the beginning of section 3 to give the relevant background and to show the peculiarities of our development. The end of section 3 and sections 4 and 5, form the main contribution of this paper, presenting for the first time systematic analyses of the system. These evaluations cover both, the possibilities given to authors with regard to content as well as the quality of the automatic translations, as compared to the old, manually written and translated danger descriptions.

2   Background

The languages generated by our catalogue system can be considered Controlled Natural Languages (CNL) [7]. The first CNLs with the goal to improve translation appeared around 1980, such as Multinational Customized English [14] and Perkins Approved Clear English [11]. Further languages were developed in the 1990s, including KANT Controlled English [9] and Caterpillar Technical English [5]. The goal was always to improve the translation by either making the work of translators easier by providing more uniform input texts or by producing automated translations of sufficient quality to be transformed into the final documents after manual correction and careful post-editing. Adherence to typical CNL rules has been shown to improve quality and productivity of computer-aided translation [1, 10]. For the Controlled Language for Crisis Management, it has been shown that texts are easier to translate and require less time for post-editing [16].

In contrast, the Grammatical Framework (GF) [12] is a general framework for high-quality rule-based machine translation. It is usable in narrow domains without the need for post-editing, such as the one presented in this paper. GF applies deep linguistic knowledge about morphology and syntax and has been used in prototypes such as AceWiki-GF [6] and a system enhanced by statistical machine translation to translate patents [3], but it does not yet have applications in productive use that match the complexity of texts of our problem domain of avalanche bulletins.

With PILLS [2], as a further comparable system, master documents containing medical information can be automatically transformed into specific documents for different user groups and translated into different languages. As the outcome of a one-year research project, PILLS was a prototype and was – to our knowledge – never applied operationally.

In terms of the PENS categorization scheme for CNLs [7], the languages presented here fall into the category P=2, E=2, N=5, S=4: They have relatively low precision and expressiveness (seen from a formal semantics point of view), but are maximally natural and comparatively simple.

3   Catalogue-Based Translation System

In this section, we give a summary of the methods which we described in our previous paper [17]. In general, a catalogue-based translation system is a collection of predefined phrases (or sentence templates) and therefore cannot be used to translate arbitrary sentences. The phrases in our system were created in the source language

German, translated manually into the target languages French, Italian and English, and stored in a database. The editing tool for the creation of the phrases follows an approach similar to conceptual authoring [4, 13]: sentences are created by first selecting a general sentence pattern from a list and then gradually specifying and expanding the different sentence components. Once a phrase is chosen, it is immediately available in the target languages.

The individual sentences are not static but consist of a succession of up to ten segments. For each segment, the authors can select from a pull-down menu of predetermined options. These options can likewise consist of a series of sub-segments with selectable options, and, as part of the sub-segments, even sub-sub-segments are possible. Theoretically, the 110 predefined phrases could be used to generate several trillion different sentences. Not all possible sentences are meaningful, but all those that make sense must have correct translations in all languages. As no proofreading is possible in operational use, the translations in the catalogue must be guaranteed to be of high quality.

3.1   Creating the Phrases in the Source Language

The sentences were created by an experienced avalanche forecaster whose native language is German and who has a good knowledge of all the target languages. Numerous avalanche bulletins from the past 15 years were consulted in order to cover as many situations as possible. No phrases were taken directly: their content was always generalized and the phrase structure was simplified wherever possible. The challenge was to find sentences that were universal enough to describe all the possible danger situations and simple enough to be translated. No explicit simplified grammar was used in any language. As a sentence can only be used when it works in the source language as well as in all target languages, the original German sentences had to obey the following rules:

- In each individual language, adjectives can only be used when they refer to subjects with the same gender and number in all the options.
- Articles depend on number and – in most of the languages used – gender and must therefore usually be included in the same option as the noun.
- Prepositions often change with the noun and must therefore also be included in the same option as the noun, e.g. 'in' Ticino (a region), but 'on the' Rigi (a mountain).
- As German has four grammatical cases, this sometimes necessitated splitting certain phrases into additional segments and sub-segments. E.g. "Fresh snow drifts require caution / are to be avoided" must be separated from "Fresh snow drifts represent the main danger", because in German the case of "fresh snow drifts" turns "Frischen Triebschnee beachten / umgehen" into "Frischer Triebschnee ist die Hauptgefahr".
- Demonstrative pronouns are only allowed to substitute one specific noun. Thus, e.g. the German "diese" is listed twice in the same pulldown, once for "the avalanches" (in Italian the feminine "queste ultime") and once for "the snow drifts" (in Italian the masculine "questi ultimi"). As there is no difference in the source language German, the substituted noun is indicated in the bulletin editor beside the pronoun, which allows the avalanche forecasters to choose correctly.

3.2   Translation of the Catalogue

Translations take place on the segment level. Although German, French, Italian and English are all Indo-European languages, the differences in word order, gender, declension and so on make segmented translation difficult. Thus, specific editing and visualization software had to be developed by a translation agency to prepare the phrase translations. The translations themselves were performed manually by professional translators familiar with the topic and applying our text corpus. In addition to the omnipresent problem of inflection, ensuring the correct word order also proved difficult. Other problems included:

- clitics, apostrophes and elisions to avoid hiatus, especially in French and Italian;
- the Italian impure 's' ("*i grandi* accumuli" but "*gli spessi* accumuli");
- the split negation in French ("ne ... pas").

When translating the individual sentences and options, no logical functions, distinction of cases or post processing were used, except for a check to ensure the presence of a space between the different segments and a capital letter at the beginning of each sentence. In comparison with the source language, only two changes were allowed in the target languages (Fig. 2): (1) the segment order could vary between the languages (but is fixed for any given language and thus independent from the chosen options) and (2) each segment could be split in two (into ...a, ...b, Fig. 2). The latter facility was widely used, mainly to construct idiomatic word orders. This splitting is only used in the target languages and limits the use of our system to translations from German into the other languages but not backwards. Technically, the system could be used from any language to any other in the language matrix, but when producing the input it would be difficult for forecasters to find the correct sentences in a source language with segment splits.

Apostrophes, elisions, clitics and the impure 's' were handled by using pulldown splits or by taking all together into the same option. The latter required sometimes splits across the constituent units. As splits are invisible, this did not detract the output.

Segment 1	Segment 2	Segment 3	Segment 4	Segment 5
die Lawinen	können			gross werden.
nasse Lawinen		auch	oft	weit vorstossen.
diese		{on_steep} Sonnenhängen	weiterhin	bis in die aperen Täler vorstossen.
		in diesen Gebieten		bis in tiefe Lagen vorstossen.

Segment 3a	Segment 1	Segment 2	Segment 3b	Segment 4	Segment 5
	the avalanches	can			reach large size.
	wet avalanches		also	in many cases	reach a long way.
{on_steep} sunny slopes	they			as before	reach the bare valleys.
in these regions					reach low altitudes.

Fig. 2. Schema of a phrase in the source language German (above). {on_steep} mark a subsegment with several further options. In this example, [blank] is one of the options in the third and fourth segment. In English, the order of the segments is different and segment 3 is split.

3.3   Operational Use

Since going operational, nearly 2000 danger descriptions have been produced per language. As before, the danger descriptions in German were proofread and discussed by at least two avalanche forecasters. Once the content of the German text was found to be correct, the translated texts were published without any further proofreading or corrections.

In a systematic survey we performed, all forecasters rated their satisfaction with the catalogue as "excellent". Six out of seven forecasters declared that at least "almost always" the differences between what they wanted to write and what they could write with the catalogues fell within the range of uncertainty regarding the current danger situation. "Greater limitations" never occurred. In the case of missing sentences, the system allows to add arbitrary text strings in all four languages and to use them immediately. However, no such 'joker phrases' were actually used during the first two winters of operational service.

4   Quality of the Texts

4.1   Method

To assess the language quality, we compared in a blind study texts from old, manually written and translated descriptions with the new descriptions from the catalogue.

To get a comparable set, we chose one danger description from the evening edition of the avalanche bulletin from every second calendar day, starting at the beginning of December and finishing at the end of March. The descriptions from the catalogue were taken from the 2012/13 winter season, the freely written descriptions from the issues from winter 2011/12 back to 2007/08. To avoid evaluating texts that were too short, we only used danger descriptions with more than 100 characters in German. On days with more than one danger description, we randomly chose one of them.

Table 1. Questions concerning the language quality (correctness, comprehensibility, readability and clarity)

1. Is the text correct?				
("minor error" = typing mistake, incorrect punctuation or use of upper/lower case letters...)				
Absolutely correct	1 minor error	several minor / 1 major error	several major errors	Completely wrong
2. Is the language easy to understand? (Assuming familiarity with the key technical terms)				
Very easy to understand	Easy to understand	Understandable	Difficult to understand	Incomprehensible
3. Is the text well formulated and pleasant to read?				
Very well crafted	Easy to read	Clear	Difficult to read	Barely or not at all readable
4. Is the situation described clearly?				
Clearly and precisely	Reasonably clearly	Understandably	Unclearly, meaningless	Incomprehensibly, contradictory

As 120 descriptions per language are too much for a survey, we divided them into 6 different sets, containing 10 descriptions from the old and new bulletin each. We divided the descriptions into the different sets in such a way that different avalanche situations were distributed as uniformly as possible. The order of the descriptions was chosen randomly for each dataset, but identical across all languages.

For every description, we asked four questions about the language quality (Tab. 1) and, additionally, in what manner the participant assumed the text was produced.

The survey was posted on www.slf.ch, on the website of the Swiss avalanche warning service, from 18 February to 5 March 2014. Each participant randomly received one out of the six data sets, in the same language as the website was visited. After a quality check, we had usable data from 204 participants.

93% of the participants were native speakers, 81% were men. The mean age was 43 years. Reflecting the languages of the visitors of our website, we received the most answers for German (76) and the least for English (18). With a median between "medium" and "high", English participants rated their experience in evaluating avalanche dangers slightly higher than the other participants with "medium". Other particularities when comparing the participants using the different languages were not found.

Table 2. Participants in the survey, divided into languages and allotted datasets

Language, n per set (1/../6)	German, 76 14/11/13/10/16/12	English,18 3/2/3/5/4/1	French, 55 10/12/9/6/6/12	Italian, 55 9/9/7/12/8/10

4.2   Analysis

The age of the participants shows normal distribution permitting the use of the t-test. To analyse the detection rate of the origin of a description within a language, the data were cross-tabulated and the chi-square statistic was calculated. All differences between categorical variables were tested with the Mann-Whitney U-test for statistical significance (using $p = 0.05$).

When comparing the language quality of old and new descriptions, we could only find differences in isolated cases by using common parameters for ordinal data as median or mode. As we did not wish to jump to the conclusion that there was no difference at all, we assumed the predefined responses to be equal in distance and allocated numerical values to the different categories, starting with 5 for the best rating and 1 for the worst. We only used these numerical values to calculate mean values in order to show differences between different languages and between the old and the new descriptions.

Not all of the 6 datasets of a particular language had the same number of usable answers (Tab. 2). We therefore checked our data in every language for anomalies in distribution between the different datasets. As we did not find any, we pooled all the answers together.

To test significances between different languages, as well as to analyze the overall rating over all the languages, we used a balanced dataset. This contained all the English answers and in each of the other languages randomly chosen ratings of 180 descriptions from the old and the new bulletin each.

4.3   Results

The evaluators detected the origin of a given text in 59% of the German descriptions (Tab. 3). In the target languages, the rate of correct recognition was lower, with 55% in French and 52% in Italian and English. The recognition rate was significantly better than random only for German and French.

Table 4 shows answers to questions regarding the real origin of the danger descriptions. Differences between old and new descriptions are small and vary from language to language. Thus, with our balanced dataset we only get a significant decrease taking all languages and all questions together ($p = 0.02$), but not for individual questions.

Table 3. Correct ratings of the origin of the descriptions. Significant values are highlighted.

	German	English	French	Italian
n (equally balanced old/new)	1520	360	1100	1100
detection rate	**0.59**	0.52	**0.55**	0.52
p - value	$p < 0.001$	$p = 0.40$	$p < 0.001$	$p = 0.13$

Table 4. Rating for the new descriptions from the catalogue of phrases and difference between new and old descriptions. Better ratings for the new descriptions are marked green, lower ratings red. Significant differences are highlighted. *are calculated from the balanced dataset.

		correct	comprehensible	readable	clear	all
German	mean	4.75	4.30	3.93	4.29	4.32
(n=1520)	difference	0.03	**0.13**	0.05	**0.16**	**0.09**
	(new-old)	(p=0.22)	(p=0.003)	(p=0.25)	(p=0.001)	(p<0.001)
English	mean	3.89	3.74	3.51	3.73	3.72
(n=360)	difference	-0.01	0.01	0.03	-0.05	-0.003
	(new-old)	(p=0.61)	(p=0.90)	(p=0.95)	(p=0.45)	(p=0.54)
French	mean	4.57	4.30	4.07	4.34	4.32
(n=1100)	difference	**-0.12**	-0.04	**-0.11**	0.01	**-0.07**
	(new-old)	(p=0.001)	(p=0.42)	(p=0.01)	(p=0.47)	(p=0.001)
Italian	Mean	4.35	4.21	3.99	4.28	4.21
(n=1100)	difference	**-0.16**	-0.09	-0.08	**-0.12**	**-0.11**
	(new-old)	(p=0.001)	(p=0.08)	(p=0.12)	(p=0.01)	(p<0.001)
all languages	mean	4.39	4.14	3.87	4.16	4.14
	difference	-0.06	0.004	-0.03	0.001	**-0.02**
	(new-old)	(p=0.08)*	(p=0.21)*	(p=0.10)*	(p=0.08)*	(p=0.02)*

5   Discussion

According to the avalanche forecasters, the catalogue of phrases always allowed an adequate description of the danger situation. The translations in the catalogue were checked extensively by the developer, an experienced avalanche forecaster with knowledge in all four languages. The catalogue proved to be even more exact with regard to content, as the manual translation method used for old avalanche bulletins lacked the necessary time to correct smaller inconsistencies.

The detection rate was statistically significant above the random value, but the number of correctly recognized descriptions was small with 55% on average for all languages. This corresponds to, for example, correctly recognizing 2 out of 20 descriptions and then tossing a coin for the remaining 18 descriptions.

French and German speaking participants rated the language quality best with an overall value of 4.32. Italian was nearly as good with a value of 4.21. English ratings were significantly lower and this in both, the old and the new descriptions with a mean of 3.75 and 3.72 respectively. Perhaps this is due to the fact that our translators are British and by using the glossary of the European Avalanche Warning Services (www.avalanches.org) which differs substantially from terminology used in North America, where at least some of the participants of the survey live.

In addition, the large variance between different participants in assessing the same dataset shows that the absolute value of the rating is not only a question of the sentences, but also possibly affected by varying interpretations of the given texts or some other habit of the individual participant. To understand this anomaly, further research would be needed. In our survey, we are much more interested in the changes in language quality due to the introduction of the catalogue of phrases than in the absolute value of quality. Our purpose is hardly affected by these anomalies, thanks to a symmetrical dataset with always contains the same number of descriptions from each origin.

Compared to the differences between the languages, the differences between old and new descriptions are small. This is surprising because the introduction of the catalogue of phrases was a fundamental change and the catalogue itself was mostly translated by different translators.

Of all properties, the correctness reaches the best rating (Tab. 4), whereas the comprehensibility and the clarity of the formulations lie ex aequo in the middle of the investigated parameters about the language quality. The catalogue of phrases leads to a standardized language. As Swiss avalanche forecasters believe that this kind of simple and unambiguous language is well suited to communicate warnings, they wrote the "old" danger descriptions in a similar way as well. In this context, it is not surprising that of all the quality criteria, the pleasure to read was assessed lowest.

In German the descriptions generated with the catalogue of phrases were rated even better, for all four criteria (correctness, comprehensibility, readability and clarity). Note that German is the source language of both, the manually written texts and the catalogue of phrases. In Italian and French, descriptions from the catalogue of phrases were rated lower, for all four criteria in Italian and for three criteria in French. However, the differences are small and in many cases not significant (Tab. 4). In English, no noteworthy change was found.

Statistical significance is a question related to the number of trials, and with the more than 5,500 assessments used in our balanced dataset we can test for even slight differences. Consequently, the decrease of the language-weighted mean values over all questions is statistically significant, even when numerical values for our ordinal data shows, that the decrease was marginal with a value falling from 4.16 to 4.14.

Given the only marginal change in ratings from old to new, and the poor recognition rate, we conclude that in the majority of cases, users did not notice a decrease in the language quality with the introduction of the catalogue. Thus, the language quality from the catalogue of phrases can be judged as virtually equivalent to the text written from scratch and translated by topic-familiar professionals.

6   Conclusions

The catalogue-based system proved to be well-suited to generate the Swiss avalanche bulletin. After two years of operational use, all forecasters declared that within the limited time available to produce forecasts, it was possible to describe the different avalanche situations with precision and efficiency.

The system also proved to be well-suited for fully automatic and instantaneous translation of danger descriptions from German into the target languages French, Italian and English. The translations do not need to be proofread or corrected, and they turned out to be even better with respect to their content than the manual translations of the old avalanche bulletin.

The quality of the language was assessed in a blind study, comparing old, manually translated danger descriptions with new, catalogue-based danger descriptions. Recognizing the difference proved to be difficult; the mean detection rate was only 55%. Based on four criteria the quality of danger description was rated good with some differences between languages. With the introduction of the catalogue of phrases, there were only marginal changes in the different quality ratings. Depending on the language, they show a small improvement or a slight decrease in quality. Thus the bulletins produced by the catalogue of phrases were virtually equivalent in language quality to those produced using the old method of ad hoc translation.

As using a phrase catalogue requires experience, frequent operational use is necessary. It is crucial that users find the phrases matching the given danger situation quickly enough, which has shown to be the case for our system. The implemented search engine was essential. Our experience has shown that the number of phrases should be kept to a minimum by reusing individual phrases in multiple contexts, and that the presented approach is particularly well-suited if the problem domain can be described by a small sublanguage, as is the case for the highly specific topic of avalanche forecasting.

With respect to financial aspects, the cost-benefit ratio of our system turned out to be excellent. The savings from not needing manual translations are expected to exceed the initial development costs within a few years. Applying the database to other multi-lingual countries or extending it to topics such as weather forecasting is conceivable. An adaption to very different languages seems difficult due to differences in grammar and language usage.

The construction of the catalogue and the translations had both been done in an empirical way. We gladly place them at the disposal for further investigations.

Acknowledgments. We thank Martin Bächtold from www.ttn.ch and his translators for the courage to translate the catalogue of phrases and for maintaining a high quality standard. Furthermore, we thank Eva Knop, Nico Grubert, Frank Techel and Curtis Gautschi for valuable input and the participants of the survey.

References

1. Aikawa, T., Schwartz, L., King, R., Corston-Oliver, M., Lozano, C.: Impact of controlled language on translation quality and post-editing in a statistical machine translation environment. In: Proceedings of the MT Summit XI, pp. 1–7. European Association for Machine Translation (2007)
2. Bouayad-Agha, N., Power, R., Belz, A.: PILLS: Multilingual generation of medical information documents with overlapping content. In: Proceedings of the Third International Conference on Language Resources and Evaluation (LREC), pp. 2111–2114 (2002)
3. España-Bonet, C., Enache, R., Slaski, A., Ranta, A., Màrquez, L., Gonzàlez, M.: Patent translation within the MOLTO project. In: Proceedings of the 4th Workshop on Patent Translation, MT Summit (2011), http://www.molto-project.eu/sites/default/files/patentsMOLTO4.pdf
4. Hallett, C., Scott, D., Power, R.: Composing questions through conceptual authoring. Computational Linguistics 33(1), 105–133 (2007)
5. Hayes, P., Maxwell, S., Schmandt, L.: Controlled English advantages for translated and original English documents. In: Proceedings of CLAW 1996, pp. 84–92 (1996)
6. Kaljurand, K., Kuhn, T.: A Multilingual Semantic Wiki Based on Attempto Controlled English and Grammatical Framework. In: Cimiano, P., Corcho, O., Presutti, V., Hollink, L., Rudolph, S. (eds.) ESWC 2013. LNCS, vol. 7882, pp. 427–441. Springer, Heidelberg (2013)
7. Kuhn, T.: A Survey and Classification of Controlled Natural Languages. Computational Linguistics 40(1) (2014)
8. Lepsus, T., Langlais, P., Lapalme, G.: A corpus-based Approach to Weather Report Translation. Technical Report, University of Montréal, Canada (2004)
9. Mitamura, T., Nyberg, E.H.: Controlled English for knowledge-based MT: Experience with the KANT system. In: Proceedings of TMI 1995, pp. 158–172 (1995)
10. O'Brien, S., Roturier, J.: How portable are controlled language rules? A comparison of two empirical MT studies. In: Proceedings of MT Summit XI, pp. 345–352. European Association for Machine Translation (2007)
11. Pym, P.J.: Pre-editing and the use of simplified writing for MT: an engineer's experience of operating an MT system. In: Translating and the Computer 10: The Translation Environment 10 Years on, number 10, pp. 80–96. Aslib (1990)
12. Ranta, A.: Grammatical Framework: Programming with Multilingual Grammars. CSLI Publications, Stanford (2011)
13. Ruesch, M., Egloff, A., Gerber, M., Weiss, G., Winkler, K.: The software behind the interactive display of the Swiss avalanche bulletin. In: Proceedings ISSW 2013. International Snow Science Workshop, Grenoble, France, pp. 406–412. ANENA, IRSTEA, Météo-France (2013)
14. Ruffino, J.R.: Coping with machine translation. In: Lawson, V. (ed.) Practical Experience of Machine Translation, pp. 57–60. North-Holland Publishing Company (1982)
15. Schug, J.: Personal communication, Meteomedia, Gais, Switzerland (May 14, 2010)
16. Temnikova, I.: Text Complexity and Text Simplification in the Crisis Management Domain. Ph.D. thesis, University of Wolverhampton (2012)
17. Winkler, K., Bächtold, M., Gallorini, S., Niederer, U., Stucki, T., Pielmeier, C., Darms, G., Dürr, L., Techel, F., Zweifel, B.: Swiss avalanche bulletin: automated translation with a catalogue of phrases. In: Proceedings ISSW 2013. International Snow Science Workshop, Grenoble, France, pp. 437–441. ANENA, IRSTEA, Météo-France (2013)

Towards an Error Correction Memory to Enhance Technical Texts Authoring in LELIE

Juyeon Kang[1] and Patrick Saint-Dizier[2]

[1] Prometil
Toulouse, France
[2] IRIT - CNRS
Toulouse, France
stdizier@irit.fr, j.kang@prometil.com

Abstract. In this paper, we investigate and experiment the notion of error correction memory applied to error correction in technical texts. The main purpose is to induce relatively generic correction patterns associated with more contextual correction recommendations, based on previously memorized and analyzed corrections. The notion of error correction memory is developed within the framework of the LELIE project and illustrated on the case of fuzzy lexical items, which is a major problem in technical texts.

1 Introduction

Technical documents form a linguistic genre with specific linguistic constraints in terms of lexical realizations, including business or domain dependent aspects, grammar and style. These documents are designed to be easy to read and as efficient and unambiguous as possible for their users and readers. For that purpose, they tend to follow relatively strict controlled natural language principles concerning both their form and contents. Guidelines for writing in controlled languages have been elaborated in various sectors, they are summarized in e.g. (Alred 2012), (Umwalla 2004), (O'Brian 2003), (Weiss 2000), and (Wyner et al. 2010). Besides guidelines, the boilerplate technique is also used for simple texts or for requirement authoring.

Authoring principles and guidelines, in the everyday life of technical writers, are often only partly observed, for several reasons including workload and the large number of revisions made by several actors on a text. Table 1 below shows some major errors found by the LELIE system over 300 pages of technical documentation for companies A, B and C (kept anonymous) in spite of the strict guidelines they impose. These results show that there are still many errors of various types and space for correction strategies.

In the LELIE project (Barcellini et al. 2012), we developed a system that detects several types of errors in technical documents and produces **alerts**. The LELIE system makes local parses of technical texts in order to detect writing errors. Parses ranges from finding fuzzy terms to complex structures that must be revised (e.g. discourse structures, coordinations of NPs). In both cases,

B. Davis et al. (Eds.): CNL 2014, LNAI 8625, pp. 55–65, 2014.
© Springer International Publishing Switzerland 2014

it is necessary to develop some kind of 'local' grammar to recognize ill-formed constructions, but also to filter out others which are correct (e.g. fuzzy terms in business terms are correct).

The alerts produced by the LELIE system have been found useful by most technical writers that tested the system. However, to be really helpful to technical writers, it turns out that (1) false positives (about 30% of the alerts) must be filtered out and (2) help must be provided to technical writers under the form of correction patterns and recommendations whenever possible. Our on-going research aims at specifying, developing and testing several facets of an **error correction memory** system that would, after a period of observation of technical writers making corrections from the LELIE alerts, (1) memorize errors which are not or almost never corrected so that they are no longer displayed in texts in the future and (2) memorize corrections realized by writers and propose typical correction recommendations. Our approach is aimed at being very flexible w.r.t. the writer's practices. It is more flexible than systems such as RAT-RQA, Rubric, Attempto, Peng, or Rabbit which are based the recognition of fixed erroneous structures.

Table 1. Errors found in technical texts for companies A, B and C

error type	frequency / 1000 lines	A	B	C
fuzzy lexical items	66	44	89	49
modals in instructions	5	0	12	1
pronouns with unclear reference	22	4	48	2
negation	52	8	109	9
complex discourse structures	43	12	65	50
complex coordinations	19	30	10	17
heavy N+N or noun complements	46	58	62	15
passives	34	16	72	4
sentences too complex	108	16	221	24
incorrect references	13	33	22	2

In this paper, we develop elements of a method that shows how to construct (1) relatively generic **correction patterns** paired with (2) accurate **contextual correction recommendations**, based on previously memorized and analyzed corrections. The approach of a correction memory that helps technical writers by providing them with error corrections validated and made homogeneous over a whole team of technical writers, via discussion and mediation, seems to be new to the best of our knowledge.

This notion of error correction memory originates from the notion of translation memory, it is however substantially different in its principles and implementation. An in-depth analysis of memory-based language processing is developed (Daelemans et al. 2005) and implemented in the TiMBL software. This work develops several forms of statistical means to produce generalizations in syntax, semantics and morphology. It also warns against excessive forms of generalizations. (Buchholz, 2002) develops an insightful memory-based analysis on how grammatical constructions can be induced from samples. Memory-based systems are also used to resolve ambiguities, using notions such as analogies (Schriever et al. 1989). Finally, memory-based techniques are used in programming languages support systems to help programmers to resolve frequent errors.

2   The Case of Fuzzy Lexical Items

The LELIE system (features and performances are given in (Barcellini et al. 2012), (Saint-Dizier 2014)) detects several types of errors, lexical, syntactic and related to style. It also allows to specify business constraints such as controls on style and the use of business terms. The errors detected by LELIE are typical errors of technical texts (e.g. Table 1), they would not be errors in ordinary language. Error detection in LELIE depends on the discourse structure: for example modals are the norm in requirements but not in instructions. Titles allow deverbals which are not frequently admitted in instructions or warnings. The output of LELIE is the original text with annotations. LELIE is parameterized and offers several levels of alerts depending on the a priori error severity. LELIE and the experiments reported below are developed on the logic-based <TextCoop> platform (Saint-Dizier 2012). Lelie is fully implemented and is freely available.

Let us now focus in this short article on the case of fuzzy lexical items which is a major type of error, quite representative of what an error correction memory could be. Roughly, a fuzzy lexical item denotes a concept whose meaning, interpretation, or boundaries can vary considerably according to context, readers or conditions, instead of being fixed once and for all. It is important to note that (1) that it is difficult to precisely define and identify what a fuzzy lexical item is (to be contrasted in our context with vague and underspecified expressions, which involve different forms of corrections) and (2) that there are several categories of fuzzy lexical items. These categories include adverbs (manner, temporal, location, and modal adverbs), adjectives (*adapted, appropriate*) determiners (*some, a few*), prepositions (*near, around*), a few verbs (*minimize, increase*) and nouns. These categories are not homogeneous in terms of fuzziness, e.g. determiners and prepositions are always fuzzy. The degree of fuzziness is also quite different from one term to another in a category. Note that a verb such as *damaged* in *the mother card risks to be damaged* is not fuzzy but vague because the importance and the nature of the damage is unknown; *heat the probe to reach 500 degrees* is not fuzzy but underspecified because the means to heat the probe are not given: an adjunct is missing in this instruction.

The context in which a fuzzy lexical item is uttered may also have an influence on its severity level. For example 'progressively' used in a short action (*progressively close the water pipe*) or used in an action that has a substantial length (*progressively heat the probe till 300 degrees Celsius are reached*) may entail different severity levels because the application of 'progressively' may be more difficult to realize in the second case. This motivates the need to memorize the context of the error to establish an accurate error diagnosis.

In average, a fuzzy lexical item is found every 4 sentences in our corpus. In our test corpus, from 420 manually annotated fuzzy lexical items, LELIE has a detection precision of 88% with 11% of noise. Then, on a smaller experiment with two technical writers from the 'B' company, considering 120 different fuzzy lexical items used in different contexts, 36 have been judged not to be errors (30%): they are noise or minor problems. Among the other 84 errors, only 62 have been corrected. The remaining 22 have been judged problematic and very difficult to correct. It took between 2 and 10 minutes to correct each of the 62 errors, with an average of about 6 minutes per error. Correcting fuzzy lexical items indeed often requires domain documentation and expertise.

In our experimentation, the following questions, crucial to controlled natural language systems, have been considered:

- What are the strategies deployed by technical writers when they see the alerts? what do they think of the relevance of each alert? how do they feel about making a correction? How much they interact with each other ?
- Over large documents, how is it possible to produce stable and homogeneous corrections?
- How much of the sentence is modified, besides the fuzzy lexical item? Does the modification affect the sentence content?
- How difficult is a modification and what resources does this requires (e.g. external documentation, asking someone else)? How many corrections have effectively been done? How many are left pending and why?

3   A Method for the Definition of an Error Correction Memory

Our analysis is based on a corpus of technical texts coming from seven companies, kept anonymous at their request. Our corpus contains about 120 pages from 27 documents. The main features considered to validate our corpus are: (1) texts corresponding to various professional activities: product design, maintenance, production launch, specifications, regulations and requirements, (2) texts following various kinds of business style and format guidelines imposed by companies, (3) texts coming from various industrial areas: finance, telecommunications, transportation, energy, computer science, and chemistry.

The main principle is to observe technical writers when they make corrections from LELIE's alerts and to memorize any error with its final correction together with its precise context of utterance. The absence of a correction is also memorized. After a certain period of observation, there is sufficient material to develop the error correction memory. In addition, correctly realized utterances in the same context (i.e. without any alert) are also considered as a correction guide.

The main features and advantages of an error correction memory in the context of LELIE are:

- Corrections take into account the utterance context and the company's authoring practices,

- Corrections which are proposed after observation result from a consensus among technical writers in a group since an administrator (possibly via mediation) determines the best corrections to be kept given a context. These corrections are then proposed in future correction tasks in similar situations.
- Corrections are directly accessible to technical writers: as a result, a lot of time is saved; furthermore, corrections become homogeneous over the various documents of the company,
- Corrections reflect a certain know-how of the authoring habits and guidelines of a company, therefore they can be used to train novices.

This introduces a more dynamic and flexible view of implementing controlled natural language principles as suggested e.g. in (Ganier et al. 2007) than in standard authoring guidelines or boilerplates.

3.1   A Lexicon of Fuzzy Lexical Items

In the Lelie system, a lexicon has been implemented that contains the most common fuzzy lexical items found in our corpus (about 450 terms). Since some items are a priori more fuzzy than others, a mark, between 1 and 3 (3 being the worse case) has been assigned a priori. This mark is however not fixed, it may evolve depending on technical writers' behavior. For illustrative purposes, Table 2 below gives figures about some types of entries of our lexicon for English.

Table 2. Main fuzzy lexical classes

category	number of entries	a priori severity level
manner adverbs	130	2 to 3
temporal and location adverbs	107	in general 2
determiners	24	3
prepositions	31	2 to 3
verbs and modals	73	1 to 2
adjectives	87	in general 1

3.2   Memorizing Technical Writers' Behavior

An observation on how technical writers proceed was then carried out. The tests we made do not include any temporal or planning consideration (how much time it takes to make a correction, or how they organize the corrections) or any consideration concerning the means and the strategies used by technical writers. At this stage, we simply examine the correction results, which are stored in a database. At the moment, since no specific interface has been designed, the initial and the corrected texts are compared once all the corrections have been made. The protocol to memorize corrections is the following:

- for a new fuzzy lexical item that originates an alert, create a new entry in the database, include its category and a priori severity level,

- for each alert concerning this item, include it in its database entry with its context (see below) and the correction made by the technical writer. Indicate who made the correction (several writers often work on similar texts). Tag the term on which the alert is in the input text and tag the text portion that has been changed in the resulting sentence.
- If the initial sentence has not been corrected then it is memorized and no correction is entered.

The database is realized in Prolog as follows:

```
fuzzyitem([term], [category], [severity],
[[text fragment with alert, text after correction with tags,
ID of writer], ....] ).
```

For example:

```
fuzzyitem([progressively], [adverb], [3],
[[[<fuzzy>, progressively, </fuzzy>, heat, the, probe],
    [[heat, the, probe, <revised>, progressively,
            in, 5, seconds, </revised>]], [John] ] .... ]
```

3.3   Error Correction Memory Scenarios

Considering technical writers corrections, error correction memory scenarios include the following main situations, which have been developed a priori and intuitively before evaluating their operational adequacy:

1. A fuzzy lexical item that is **not corrected** over several similar cases, within a certain word context or in general, no longer originates an alert. We are evaluating at the moment a threshold (e.g. 5 not corrected alerts) before this decision can be validated by technical writers. The corresponding fuzzy lexical item in the LELIE lexicon becomes inactive for that context, e.g. in *to minimize fire alarms*, 'minimize' describes a general behavior, not something very specific, it is therefore no longer displayed as an error. Same situation for 'easy' in *a location that allows easy viewing during inspection.*

2. (2a) A fuzzy lexical item that is **replaced or complemented by a value, a set of values or an interval**, may originate, via generalizations, the development of correction patterns that require e.g. values or intervals. For example, from examples such as:
   progressively close the pipe → progressively close the pipe in 30 seconds.
   Progressively heat the probe → heat the probe progressively over a 2 to 4 mns period.
   The power must be reduced progressively to 65% to reach 180 knots → reduce the power to 65% with a reduction of 10% every 30 seconds to reach 180 knots.
   A correction pattern could be the association of progressively (to keep the manner and its continuous character) with a time interval, possibly complex, as in the third example:

progressively → *progressively [temporal indication, type: value, interval, ...].*
This pattern is composed of two facets: a relatively generic correction pattern
that suggests a revised formulation (e.g. the adverb followed by an interval
of values) and a **correction recommendation** that proposes, in context
and when relevant, one or more typical precise values for the subfield 'value'.
The pairing of these two levels generic / instantiation seems to be a good
compromise between adequacy and efficiency of the correction.

(2b) In parallel with generalizing over corrections, the above item can be
complemented by the **observation of correctly realized utterance with
the same context** (but no fuzzy term: e.g. *heat the probe in 2 to 4 mns*) via
a direct search in related texts. The idea is that errors are not systematic
and that it may be possible to find correct realizations that may be used
consistently with the corrections that have been observed.

3. A fuzzy lexical item that is simply **erased** in a certain context (probably
   because it is judged to be useless, of little relevance or redundant) originates
   a correction recommendation that specifies that it may not be necessary in
   that context. For example: *any new special conditions* → *any new conditions;
   proc. 690 used as a basic reference applicable to airborne* → *proc. 690 used
   as a reference....* In these examples, 'special' and 'basic' are fuzzy, but they
   have been judged not to convey a very heavy meaning, therefore they can
   be erased.

4. A fuzzy lexical item may be **replaced by another term or expression
   in context that is not fuzzy**, e.g. *aircraft used in normal operation* →
   *aircraft used with side winds below 35 kts and outside air temperature be-
   low 50 Celsius*, in that case the suggestion to revise 'normal' in context is
   memorized and then proposed in similar situations.

5. Finally a fuzzy lexical item may involve a complete rewriting of the sentence
   in which it occurs. This is the worst case, it should be avoided whenever
   possible because it often involves changes in the utterance meaning.

In a given domain, errors are very reccurent, they concern a small number of
fuzzy terms, but with a large diversity of contexts. A rough frequency indication
for each of these cases, based on 52 different fuzzy lexical items with 332 observed
situations can be summarized as follows:

Table 3. Correction situations distribution

case nb.	number of cases	rate (%)
1	60	18
2	154	46
3	44	13
4	46	14
5	28	9

3.4   Error Contexts

Let us now define the parameters of these scenarios, namely: (1) definition of contexts and (2) definition of generic patterns and specific correction recommendations. In our first experiment, **Contexts** are words which appear either before or after the fuzzy lexical item that characterize its context of utterance. In the case of fuzzy lexical items, a context is composed of nouns or noun compounds (frequent in technical texts) N_i, adjectives A_k and action verbs V_j. Our strategy is to first explore the simple case of a fixed number of terms to unambiguously characterize a context, independently of the fuzzy lexical item category and usage. In our expriment, the context is composed of (1) a main or head word which is the word to which the fuzzy item applies (e.g. 'fire alarms' in 'minimize fire alarms') and (2) additional words that appear either before or after the main one. The closest words in terms of word distance are considered.

In the context definition, morphological variants are included and close words (sisters) if an ontology exists. The approach has the advantage of not including any syntactic consideration. To evaluate the number of additional words which are needed in the context besides the head word, we constructed 42 contexts from 3 different texts composed of 2, 3, 4 and 5 additional words. We then asked technical writers to indicate from what number of additional words each context was stable, i.e. adding a new words does not change what it means or refers to. Over our small sample, results are the following:

Table 4. Size of context

number of additional words	stability from previous set
3	85%
4	92%
5	94%

From these observations, a context of 4 additional words (if these can be found in the utterance) and the main words is adopted.

3.5   Error Correction Patterns

Automatically defining **correction patterns** from the different sets of samples in the database via generalization(s) would be the most straightforward approach. However, we first want to evaluate the form and contents of patterns and recommendations that would be the most appropriate for efficiently correcting errors. The cooperation between correction patterns and correction recommendations needs to be investigated. By efficiently correcting errors, we mean adequacy w.r.t. (1) the error analysis and type of alert and (2) correction feasibility for the technical writer.

For this first experiment, correction patterns have been defined manually considering (1) the syntactic category of the fuzzy item and (2) the correction samples collected in the database. A pattern is viewed as a guide which requires the expertise of the technical writer. It is not imperative. Here are a few relevant and illustrative types of patterns, given in a readable form:

- **fuzzy determiners:** specification of an upper or a lower boundary (N) or an interval, e.g. pattern: [a few X] → [less than N X], [most X] → [more than N X]. Besides patterns, which are generic, the context may induce a correction recommendation for the value of X: depending on X and its usage (context) a value for X can be suggested, e.g. '12' in *take-off a few knots above V1* → *take-off less than 12 knots above V1*, with Context = main term: knots, additional: take-off, above V1.
- **temporal adverbs**, combined with an action verb, such as *frequently, regularly*: specification of a temporal value with an adequate quantifier, e.g.: [regularly Action] → [every Time Action], where Time is a variable that is instantiated on the basis of the context or the Action. An adverb such as *progressively* is associated with a Time interval when it modifies a durative verb: [progressively verb(durative)] → [progressively verb(durative) in Time], e.g. *progressively close the pipe in 10 seconds.* Time is suggested by the correction recommendation level.
- **manner adverbs**, such as *carefully* which do not have any direct measurable interpretation, the recommendation is (1) to produce a warning that describes the reasons of the care if there is a risk, or (2) to explain how to make the action in more detail, via a kind of 'zoom in', or (3) to simply skip the adverb in case it is not crucial. For example, [carefully Action] → [carefully Action Warning], e.g. *carefully plug-in the mother card* → *carefully plug-in the mother card otherwise you may damage the connectors.*
- **prepositions** such as *near, next to, around, about* require the specification of a value or an interval of values that depends on the context. A pattern is for example: [near noun(location)] → [less than Distance from noun(location)], where Distance depends on the context, e.g. *park near the gate* → *park less than 100 meters from the gate*. The variable Distance is contextual and constitutes the correction recommendation, making the pattern more precise.
- **adjectives** such as *acceptable, convenient, specific* as in *a specific procedure, a convenient programming language* can only be corrected via a short paraphrase of what the fuzzy adjective means. For example, *convenient* may be paraphrased by *that has debugging tools*. Such paraphrases can be suggested to technical writers from the corrections already observed and stored in the database that implements the error correction memory.

At the moment, 27 non-overlapping patterns have been defined to correct fuzzy lexical items. Some patterns refer to frequent errors, with stable corrections: they can be induced and validated after about 80 pages of corrected text. Others are less frequent and require much larger text volumes. Error correction recommendations are more difficult to stabilize because contexts may be very diverse. At the moment, (1) either a precise recommendation has emerged or has been found in correct texts and has been validated and is proposed or (2) the system simply keeps track of all the corrections made and displays them by decreasing frequency.

We are now defining a protocol to evaluate the adequacy of these patterns w.r.t. the document contents and their usability by technical writers. Adequacy is related to the linguistic and contents level: the principle is that the meaning of the corrected utterances must not be affected or in a very minimal way by the changes suggested by correction patterns. Usability means that the patterns and the correction recommendations that make them more precise can be understood and used by technical writers after a short training period and that they really use them in the long range, over several types of documents.

4   Perspectives

In this paper, we have explored the notion of error correction memory, which, paired with the LELIE system that detects specific errors of technical writing, allows both the detection and the correction of errors. Correction scenarios are based on an architecture that develops an error correction memory based on (1) generic correction patterns and (2) correction recommendations for elements in those patterns which are more contextual. Both levels are acquired from the observation of already realized corrections and correct texts. This approach is quite new, it needs an in-depth evaluation in terms of linguistic adequacy and usability for technical writers.

In parallel with fuzzy items, we are exploring other facets of an error correction memory for other major types of errors such as negation or complex sentences. For complex sentences there are situations which can be handled quite straightforwardly because they reflect a stable writing practice. For example, illustrations, exceptions, purposes or circumstances can be realized in one or more additional sentences instead of being inserted into the main one. For example, roughly, a pattern for purpose clause 'externalization' can be for a requirement: [X shall Y conj(purpose) Z] → [X shall Y. The goal is to Z]. We believe that a similar technique could be used for heavy sequences of N+N or noun complements and heavy sequences of coordination or relatives.

References

1. Alred, G.J., Charles, T.B., Walter, E.O.: Handbook of Technical Writing. St Martin's Press, New York (2012)
2. Barcellini, F., Albert, C., Saint-Dizier, P.: Risk Analysis and Prevention: LELIE, a Tool dedicated to Procedure and Requirement Authoring. LREC, Istanbul (2012)
3. Buchholz, S.: Memory-based grammatical relation finding, PhD, Tilburg (2002)
4. Daelemans, W., van Der Bosch, A.: Memory-Based Language Processing, Cambridge (2005)
5. Ganier, F., Barcenilla, J.: Considering users and the way they use procedural texts: some prerequisites for the design of appropriate documents. In: Alamargot, D., Terrier, P., Cellier, J.-M. (eds.) Improving the Production and Understanding of Written Documents in the Workplace. Elsevier Publishers (2007)

6. O'Brien, S.: Controlling Controlled English. An Analysis of Several Controlled Language Rule Sets. Dublin City University report (2003)
7. Saint-Dizier, P.: Processing Natural Language Arguments with the <TextCoop> Platform. Journal of Argumentation and Computation 3(2) (2012)
8. Saint-Dizier, P.: Challenges of Discourse Processing: the case of technical documents. Cambridge Scholars, UK (2014)
9. Schriver, K.A.: Evaluating text quality: The continuum from text-focused to reader-focused methods. IEEE Transactions on Professional Communication 32, 238–255 (1989)
10. Unwalla, M.: AECMA Simplified English (2004),
    http://www.techscribe.co.uk/ta/aecma-simplified-english.pdf
11. Weiss, E.H.: Writing remedies. Practical exercises for technical writing. Oryx Press (2000)
12. Van der Linden, K.: Speaking of Actions: choosing Rhetorical Status and Grammatical Form in Instructional Text Generation. PhD, Univ. of Colorado, USA (1993)
13. Wyner, A., et al.: On Controlled Natural Languages: Properties and Prospects (2010)

RuleCNL: A Controlled Natural Language for Business Rule Specifications

Paul Brillant Feuto Njonko[1], Sylviane Cardey[1], Peter Greenfield[1],
and Walid El Abed[2]

[1] Centre Tesnière - Équipe d'Accueil 2283
Université de Franche-Comté - UFR SLHS
30, rue Mégevand, 25030 Besançon Cedex, France
{paul.feuto_njonko,sylviane.cardey,peter.greenfield}@univ-fcomte.fr
[2] Global Data Excellence Ltd.
Geneva, Switzerland
walid.elabed@globaldataexcellence.com

Abstract. Business rules represent the primary means by which companies define their business, perform their actions in order to reach their objectives. Thus, they need to be expressed unambiguously to avoid inconsistencies between business stakeholders and formally in order to be machine-processed. A promising solution is the use of a controlled natural language (CNL) which is a good mediator between natural and formal languages. This paper presents RuleCNL, which is a CNL for defining business rules. Its core feature is the alignment of the business rule definition with the business vocabulary which ensures traceability and consistency with the business domain. The RuleCNL tool provides editors that assist end-users in the writing process and automatic mappings into the Semantics of Business Vocabulary and Business Rules (SBVR) standard. SBVR is grounded in first order logic and includes constructs called semantic formulations that structure the meaning of rules.

Keywords: Business Rule, Controlled Natural Language, Automatic Mapping, Semantics of Business Vocabulary and Business Rules.

1 Introduction

Nowadays, companies are facing much pressure due to competition and growth, which requires frequent adaptation of their business rules. However, for a couple of decades, business rules have been hard-coded in automated business processes, information systems and often inconsistently so. Thus, changing or modifying business rules inevitably requires software engineers' intervention because they are inaccessible to business experts (e.g. healthcare experts, finance experts, etc.) who understand the actual problem domain and are responsible for finding solutions. As a result, companies cannot keep pace with the changing business environment.

The business rule approach (BRA) has evolved over the years in order to solve the deficiency described above [5] [1]. It claims that all business rules should be

B. Davis et al. (Eds.): CNL 2014, LNAI 8625, pp. 66–77, 2014.

collected and explicitly represented in a centralized application called business rule management system (BRMS). Many formal business rule languages have been devised allowing companies to define their business rules explicitly and formally. However, since such rules have to be created and/or verified by domain experts who are mostly not familiar with formal notations, a promising solution is the use of a controlled natural language (CNL) that can serve as a front-end interface and provide automatic mappings into formal notations. Thus, this paper presents RuleCNL for expressing business rules. Its core feature is the alignment of the business rule definition with the business vocabulary which ensures traceability and consistency with the business domain. The underlying natural language (NL) in this paper is English but RuleCNL also works with French. The RuleCNL tool provides editors that assist end-users in the writing process and provides automatic mappings into the Semantics of Business Vocabulary and Business Rules (SBVR) standard. SBVR is grounded in first order logic and includes constructs called semantic formulations that structure the meaning of rules.

The rest of the paper is structured as follows: In Section 2, we introduce the notion of business rules and CNLs. Section 3 presents some related work on CNLs for business rules and in Section 4, we describe the RuleCNL in detail. Section 5 presents the RuleCNL tool and Section 6 the conclusions and future work.

2   Business Rules and Controlled Natural Languages

2.1   Business Rules

In the literature, we find numerous definitions of business rules. However the most used definition is given by the Business Rule Group (BRG) [2] as follows:

"a business rule is a statement that defines or constrains some aspect of the business. It is intended to assert business structure, or to control or influence the behavior of the business."

E.g. *A loan must be approved if its value is less than 10,000 Euros.*

One challenge with the BRA is to find the characteristics of a good business rule. Some workers [3] [4] have proposed a set of characteristics for a business rule statement to be deemed as good. Among them, we can cite that a business rule should be atomic, declarative, business related, consistent, unambiguous, etc.

In the context of the BRA [1] [5], many formal languages have been proposed by many vendors for business rules modeling. These languages have a well-defined syntax, an unambiguous semantics and support automated reasoning over rules. [6] provides a state of the art on business rule languages and concludes that most of them are hard to use for business people without training in formal methods, but are rather easy for software engineers. We contend that business rules should be expressed declaratively in NL sentences for the business audience. Thus, CNLs are good solutions for bridging the gap between natural and formal languages [7].

2.2   Controlled Natural Languages

CNLs are engineered subsets of natural languages whose grammars and vocabularies have been restricted in a systematic way in order to reduce both the ambiguity and complexity of full NLs (e.g. English, French, etc.) [8].

In general, CNLs fall into two broad categories: human-oriented CNLs and machine-oriented CNLs. Human-oriented CNLs are intended to improve the communication among people for specific purposes and the readability and comprehensibility of technical documentations. They have no formal semantics and are usually defined by informal guidelines [9]. Machine-oriented CNLs are designed to improve the communication between humans and computers. They are completely unambiguous and can be defined by formal grammars with a direct mapping to formal logic [9].

Machine-oriented CNLs can be used in various domains and applications such as CNL for knowledge representation (Attempto Controlled English [10], Processable English [11], Computer Processable Language [12], etc.), CNL for ontologies [13], CNL for semantic web [14], CNL for machine translation [15], CNL for business rules like RuleCNL as presented in this paper, etc.

3   Related Work

The idea of verbalizing rules that already exist in a formal representation [16] [17] has led the domain of business rules to become an interesting application of CNLs. Because business rules need to be approved and followed by people with no particular background in formal or logic representation, it is important to have an intuitive representation that CNLs can offer. There are some CNLs that have been defined for this particular problem area.

In the business context, the Object Management Group (OMG)[1] has published a standard called SBVR [20] which provides a means for describing the structure of the meaning of rules expressed in the natural language that business people use. However, SBVR is not itself a CNL so it is up to each SBVR-implementing language or notation to specify its formal mechanisms [19]. SBVR claims to be restricted to semantics leaving apart a key functionality of NLs, which is syntax. Thus, for various reasons, the SBVR standard did not include a normative specification of the language to be used by business people to express their vocabulary and rules.

SBVR-Structured-English (SE) [20] and RuleSpeak [21] are both defined in the SBVR specification as CNLs to express business rules in a restricted version of English. However, these CNLs are not languages per se, but rather a set of best practices for human speakers. They are defined informally by sets of guidelines based on experiences of best practice in rule systems [9]. They are not normative and have no formal grammar but can be mapped to the semantics formulation of the SBVR meta-model. They are not supported by any tooling and cannot be processed in a fully automatic way [18]. The syntax is achieved by

---

[1] http://www.omg.org/

text formatting and coloring, which could be used to aid understanding by the domain expert user. However, a CNL requires a formal definition of its syntax (the language's grammar), which can be used to support business users in the process of entering syntactically correct inputs. This limitation is avoided by our RuleCNL controlled natural language.

4   RuleCNL: A Controlled Natural Language for Business Rules Specifications

4.1   Introduction

In this section, we present our RuleCNL for expressing business rules. As mentioned in the introduction, its methodology is based on the alignment of the business rule definitions with the business vocabulary. Thus, business rules are semantically connected to the business domain and readily understandable by domain experts. The methodology is derived from the core idea of the BRA advocated by the BRG as follows: *"Rules build on facts, and facts build on concepts as expressed by terms."*[3]. In order to overcome the limitations highlighted in the previous section, we defined a formal grammar and therefore a parser that can be used for the syntax analysis of rules. The writing process of a business rule is fully supported by the consistency check imposed by the methodology. Its semantics is defined by automatic mappings into the SBVR semantic formulations. This enables a language-independent way of describing the semantic structure of rule statements and is grounded on a sound theoretical foundation of formal logic. Fig. 1 shows the general architecture of the RuleCNL.

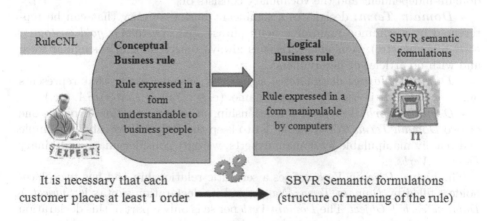

Fig. 1. General architecture of the RuleCNL

For the sake of readability, the SBVR semantic formulations of the example of the Fig. 1 is shown at the Fig. 2.

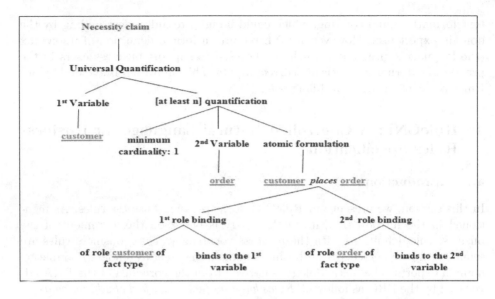

Fig. 2. SBVR semantic formulations of the rule shown in the Fig. 1

4.2   RuleCNL Vocabulary

The RuleCNL vocabulary represents the conceptual model of the business domain which defines a cohesive set of interconnected concepts (domain terms and their relations) that a given company uses in its talking or writing in the course of doing business. It is defined in a structured way by a business user and represents the knowledge that the company knows about itself. The RuleCNL is domain-independent and the vocabulary consists of:

- **Domain Term**: designates a significant business entity that can be represented by a common noun or a noun phrase. (e.g. *customer*, *gold customer*, *bank account*, etc.). A *Domain Term* is always represented in a singular form and with no articles or determiners.

- **Domain Name**: designates a significant business entity that represents only one thing. It is usually a proper name. (e.g. *France*, *Euro*, *USA*, etc.)

- **Domain Verb**: designates a relationship, situation, or action involving one or two *Domain Terms/Names*. In order to keep the RuleCNL vocabulary simple and readily manipulable by domain experts, we only consider unary and binary *Domain Verbs*.

The binary *Domain Verb* defines a semantic relationship and has two placeholders filled by *Domain Terms/Names* and its declaration syntax is *Subject + Domain Verb + Object*. The *Domain Verb* per se is only a part of this declaration syntax and has no meaning in isolation, but only within the relationship.

For instance: Let us consider the verb *to run*, it has different meanings within the following relationships:

<u>manager</u> *runs* <u>company</u>; <u>horse</u> *runs* <u>race</u>; <u>computer</u> *runs* <u>program</u>

A *Domain Verb* can be written both in active or passive form. (e.g. *customer places order*; *order is placed by customer*). The *Domain Verb* can be a linguistic verb (in this case, it is conjugated in the third-person singular) or a combination of a verb with some functional words (preposition, etc.).

The unary *Domain Verb* defines a characteristic or a state of a *Domain Term/Name* and its declaration syntax is *Subject + Domain Verb*. Its evaluation leads to a Boolean value. (e.g. *order shipped, customer smokes*)

There are no additional words or functional words in the relationship. This leads to a great flexibility and any constraints or restrictions will be added when defining business rules. The RuleCNL vocabulary includes some built-in relationships as comparison verbs (equality/inequality) that are not defined by domain users. Domain users define or import their vocabulary with the help of the vocabulary editor.

4.3   RuleCNL Grammar

RuleCNL grammar defines syntax rules and constrains for business rules. It assumes the existence of RuleCNL vocabulary and makes reference to *Domain Terms/Names* and *Domain Verbs* defined in the vocabulary. The general structure of a rule is: *Modality + Statement*. The *Modality* carries the sense of operational or structural rules. (e.g. *It is obligatory that, It is necessary that,* etc.). The *Statement* is a declarative sentence that regulates the structure of the rule. Its general pattern is a set of clauses which can go from a simple to a very complex/compound (linked by connectives and conditionals) structure. Each clause is always based on exactly one *Domain Verb* defined in the vocabulary. Subsequently, it combines many linguistic particles (function words, adverbs, etc.) in order to form a grammatically correct sentence. The grammar supports the use of complex noun phrases involving quantifications, instantiations and qualifications of *Domain Terms*. It also supports verb phrases involving verbs and prepositional phrases and can be used to define simple, compound and conditional sentence structures. The following examples show some statement structures. In these examples, *Domain Terms* are underlined; *Domain Verbs* are in italic font and other linguistic particles are in bold font.

Simple statement: It is based on only one clause.

E.g. each <u>customer</u> *places* **at least one** <u>order</u>

This statement follows the structure: *Subject + BinaryVerb + Object* and is based on the clause (*Domain Verb*) <u>customer</u> *places* <u>order</u>

Subject and *Object* are noun phrases with determiners which in this case are quantifiers (each, at least). In general, a determiner can also map to an article (a, an, the) or nothing. *Subject* and *Object* make reference to *Domain Terms* visible in the vocabulary. The *BinaryVerb* also makes reference to a *Domain*

Verb of the vocabulary. In this example, *Subject*, *Object* and *Domain Verb* are unqualified, and then the rule will be applied to any instance of the related *Domain Terms*. However, they can be qualified by other descriptive elements, such as their existence in a particular state, in order to specify the applicability of the rule with enough precision.

Compound/complex statement: this is recursively built from simpler statements through coordinators (and, or) and subordinators (if, who, that, which).

E.g. each <u>order</u> *is shipped* if the <u>customer</u> **who** *places* **the** <u>order</u> *is adult* **and** *holds* **an** <u>account</u> **that** *has* **a** <u>outstanding balance</u> **that** *is greater than* **0** This statement is based on the following *Domain Verbs*:

<u>order</u> *shipped*;
<u>customer</u> *adult*;
<u>customer</u> *places* <u>order</u>;
<u>customer</u> *holds* <u>account</u>;
<u>account</u> *has* <u>outstanding balance</u>
defined in the vocabulary
and the built-in comparison verb <u>quantity1</u> *is greater than* <u>quantity2</u>

4.4   Formalization of the Grammar

In order to build a parser for the RuleCNL, we have formalized our grammar rules using Extended Backus-Naur Form (EBNF) which is a notation for specifying context free grammars. The RuleCNL grammar consists of a set of rewriting rules used to restrict the syntax of rule statements. An excerpt of the general rule pattern is shown at Fig. 3. The vertical bar (|) is the disjunction and the comma character (,) is the conjunction. The symbol ( )+ means that at least one occurrence of rule element enclosed in the bracket must appear at that point.

```
Statement = (Base_Statement | Implication_Statement) ;
Implication_Statement = Consequent, "if", Antecedent ;
Consequent = Base_Statement;
Antecedent = Base_Statement;
Base_Statement = (Simple_Statement | Compound_Statement) ;
Compound_Statement = (Connector, Simple_Statement)+;
Connector = ("and" | "or");
Simple_Statement = Clause ;
Clause = (Binary_Clause | Unary_Clause) ;
Binary_Clause = (Subject, Binary_Verb, Object) ;
Unary_Clause = (Subject, Unary_Verb) ;
Subject = Noun_Phrase ;
Object = Noun_Phrase ;
Binary_Verb = Verb_Phrase ;
Unary_Verb = Verb_Phrase ;
```

Fig. 3. General rule pattern

4.5   RuleCNL Semantics

The RuleCNL semantics is defined by automatic mappings from RuleCNL rules to the SBVR semantic formulation (SF) description. SF is a part of the SBVR specification [20] that provides a means for describing the structure of the meaning of rules expressed in NL that business people use. SF is an abstract and language independent syntax to represent the meaning of a rule in a set of logic structures so that it can be machine processed. The full SBVR SF is not presented in this paper, but can be found in [20].

Fig. 4 shows the resulting SF in the XML form generated by the RuleCNL tool from the example of Rule 1 below

Rule 1: It is obligatory that the customer "John" places at least one order

```
<sbvr:rule  ruleID = "Rule1"/>
<sbvr:guidanceStatement xmi:id="stmt-formal" expression="stmt-formal-t" meaning="stmt-formal-p"/>
<sbvr:obligationFormulation xmi:id="obligation"/>
<sbvr:universalQuantification formulationEmbedsuniversalQuantification "the"/>
<sbvr:QuantificationIntroducesVariable  variableRangesOverConcept " ref= xmi:customer"/>
<sbvr:projectionIsOnVariable variable ="ref= xmi:customer/>
<sbvr:closedProjectionDefinesInstanceofNounConcept "John"/>
<sbvr:QuantificationScopesOverAtomicFormulation/>
<sbvr:atomicFormulation  atomicFormulationIsBasedOnBinaryFactType " ref= xmi:places"/>
 <sbvr:existentialQuantification formulationEmbedsexistentialQuantification "at_least" cardinality ="1"/>
<sbvr:QuantificationIntroducesVariable  variableRangesOverConcept " ref= xmi:order"/>
```

Fig. 4. Mapping of a RuleCNL rule to SBVR semantic formulation

Domain Terms are mapped to Noun concepts, determiners are mapped to quantifications, *Domain Names* are mapped to Individual concepts, *Domain Verbs* are mapped to Fact types, coordinators are mapped to logical operators, relative clauses are mapped to Projections, etc.

5   RuleCNL Tool

5.1   Implementation

An important feature of a reliable CNL is its tool support because one of the biggest problems (if not the biggest problem) of CNLs is the usability of a new CNL by end-users [9]. In reality, the limited expressiveness due to the restriction on vocabulary and grammar of CNLs leads to the difficulty in writing statements that comply with the imposed restriction. Writing syntactically correct statements without tool support is much more complicated because the user

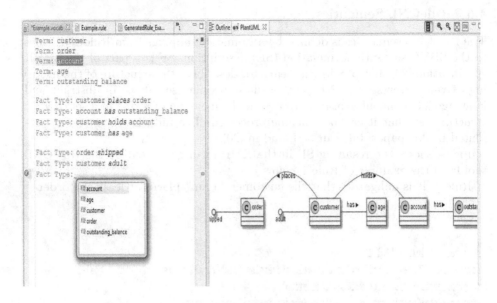

Fig. 5. Vocabulary editor

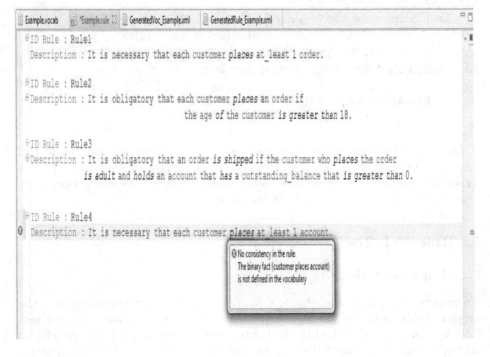

Fig. 6. Rule editor

needs to learn syntax restrictions, which are in many cases not trivial to explain. Thus, we have developed editors that make the writing process and the usability of the RuleCNL as effortless as possible. There are two editors: a vocabulary editor (Fig. 5) and a rule editor (Fig. 6).

The vocabulary editor assists the users to specify their vocabulary. It has two customized and dynamic views on the vocabulary in use: an outline view (tree-like) and a graphical view (UML-like notation). The rule editor assists the users to specify the business rule statements.

Both editors offer high level features such as auto-completion, error-handling, automatic highlighting and validation.

5.2   Evaluation

An ideal CNL should be effortless to learn and expressive enough to describe the domain problem. Thus, we have evaluated the RuleCNL with respect to its expressivity and comprehensibility. For the experiment, we collected about 50 business rules from real-life case studies of two companies written in the English and French languages. The first company operates in the domain of banking and insurance whereas the second is a parastatal. The evaluation was carried out by four end-users divided into two groups: group 1 is made up of two business experts with no background in formal notations of business rules and group 2 is made up of two business users with a background in information system technology. Our objective was twofold and consisted in finding how many business rules the RuleCNL could formalize in a natural way and how easy the users could understand the formalization. Thus, the evaluation's metrics are the expressiveness and the users comprehension of the RuleCNL. One could have also added the readability, but as RuleCNL is close to NL, statements written in RuleCNL are read in the same way as in the underlying NL. Table 1 shows the result of the experiment with the agreement of the two users of each group. This result is the same both for English and French.

Table 1. Evaluation

Measures/Users	Group 1	Group 2
Expressiveness	84%	84%
Comprehensibility	90%	100%

As we can see in the Table 1, the expressiveness is 84% for both groups. The remaining 16% was because of syntactic and semantic ambiguities in some rules. However, with more training, the users rephrased these rules so that the tool was able to formalize. Regarding the comprehensibility, group 1 confirmed that it understood 90% of the formalized rules in a natural way and group 2 understood all the rules. This result is not surprising because group 1 users do not have a background in formal notations. Thus, the 10% remaining consisted of complex rules, which require much constrains imposed by the grammar.

6 Conclusions and Future Work

The ultimate goal to bridge the gap between natural and formal languages has brought interesting research challenges in the area of CNL. In this paper, we have presented the RuleCNL which is a CNL for business rule specifications. The aim of RuleCNL is to help business experts formalize their business rules in a business-friendly way that can be understood by computers. The RuleCNL syntax is defined by a formal grammar and its semantics is defined by automatic mappings of RuleCNL rules to SBVR semantic formulations. The RuleCNL tool provides editors that assist end-users in the writing process. RuleCNL along with its tool have been evaluated with satisfactory results from business experts. We are currently improving the tool and extending evaluation to many other companies. The future work will be to go from the SBVR SF to some production rules for rule engines or software components.

References

1. Barbara, V.H.: Business Rules Applied: Building Better Systems Using the Business Rules Approach. John Wiley & Sons, Inc., New York (2001)
2. Business Rule Group, http://www.businessrulesgroup.org/defnbrg.shtml
3. Business Rule Approach, http://www.businessrulesgroup.org/bra.shtml
4. Tony, M.: Business Rules and Information Systems: Aligning IT with Business Goals. Addison-Wesley Professional (2002)
5. Ross, R.G.: Principles of the Business Rule Approach. Addison-Wesley Professional, USA (2003)
6. Lucie, B., Sophie, R., Bertrand, G., Stefan, L., Michael, S.: Report on State of the Art and Prospective Evolution of Formal Languages for Business Rules. Public Research Centre Henri Tudor, Luxembourg (2006)
7. Lévy, F., Nazarenko, A.: Formalization of Natural Language Regulations through SBVR Structured English (Tutorial). In: Morgenstern, L., Stefaneas, P., Lévy, F., Wyner, A., Paschke, A. (eds.) RuleML 2013. LNCS, vol. 8035, pp. 19–33. Springer, Heidelberg (2013)
8. Rolf, S.: Controlled Natural Languages for Knowledge Representation. In: COLING 2010 Proceedings of the 23rd International Conference on Computational Linguistics, pp. 1113–1121 (2010)
9. Kuhn, T.: Controlled English for Knowledge Representation. Doctoral thesis, Faculty of Economics, Business Administration and Information Technology of the University of Zurich (2010)
10. Fuchs, N.E., Kaljurand, K., Kuhn, T.: Attempto Controlled English for Knowledge Representation. In: Baroglio, C., Bonatti, P.A., Małuszyński, J., Marchiori, M., Polleres, A., Schaffert, S. (eds.) Reasoning Web. LNCS, vol. 5224, pp. 104–124. Springer, Heidelberg (2008)
11. White, C., Rolf, S.: An Update on PENG Light. In: Proceedings of ALTA 2009, pp. 80–88 (2009)
12. Clark, P., Harrison, P., Jenkins, T., Thompson, J., Wojcik, R.: Acquiring and Using World Knowledge using a Restricted Subset of English. In: The 18th International FLAIRS Conference (FLAIRS 2005) (2005)

13. Hart, G., Johnson, M., Dolbear, C.: Rabbit: Developing a Controlled Natural Language for authoring ontologies. In: Bechhofer, S., Hauswirth, M., Hoffmann, J., Koubarakis, M. (eds.) ESWC 2008. LNCS, vol. 5021, pp. 348–360. Springer, Heidelberg (2008)
14. Rolf, S.: Controlled Natural Language as Interface Language to the Semantic Web. In: 2nd Indian International Conference on Artificial Intelligence (IICAI 2005), Pune, India (2005)
15. Cardey, S.: Machine Translation of Controlled Languages for more Reliable Human Communication in Safety Critical Applications. In: Proceedings of the 12th International Symposium on Social Communication, Cuba, pp. 953–958 (2011)
16. Terry, H.: Business Rule Verbalization. In: Proceedings of the 3rd International Conference ISTA 2004, Germany. Lecture Notes in Informatics, vol. P-48, pp. 39–52 (2004)
17. Sergey, L., Gerd, W.: Verbalization of the REWERSE I1 Rule Markup Language. Deliverable I1-D6, REWERSE (September 2006)
18. Ruth, R.P.: An object-oriented approach to the translation between mof metaschemas application to the translation between UML and SBVR. Doctoral thesis, Polytechnic University of Catalonia, Barcelona (2009)
19. Anderson, K., Spreeuwenberg, S.: SBVR's Approach to Controlled Natural Language. In: Proceedings of the Workshop on Controlled Natural Language, Italy, pp. 155–169 (2009)
20. Semantics of Business Vocabulary and Business Rules (SBVR), v1.0. Object Management Group (2008), http://www.omg.org/spec/SBVR/1.0/
21. RuleSpeak, http://www.rulespeak.com/en/

Toward Verbalizing Ontologies in isiZulu

C. Maria Keet[1] and Langa Khumalo[2]

[1] Department of Computer Science, University of Cape Town, South Africa
mkeet@cs.uct.ac.za
[2] Linguistics Program, School of Arts, University of KwaZulu-Natal, South Africa
Khumalol@ukzn.ac.za

Abstract. IsiZulu is one of the eleven official languages of South Africa and roughly half the population can speak it. It is the first (home) language for over 10 million people in South Africa. Only a few computational resources exist for isiZulu and its related Nguni languages, yet the imperative for tool development exists. We focus on natural language generation, and the grammar options and preferences in particular, which will inform verbalization of knowledge representation languages and could contribute to machine translation. The verbalization pattern specification shows that the grammar rules are elaborate and there are several options of which one may have preference. We devised verbalization patterns for subsumption, basic disjointness, existential and universal quantification, and conjunction. This was evaluated in a survey among linguists and non-linguists. Some differences between linguists and non-linguists can be observed, with the former much more in agreement, and preferences depend on the overall structure of the sentence, such as singular for subsumption and plural in other cases.

1 Introduction

While South Africa has been celebrated as having the most enabling constitution in the protection and advancement of African languages and has had a stable democracy for two decades, there is a glaring limitation in the investment in computational linguistics and human language technologies (HLT). Although the imperative in HLT exist, there has been a lack of coordination in the development of HLT in African languages and a total lack of commitment from government and related institutions to invest and advance HLTs. However, the need for them is voiced; e.g., the "National Recordal System" project by the National Indigenous Knowledge Systems Office (NIKSO) of the South African Department of Science and Technology, and the University of KwaZulu-Natal, which recently made a ground-breaking introduction of mandatory isiZulu module for all its students, and is driving the development of scientific terminology in isiZulu. Visible advances are those that have been made by large companies such as Google and Microsoft, which have seen the localization of the user interfaces of their software, and an error-full Google Translate English-isiZulu. These and related endeavours require natural language generation and machine translation,

B. Davis et al. (Eds.): CNL 2014, LNAI 8625, pp. 78–89, 2014.

and multilingualism in knowledge representation (e.g., [7,1]) with end-user and domain expert interfaces, which do not exist.

Multilingual systems are being developed elsewhere (among many, [2,10,6]), and there are larger projects, such as Monnet (http://www.monnet-project.eu) for foundational aspects and Organic.Lingua (http://www.organic-lingua.eu) as applied project. As it appeared during our investigation, these advances are not immediately applicable with Nguni languages. Starting from the base and defining a grammar alike described in [12], is a rather daunting task, because the still important reference for linguistic work for isiZulu and Southern Bantu languages are old and outdated [4,5] and it will take many years to update. In the meantime, it is prudent to commence with the basics of NLG in such a way to serve linguists, computer scientists, and domain experts to show relevance. To this end, we take common language constructs of a practical logic language, such as the OWL 2 EL profile [14] that is also used for the SNOMED CT medical terminology, as a starting point to focus on CNL and verbalizations of logical theories. Concerning verbalizations for OWL ontologies, it is already known that there are variations for verbalizations within English [15] and good English-OWL systems exist, notably ACE [8] and SWAT [16]. The main results for logic-based conceptual models have been obtained also for monolingual English verbalizations [3], whereas limitations of the so-called template-based approach have been investigated for the multilingual setting [9].

Overall, this raises several questions: 1) what are the verbalization patterns for isiZulu for the basic constructs? 2) what does that entail for an implementation of a verbalization? 3) are there theoretical options one can choose from, like in other languages, and which ones are preferred among isiZulu speakers? We devised the high-level patterns for verbalization of subsumption, disjointness, existential and universal quantification, and conjunction. The grammar rules for isiZulu are complex to the extent that a template-based approach is not feasible for either of the constructs investigated. This is due to, mainly, the semantics of the noun that affects several other components in a sentence, and the highly agglutinative nature of isiZulu. This also means existing multilingual and verbalization models and infrastructures cannot be transposed and translated to the Nguni languages. There are verbalization options, and we have conducted a survey to elicit both linguist and non-linguist preferences to inform algorithm development for a NLG-focussed grammar engine.

The remainder of this paper is organised as follows. Section 2 describes some basic aspects of isiZulu and Section 3 summarizes the results of the verbalization patterns. The user evaluation is presented in Section 4. We discuss in Section 5 and conclude in Section 6.

2   Some Very Basic Aspects of isiZulu

IsiZulu is the most populous language in South Africa spoken as a first (home) language by about 23% of the over 50 million population. It has been documented for over a hundred and seventy years with the first booklet *Incwadi Yokuqala*

Yabafundayo having been produced in 1837. It is a Bantu language that belongs to the Nguni sub-group of languages comprising of isiXhosa, isiNdebele, siSwati and isiZulu. Bantu languages have characteristically agglutinating morphology, which makes them rich and complex in their structure and one of the salient features of isiZulu is the system of noun classes. Each noun in isiZulu belongs to a noun class. It is the noun class that controls the concordance of all words in a sentence whose structure is typically subject verb object (SVO), although variations are attested to exist. The isiZulu noun class prefixes, based on Meinhoff (1948), are mostly coupled in terms of singular/plural, and the classes are listed in Table 1.

The noun comprises of two formatives, the prefix and the stem; its structure is depicted in Fig. 1. Prefixes express number and indicate the class to which a particular noun belongs. A prefix can be characterized as full or incomplete. The full prefix has the augment (pre-prefix) followed by a prefix proper and an incomplete prefix only has the augment respectively illustrated as $i_{augment}$ $mi_{prefix\ proper}$ $fula_{stem}$ (*imifula* = rivers) and $o_{augment}$ $gogo_{stem}$ (*ogogo* = grandmothers). Because of the agglutinating nature of isiZulu, a number of prefixes are phonologically conditioned and yet others are homographs. As stated earlier, the morphology of the head noun in the subject position will then influence the agreement pattern as shown in following the example.

Amantombazana amadala adlala ibhola elimhlophe
ama-ntombazana **ama**-dala **a**-dlal-a   **i**-bhola **e-li**-mhlophe
6.-girls   **6.**big   **6.SUBJ**-play **5.**-ball **REL-5.**-white
'The big girls are playing with the white ball'

The abbreviations by convention refer, respectively, to SUBJ = subject, REL = relative and 6./5. = noun class 6 and 5 respectively. The complex agreement system presents interesting challenges in the development of computational technologies in isiZulu. The understanding of the basic morphological structure of isiZulu is crucial in the formulation of the technologies.

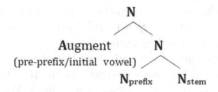

Fig. 1. The structure of isiZulu Nouns

3   Summary of the Relevant Grammar Rules

Due to space limitations, we describe the patterns and important features, not the analysis we have conducted and (elaborate) algorithms developed.

Table 1. Zulu noun classes, with examples. The noun class prefix of classes 1 and 3 is conditioned by the morphology of the stem to which it attaches: -*mu*- before monosyllabic stems and -*m*- for other stems. C: Noun class, AU: augment, PRE: prefix, NEG SC: negative subject concord, PRON: pronomial.

C	AU	PRE	Stem (example)	NEG SC	PRON	Meaning	Example	
1	u-	m(u)-	-fana	aka-	yena	humans and other	umfana	boy
2	a-	ba-	-fana	aba-	bona	animates	abafana	boys
1a	u-	-	-baba	aka-	yena	kinship terms and	ubaba	father
2a	o-	-	-baba	aba-	bona	proper names	obaba	fathers
3a	u-	-	-shizi	aka-	wona	nonhuman	ushizi	cheese
(2a)	o-	-	-shizi	aba-	bona		oshizi	cheeses
3	u-	m(u)-	-fula	awu-	wona	trees, plants, non-	umfula	river
4	i-	mi-	-fula	ayi-	yona	paired body parts	imifula	rivers
5	i-	(li)-	-gama	ali-	lona	fruits, paired body	igama	name
6	a-	ma-	-gama	awa-	wona	parts, natural phe-nomena	amagama	names
7	i-	si-	-hlalo	asi-	sona	inanimates and	isihlalo	chair
8	i-	zi-	-hlalo	azi-	zona	manner/style	izihlalo	chairs
9a	i-	-	-rabha	ayi-	yona	nonhuman	irabha	rubber
(6)	a-	ma-	-rabha	awa-	wona		amarabha	rubbers
9	i(n)-	-	-ja	ayi-	yona	animals	inja	dog
10	i-	zi(n)-	-ja	azi-	zona		izinja	dogs
11	u-	(lu)-	-thi	alu-	lona	inanimates and	uthi	stick
(10)	i-	zi(n)-	-thi	azi-	zona	long thin objects	izinthi	sticks
14	u-	bu-	-hle	abu-	bona	abstract nouns	ubuhle	beauty
15	u-	ku-	-cula	aku-	khona	infinitives	ukucula	to sing
17		ku-				locatives, remote/general		locative

The essence of possible verbalizations of the quantifiers and the main connectives are shown in Table 2. The enumerations in the isiZulu column indicate that its use *depends on the context*, which may be the category or noun class it applies to, or other aspects in the axiom before or after the symbol, and the additional "/" within an item refers to the fact that one of them has to be chosen, depending on the noun class or first letter of a term. The main variables that affect verbalization in isiZulu for the cases we investigated are the noun class of the name of the OWL class and category of the OWL class, whether the OWL class is an atomic class or a class expression, the quantifier used in the axiom, and the position of the OWL class in the axiom.

Subsumption. There are two different ways of carving up the nouns to determine which rules apply (Table 2), but for generating good verbalizations, the main issue is to choose between singular or plural with or without the universal quantification voiced, which are illustrated in (S1). One can construct a similar

Table 2. A few constructors, their typical verbalization in English, and the basic options in isiZulu; see text for further details

DL symbol	Sample verb. English	Sample verbalization in isiZulu (see text for additional rules)

⊑	... is a ...	Depends on what is on the rhs of ⊑ and desideratum:
		 A) semantic distinction
		    i) yi/ongu/uyi/ngu (living thing)
		    ii) iyi (non-living thing)
		 B) syntactic distinction
		    iii) ng (nouns commencing with a, o, or u)
		    iv) y (nouns commencing with i)

≡	1) ... is the same as ...
	 2) ... is equivalent to ...
		I. Depends on what is on the rhs of ≡:
		    i) ufana no/ne (person)
		    ii) ifana/lifana/afana (not a person)
		 II. Depends on grammatical number on lhs of ≡:
		    ii) yinto efanayo (singular)
		    ii) zifana ne/no/nezi (plural)

⊔	... or ...	1) ... okanye ... 2) ... noma ...

⊓	... and ...	Depends on the use of the ⊓:
		    i) ... na/ne/no ... (list of things)
		    ii) 1) ... futhi ... (connective)
		       2) ... kanye ... (connective)

¬	not ...	angi/akusiso/akusona/akubona/akulona/asibona/ akalona/akuyona

∃	1) some ...
	 2) there exists ...
	 3) at least one ...
		Depends on position in axiom:
		 I. quantified over class, depends on meaning of class:
		    i) kuno (living thing)
		    ii) kune (non-living thing)
		 II. includes relation (preposition issue omitted):
		    1) ... [concords]dwa
		    2) ... noma [copulative + concord]phi ...
		    3) thize

∀	1) for all ...
	 2) each ...
		Depends on what it is quantified over:
		 A) semantic distinction
		    i) wonke/bonke/sonke/zonke (living thing)
		    ii) onke/konke/lonke/yonke (non-living thing)
		 B) another semantic distinction
		    i) use noun class (see Table 1)

set of options for generic (S2) versus determinate that has an extra *u-* (S3), but the generic is preferred for the neutral setting of verbalizations.

(S1) MedicinalHerb ⊑ Plant

ikhambi ngumuthi	('medicinal herb <u>is a</u> plant')
amakhambi yimithi	('medicinal herbs <u>are</u> plants')
wonke amakhambi ngumuthi	('<u>all</u> medicinal herbs <u>are a</u> plant')

(S2) Giraffes $\sqsubseteq$ Animals
izindlulamithi yizilwane   ('giraffes <u>are</u> animals'; generic)
(S3) Cellphone $\sqsubseteq$ Phone
Umakhalekhukhwini uyifoni   ('cellphone <u>is a</u> phone'; determinate)

The possible patterns for subsumption can be, with N=noun taken from the name of the OWL class, and NC=noun class:

a. N_1 <copulative ng/y depending on first letter of N_2>N_2.
b. <plural of N_1> <copulative ng/y depending on first letter of plural of N_2><plural of N_2>.
c. <All-concord for NC_x>onke <plural of N_1, being of NC_x> <copulative ng/y depending on first letter of N_2>N_2.

If the subsumption is followed by negation, then the copulative is omitted, and also here there are options; e.g.:

(SN1) Cup $\sqsubseteq$ ¬Glass
indebe akuyona ingilazi   ('cup <u>not a</u> glass')
<u>zonke</u> izindebe aziyona ingilazi   ('<u>all</u> cups <u>not a</u> glass')

It combines the negative subject concord (NEG SC) of the noun class of the first noun (*aku-*) with the pronomial (PRON) of the noun class of second noun (*-yona*), where each noun class has its version (see Table 1). Thus, the pattern for negation in subsumption can be:

a. <N_1 of NC_x> <NEG SC of NC_x><PRON of NC_y> <N_2 of NC_y>.
b. <All-concord for NC_x>onke <plural N_1, being of NC_x> <NEG SC of NC_x><PRON of NC_y> <N_2 with NC_y>.

We leave the more complicated cases where the inclusion axiom can be used, like $\forall R.C \sqsubseteq \exists S.(D \sqcap E)$, for future work, as well as negation in other contexts.

Conjunction. The 'and' as enumeration uses *na*, which changes into (a + i =) *ne* or (a + u =) *no*, depending on the first letter of the noun and is then prefixed to the second noun that drops its first letter (always a vowel), illustrated in (C1). Conjunction as connective of clauses has two options, being *kanye* or *futhi*, illustrated in (C2).

(C1) Butter $\sqcap$ Milk
Ibhotela <u>no</u>bisi   (*Ibhotela + na + Ubisi*)
(C2) ... $\exists$has_filling.Cream $\sqcap$ $\exists$has_Icing.Lemon_flavour ...
...kune zigcwalisa ukhilimu <u>kanye</u> nezinye uqweqwe olunambitheka_ulamula...
...kune zigcwalisa ukhilimu <u>futhi</u> nezinye uqweqwe olunambitheka_ulamula...

While this distinction is a hassle in the algorithm, the pattern is straightforward.

Existential Quantification. Option I in Table 2 refers to cases like (E0), which are not used in OWL ontologies, but that has axioms of type (E1) instead, which include the object property (verb) and for which there are several verbalization options.

(E0) Ezulwini <u>kune</u> zingilosi   ('in heaven <u>there exist</u> angels')
(E1) Giraffe ⊑ ∃eats.Twig
izindlulamithi zindla izihlamvana   ('giraffes eat twigs')
yonke indlulamithi idla ihlamvana <u>elilodwa</u>   ('each giraffe eats <u>at least one</u> twig')
zonke izindlulamithi zidla ihlamvana <u>elilodwa</u>   ('all giraffes eat <u>at least one</u> twig')
yonke indlulamithi idla <u>noma yiliphi</u> ihlamvana   ('each giraffe eats <u>some</u> twig')
zonke izindlulamithi zidla <u>noma yiliphi</u> ihlamvana   ('all giraffes eat <u>some</u> twig')
yonke indlulamithi idla ihlamvana<u>thize</u>   ('each giraffe eats <u>some</u> twig')

Thus, we have a choice between 'at least' and 'some', and singular and plural. The quantification (underlined text) is more important than verb conjugation here. For the 'at least one', the relative concord (RC) is determined by the noun class system and is attached to the quantitative concord (QC) and then suffixed with the quantitative suffix *-dwa*; e.g.:

noun	NC	RC	QC	QSuffix	copulative	EP	ESuffix
ihlamvana ('twig')	class 5	*eli-*	*-lo-*	*-dwa*			
isifundo ('module')	class 7	*esi-*	*-so-*	*-dwa*			
ushizi ('cheese')	class 3a	*o-*	*-ye-*	*-dwa*			
ihlamvana ('twig')	class 5				*yi-*	*-li-*	*-phi*
isifundo ('module')	class 7				*yi-*	*-si-*	*-phi*
ushizi ('cheese')	class 3a				*ngu-*	*-mu-*	*-phi*

There are lookup tables for that, like for the NEG SC and PRON in Table 1. For the 'some' option, it is constructed as copulative + enumerative prefix (EP) + enumerative suffix *-phi*, as illustrated above, and the conjunction *noma* collocates with the enumerative to complete the meaning 'some among many'. Also for the EP, there is a fixed concord for each noun class. Note that the *-i*, respectively *-u*, are added to the copulative, because the copulative cannot be followed by a consonant that the EP begins with. Finally, the clitic *-thize*, which has a variant form *-thile*, is another expression of the complex morphology. The clitic *-thize* attaches to the noun, which is often the object of the sentence, to express the sense that it is some among many of those objects. In (E1) *inhlamvanathize* would thus mean any one of the twigs. This is a bit borderline in meaning, but it is the only candidate for being a template for that aspect. Overall, the following three core patterns are obtained:

a. <All-concord for NC_x>onke <pl. N_1, is in NC_x> <conjugated verb> <N_2 of NC_y> <RC for NC_y><QC for NC_y>dwa;

b. <All-concord for NC_x>onke <pl. N_1, is in NC_x> <conjugated verb> noma <copulative ng/y adjusted to first letter of N_2><EP of NC_y>phi <N_2>.

c. <All-concord for NC_x>onke <N_1 in NC_x> <conjugated verb> <N_2>thize;
Verb conjugation is a separate matter, which is complicated to encode, but there are no options to choose from in a verbalization. This is also the case for the prepositions in an OWL object property name (like the 'by' in 'taught by').

4   Experimental Evaluation of the Verbalisation Patterns

The aim of the experiment is to show how the understanding of the basic structure of isiZulu can illuminate the verbalization in isiZulu. While there are various options to verbalize something in isiZulu and these options involve elaborate algorithms, the experiment sought to find out possible preferences for the verbalization of the subsumption, disjointness, and quantifiers in isiZulu from the participants. The experiment also sought to find out if variations in verbalizations mattered to different participants, in particular between linguists and non-linguists.

4.1   Survey Design

The set up of the experiment was as follows.
1) Devise a set of sentences that tests the patterns introduced in Section 3, include a few cross-checks, add an 'either' and 'neither' option, and add auxiliary question, being whether the participant is a linguist or not, optional comments and optional contact email. The sentences will be generated through manual application of the patterns. For instance, Question 1 asks the participant to choose between:
   a) *Ikhambi ngumuthi*; subsumption singular
   b) *Amakhambi yimithi*; subsumption plural
   c) *Wonke amakhambi ngumuthi*; with 'for all' quantifier, and plural
   d) *Yomithathu*; either one of them
   e) *Awukho*; neither
   Question 2 asks the same thing as in Question 1, but then with the giraffes. Question 3 offers the option for disjointness singular versus plural and the universal quantification verbalised. Question 4: also asks about disjointness:
   a) *Ihebhivo alilona ikhanivo*; singular (disjointness of herbivore and carnivore)
   b) *Amahebhivo awalona ikhanivo*; plural
   c) *Yomibili*; either one of the two
   d) *Awukho*; neither
   Questions 5 to 9 deal with existential quantification: *-dwa* versus *noma ...-phi* (Question 5); Question 6 fixes *noma ...-phi* but varies by singular vs plural; Question 7 does the same but then with *-dwa*:
   a) *Sonke isifundo sifundiswa nguSolwazi oyedwa*; singular (each course is taught by at least one professor)
   b) *Zonke izifundo zifundiswa nguSolwazi oyedwa*; plural
   c) for "either" and d) "neither"
   Question 8 pits them against each other with singular *-dwa* vs singular *noma ...-phi* vs plural *noma ...-phi*, and Question 9 requires a choice on plural *noma ...-phi* versus *-thize*. Question 10 asks about *kanye* vs *futhi*. The complete list of sentences is included in the supplementary file, and the survey is left open for people to consider, accessible at `http://limesurvey.cs.ukzn.ac.za/` `index.php?sid=25965&lang=zu` (click the button labelled 'okulandelayo' to proceed to the main set of questions).

2) Set up the survey in the locally installed Limesurvey (`http://www.limesurvey.org`). This was chosen because we had localised the relevant part of it to isiZulu in a previous research activity and no other survey software has a localization to isiZulu. Thus, all questions, answer options, autotext, and error messages are in isiZulu.
3) Invite people via email to participate.
4) Collect data after 2.5 days, and analyse it using MS Excel.

4.2 Results and Discussion

Twenty five people were invited to participate in the survey, among them students, academics (linguists), and non-linguists, such as administrators. In the short time frame, this resulted in 12 completed responses, 5 of whom self-identified as linguist and 7 as non-linguist. The results are depicted in Table 3 and the (anonymised) excel file is accessible at `http://www.meteck.org/files/CNLsurvey.xls`, which also has a copy of the questions and the full answer options; here, question "1. isa" is Question 1 as described above in the materials and methods, and "sing." corresponds to the first option *Ikhambi ngumuthi*, "pl." to *Amakhambi yimithi* and so on, and likewise for Question 4's "sing." being the *Ihebhivo alilona ikhanivo* option listed above as answer option a).

The survey results show clear preferences from linguists. Question 1 option 1 is an overwhelming choice and this is predictable because of its simple structure. Once the nominal head takes the plural form there seems to be hesitation because of the complex agreement system; e.g., the answers given to Question 2 illustrates this. In the context of negation (Questions 3 and 4), the answers were mixed overall, though there was a slight preference among non-linguists for simple singular over simple plural (not present with the nominal head, Question 3). This agreement system was unavoidable for the 'forall-exists' pattern, and there the plural is preferred over singular (Questions 7 and 8). The *-phi* and *-thize* (Question 9) seem not to have any preferences, while *-dwa* has overwhelming preference over *-phi* (Question 5).

It is an attested fact that there are dialects of isiZulu and some of the salient differences in preferences may be based on dialect variation, which also may explain the dislike for either *kanye* or *futhi* (Question 10). It is important that the survey remains open to more participants and maybe a clearer pattern of preferences may emerge. A further option could be to ask them whether the generated sentence is understandable (rather than preference), which may become more relevant when larger axioms are going to be verbalised.

5 Discussion

For languages with isolating morphology such as English, verbalization templates are known to be a good way to explore with developing a controlled natural language, or may even suffice for a use case scenario, whereas this approach breaks down for languages with richer (agglutinating) morphology [9]. So far, we have not found a single case where a plain template without supporting encodings of the

Table 3. Survey results in percentage of votes (rounded) and disaggregated by linguist (Ling.) and non-linguist (Non-Ling.); sing.: singular; pl.: plural; all: ∀ verbalised; exists: with the 'forall-exists' construction; and: the connective-and

Question		Respondent			Question		Respondent		
		Ling.	Non-Ling.	Total			Ling.	Non-Ling.	Total
1. isa	sing.	80	0	33	6. exists	sing.+noma-phi	0	29	17
	pl.	0	43	25		pl.+noma-phi	0	0	0
	all+pl.	0	0	0		either	20	0	8
	either	20	57	42		neither	80	71	75
	neither	0	0	0					
2. isa	sing.	80	86	83	7. exists	sing.+-dwa	20	14	17
	pl.	0	0	0		pl.+-dwa	20	57	42
	all+pl.	0	0	0		either	40	0	17
	either	0	14	8		neither	20	29	25
	neither	20	0	8					
3. disj.	sing.	40	29	33	8. exists	sing.+-dwa	0	14	8
	all+pl.	0	14	8		sing.+noma-phi	20	0	8
	either	40	14	25		pl.+noma-phi	80	57	67
	neither	20	43	33		either	0	0	0
						neither	0	29	17
4. disj.	sing.	40	71	58	9. exists	pl.+noma-phi	40	14	25
	pl.	0	0	0		pl.+-thize	0	29	17
	either	20	0	8		either	40	43	42
	neither	40	29	33		neither	20	14	16
5. exists	pl.+-dwa	100	57	75	10. and	kanye	0	0	0
	pl.+noma-phi	0	14	8		futhi	0	14	8
	either	0	0	0		either	20	0	8
	neither	0	29	17		neither	80	86	83

grammar suffices. The survey revealed some general preferences, such as the *-dwa* option cf *-phi*, and dislikes (*futhi/kanye*), and a few notable differences in preference between linguists and non-linguists, such as the clear preference for the singular for subsumption and the unanimous preference for *-dwa* among the linguists, and overall the linguists agreed more on their preference compared to the non-linguists. The latter may have to do also with dialect and which region the isiZulu speaker is from.

These results can already feed into the development of a verbalization tool, but it requires more research before committing to invest in something like the Grammatical Framework (http://www.grammaticalframework.org/). This paper highlights motivational use cases for further investigation that benefits both isiZulu linguistics and ICT and we will continue to extend the algorithms, add more, and implement them so that domain experts can contribute and easily access, among others, the indigenous knowledge management knowledge base and scientific terminologies in isiZulu.

As an added benefit, these results may also inform translation algorithms and tools. Take, e.g., Google Translate English-isiZulu machine translation online and enter 'all giraffes eat some twig' is translated as *yonke izindlulamithi udle igatsha* (translation obtained 27-3-2014): *izindlulamithi* is in noun class 10, so it should be *zonke* instead of *yonke*, and it misses the quantifier. This can be correctly verbalised with the pattern described in Section 3. As an aside, and looking toward additional verbalization patterns: its *udle* (2nd or 3rd person singular, imperative) is also incorrect, because the verb has to be conjugated for the noun class of the first noun, which is 3rd person plural non-human (in casu, *zidla*). Another aspect to investigate in detail is the living/non-living thing distinction, which we avoided for subsumption by using a syntax-based short-cut. This may, or may not, work for other verbalization patterns.

Last, there are other issues to consider for verbalizing in isiZulu, such as multilingual ontologies and, possibly modifying the *Lemon* model [13] to cater for annotation with, at least, the noun class, and finding ways for semi-automated ontology translations to/from isiZulu.

6   Conclusions

Verbalizing formally represented knowledge in isiZulu requires a grammar engine even for the relatively basic language constructs, which are due to, mainly, the noun classes, the agglutinative nature of isiZulu, and contextual knowledge about the position of the symbol in the axiom. The salient features peculiar to isiZulu that pose a challenge are: i) the system of noun classes, ii) the system of complex agreement, iii) phonological conditioned copulatives, and iv) verb conjugation. We developed a set of possible verbalization patterns for simple subsumption, disjoint classes, quantification, and conjunction. The survey on verbalization pattern preference revealed a clear preference for the *-dwa* option, and more variation in preference by the non-linguists.

Algorithms have been developed for the verbalizations [11], which will be extended further for other larger axioms and verb conjugation, and implemented. It will also be useful to investigate comprehension of the generated sentences and the effect of dialect on preferences.

Acknowledgements.   We thank N. Hadebe, Y. Motloung, M. Ndaba, and S. Nkosi for their initial exploration into the topic.

References

1. Alberts, R., Fogwill, T., Keet, C.M.: Several required OWL features for indigenous knowledge management systems. In: Klinov, P., Horridge, M. (eds.) 7th Workshop on OWL: Experiences and Directions (OWLED 2012), Heraklion, Crete, Greece, May 27-28. CEUR-WS, vol. 849, 12 p. (2012)

2. Bosca, A., Dragoni, M., Francescomarino, C.D., Ghidini, C.: Collaborative management of multilingual ontologies. In: Buitelaar, P., Cimiano, P. (eds.) Towards the Multilingual Semantic Web. Springer (in press, 2014)
3. Curland, M., Halpin, T.: Model driven development with NORMA. In: Proceedings of the 40th International Conference on System Sciences (HICSS-40), los Alamitos, Hawaii, p. 286a. IEEE Computer Society (2007)
4. Doke, C.: Text Book of Zulu Grammar. Witwatersrand University Press (1927)
5. Doke, C.: Bantu Linguistic Terminology. Longman, Green and Co., London (1935)
6. Dongilli, P., Franconi, E.: An Intelligent Query Interface with Natural Language Support. In: Proceedings of the Nineteenth International Florida Artificial Intelligence Research Society Conference (FLAIRS 2006), Melbourne Beach, Florida, USA (May 2006)
7. Fogwill, T., Viviers, I., Engelbrecht, L., Krause, C., Alberts, R.: A software architecture for an indigenous knowledge management system. In: Indigenous Knowledge Technology Conference 2011, Windhoek, Namibia, November 2-4 (2011)
8. Fuchs, N.E., Kaljurand, K., Kuhn, T.: Discourse Representation Structures for ACE 6.6. Tech. Rep. ifi-2010.0010, Dept of Informatics, University of Zurich, Switzerland (2010)
9. Jarrar, M., Keet, C.M., Dongilli, P.: Multilingual verbalization of ORM conceptual models and axiomatized ontologies. Starlab technical report, Vrije Universiteit Brussel, Belgium (February 2006)
10. Kaljurand, K., Kuhn, T., Canedo, L.: Collaborative multilingual knowledge management based on controlled natural language. Semantic Web J. (2013) (submitted)
11. Keet, C., Khumalo, L.: Basics for a grammar engine to verbalize logical theories in isiZulu. In: Proceedings of the 8th International Web Rule Symposium (RuleML 2014), Prague, Czech Republic, August 18-20. LNCS. Springer (accepted, 2014)
12. Kuhn, T.: A principled approach to grammars for controlled natural languages and predictive editors. Journal of Logic, Language and Information 22(1), 33–70 (2013)
13. McCrae, J., de Cea, G.A., Buitelaar, P., Cimiano, P., Declerck, T., Gómez-Pérez, A., Gracia, J., Hollink, L., Montiel-Ponsoda, E., Spohr, D., Wunner, T.: The lemon cookbook. Technical report, Monnet Project (June 2012), http://www.lemon-model.net
14. Motik, B., Grau, B.C., Horrocks, I., Wu, Z., Fokoue, A., Lutz, C.: OWL 2 Web Ontology Language Profiles. W3C recommendation, W3C (October 27, 2009)
15. Schwitter, R., Kaljurand, K., Cregan, A., Dolbear, C., Hart, G.: A comparison of three controlled natural languages for OWL 1.1. In: Proceedings of OWL: Experiences and Directions (OWLED 2008 DC), Washington, DC, USA Metropolitan Area, April 1-2 (2008)
16. Third, A., Williams, S., Power, R.: OWL to English: a tool for generating organised easily-navigated hypertexts from ontologies. poster/demo paper. In: 10th International Semantic Web Conference (ISWC 2011), Bonn, Germany, October 23-27 (2011)

FrameNet CNL: A Knowledge Representation and Information Extraction Language

Guntis Barzdins

Institute of Mathematics and Computer Science, University of Latvia,
Rainis blvd. 29, Riga, LV-1459, Latvia
guntis.barzdins@lumii.lv

Abstract. The paper presents a FrameNet-based information extraction and knowledge representation framework, called FrameNet-CNL. The framework is used on natural language documents and represents the extracted knowledge in a tailor-made Frame-ontology from which unambiguous FrameNet-CNL paraphrase text can be generated automatically in multiple languages. This approach brings together the fields of information extraction and CNL, because a source text can be considered belonging to FrameNet-CNL, if information extraction parser produces the correct knowledge representation as a result. We describe a state-of-the-art information extraction parser used by a national news agency and speculate that FrameNet-CNL eventually could shape the natural language subset used for writing the newswire articles.

Keywords: knowledge representation, information extraction, FrameNet.

1   Introduction

In the collaborative report on the properties and prospects of Controlled Natural Languages (CNL) [7] a CNL was defined as an engineered subset of natural language such as English, which facilitates unambiguous human-human or human-machine communication. Among other uses of CNL it was stated that "CNLs appear to be particularly significant with respect to *information extraction* of and reasoning with the content of documents". As the ultimate goal of the CNL unambiguity and computability the report quoted the Leibnitz's ambition "… when there are disputes among persons, we could simply say: Let us calculate, without further ado, to see who is right".

Although mainstream effort in CNL community over past years has been devoted to defining restricted subsets of natural language, for which unambiguous translation to underlying formal representation is possible (e.g. Attempto Controlled English [4]), another research direction has focused on enhancing the CNL parsing and generation techniques to/from some Abstract Knowledge Representation (AKR) format (e.g. abstract grammar in Grammatical Framework [8]) to the point where the borderline between the natural language and CNL becomes blurred. The blurring occurs, when the *information extraction* parsers become capable of extracting the correct AKR not only from CNL, but also (to substantial degree) from the natural language (NL)

B. Davis et al. (Eds.): CNL 2014, LNAI 8625, pp. 90–101, 2014.
© Springer International Publishing Switzerland 2014

documents. Meanwhile, the Grammatical Framework based text generation systems have reached the level of maturity where AKR (the result of *information extraction*) can be verbalized in the grammatically correct target language such as English.

The above overview highlights the relationship between the CNL and *information extraction* fields as illustrated in Fig. 1. In this respect the traditional formal and unambiguous CNLs can be viewed as a subset of natural language for which *information extraction* achieves 100% accuracy. The overlap between these two fields has actually been present already over several years, because FrameNet [1] – the cornerstone theory for the wide coverage *information extraction* from natural language texts, has been well represented in the CNL community already [6, 9, 11].

The purpose of this paper is to further erode the borderline between the CNL and *information extraction* approaches by defining a FrameNet CNL (FN-CNL) which actually encompasses a powerful AKR paradigm (described in Section 3) along with real-world *information extraction* system (described in Section 4). The application of FN-CNL to the real-world *information extraction* has become possible only lately (for Latvian, at least) due to the recent advances [15] in the automatic frame-semantic parsing accuracy (described in Section 2.1).

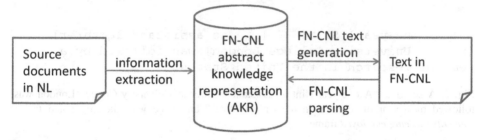

Fig. 1. The relationship between FN-CNL text, abstract knowledge representation (AKR) and information extraction from the natural language documents. This relationship is illustrated by a concrete example later in Fig. 7.

This paper is based on a practical *information extraction* system recently implemented for a national news agency in Latvia to extract and keep updated the biographical data profiles about publicly visible persons and organizations by automatically extracting this information from the multi-million document national newswire article archive. Although CNL was not the focus of the developed *information extraction* system, it was inspired by PAO-CNL [6], as both are based on the idea of merging FrameNet with Named Entity Linking (NEL) system to form the underlying AKR paradigm.

2   FrameNet

FrameNet[1] is a lexicographic database that describes word meanings based on the principles of frame semantics [1]. The central idea of frame semantics is that word

---

[1] http://framenet.icsi.berkeley.edu

meanings must be described in relation to semantic frames. Therefore, the frame and the lexical unit are the key components of FrameNet. A lexical unit is the combination of a lemma with a meaning – every new meaning of a word represents a new lexical unit. In FrameNet, each lexical unit is related to a semantic frame that it is said to evoke. The frame descriptions are coarse-grained and generalize over lexical variation. Although FrameNet addresses all parts-of-speech as frame evoking lexical units, its focus is on verbs for which the best coverage is provided.

The semantic frame describes a certain situation and the participants of that situation that are likely to be mentioned in the sentences where the evoking lexical unit (referred to as frame target) appears as illustrated by the example in Fig. 2. The semantic roles played by these participating entities are called frame elements (FE). All FrameNet frame elements are local to individual frames. This avoids the commitment to a small set of universal roles, whose specification has turned out to be controversial in the past [5]; to account for actual similarities between some frame elements (common FE such as *Time, Place*) in different frames English FrameNet includes also a rich set of frame to frame and FE to FE relations.

A [$_{Duration}$one-year] STINT^{Target} [$_{Position}$as assistant lecturer] [$_{Employer}$at University College London] was followed by a year of research in the United States.

Fig. 2. A sentence "A one-year stint as assistant lecturer at University College London was followed by a year of research in the United States" annotated with the *target* and *frame elements* of *Being employed* frame

Development of FrameNet resources for various languages is an ongoing activity [5] and in this paper Latvian and English FrameNet will be used for illustration.

2.1   Frame-Semantic Parsing

The benchmark methodology for frame-semantic parsing of natural language texts (sometimes regarded as automatic FrameNet Semantic Role Labelling to produce annotation as illustrated in Fig. 2) was set at SemEval-2007 [2] and specifically – by the best performing LTH system [3]. Further improvements to the methodology were implemented in the state-of-the-art SEMAFOR system [14].

To achieve high frame-semantic parsing accuracy for Latvian FrameNet (for which only a small training corpus is available) a new frame-semantic parser [15] based on the exhaustive search method nicknamed "C6.0" was developed[2]. The evaluation results for all mentioned frame-semantic parsers are shown in Table 1.

---

[2]   Available at http://c60.ailab.lv

Table 1. Evaluation results for frame target and frame element identification

	Target identification			FE identification		
	Preci-sion	Recall	F1	Precision	Recall	F1
LTH (English dataset SemEval'07)	66.2%	50.6%	57.3%	51.6%	35.4%	42.0%
SEMAFOR (English dataset SemEval'07)	69.7%	54.9%	61.4%	58.1%	38.8%	46.5%
C6.0 RuleSet (English dataset SemEval'07)	77.1%	53.7%	63.3%	47.3%	47.0%	47.1%
C6.0 RuleSet (Latvian Fra-meNet)	63.5%	62.7%	63.1%	65.9%	76.8%	70.9%

A distinct property of the C6.0 approach is that the frame-semantic parsing rules are generated in the human readable and editable format illustrated in Fig. 3 which is different from un-readable weight vectors of SVM or perceptron based machine learning algorithms used by the LTH and SEMAFOR frame-semantic parsing systems. The idea behind the exhaustive search based C6.0 algorithm was pioneered by the entropy based C4.5 and C5.0 decision-tree classification systems [16] which along with confidence limits for binomial distribution introduced also Laplace ratio $(n-m+1)/(n+2)$ for rule accuracy estimation, where n is the total number of training exemplars matched by the rule and m showing how many of them are false positives.

	Total matches	False positives	Laplace ratio
⌐, _, _, _, {retaliation.n.1, punish.v.1, revengeful.s.1}, _, _, _, _, ⌐	193	9	95%
⌐, _, _, {avenger, retaliated, retaliate, avenged}, _, _, _, _, _, _, ⌐	49	0	98%
⌐, MD, _, get, _, _, _, _, RB, ⌐	23	3	84%
⌐, JJ, _, sanction, _, _, _, _, _, ⌐	4	0	83%
⌐, _, _, sanction, _, NNS, _, _, IN, ⌐	5	1	71%
⌐, _, #NONE#, sanction, _, _, _, ';, _, ⌐	2	0	75%

Fig. 3. C6.0 generated RuleSet (feature value patterns) for target word identification of frame *Revenge*. The list of features appearing in the pattern are: LEMMA, POS, NER for the previous word; LEMMA, HYPERNYM, POS, NER for the current word; LEMMA, POS, NER for the next word.

The evaluation results in Table 1 show that C6.0 based English frame-semantic parser outperforms other state-of-the-art English frame-semantic parsers, while the C6.0 based Latvian frame-semantic parser performs on par with English parsers despite smaller FrameNet annotated training corpus of 4079 sentences available for Latvian compared to 139439 sentences available for English (Latvian and English comparison is only indicative due to differences in the annotation and evaluation methodologies and the reduced number of frames in the Latvian FrameNet – see Section 2.2).

Table 2. Target identification F1 scores for some FrameNet frames

Being born	100	Residence	67	Participation	40
Earnings and losses	89	Statement	67	Employment end	33
Death	80	Hiring	62	Product line	33
Education teaching	71	Membership	50	Lending	29
Being employed	70	Possession	48	Personal relationship	25
Change of leadership	67	People by vocation	46	Trial	18
Intentionally create	67	Win prize	45	People by origin	16

The further evaluation in Table 2 breaks down the target identification accuracy for some FrameNet frames. These results illustrate that the target identification accuracy varies widely between different frame types, meaning that the low-scoring frames might convey a broader concept (which can be expressed in more ways) and thus achieving high accuracy for these frames requires a larger training corpus. Meanwhile the overall target identification accuracy above 50% still results in rather efficient information extraction from the newswire archives, because the important information tends to be duplicated multiple times in news articles (see Fig. 6) thus improving the actually perceived recall rate.

2.2   "Latvian" FrameNet Subset

Latvian FrameNet was created for a practical information extraction system developed for a national news agency to automatically extract biographical data about publicly visible persons and organizations mentioned in the newswire articles.

A design decision was to use a reduced number of frames – although our methodology is applicable to any number of frames, we have selected just 26 Frames out of the 1019 frames in the English FrameNet version 1.5 (*Being born, People by age, Death, Personal relationship, Being named, Residence, Education teaching, People by vocation, People by origin, Being employed, Hiring, Employment end, Membership, Change of leadership, Giving, Intentionally create, Participation, Earnings and losses, Public procurement, Possession, Lending, Trial, Attack, Win prize, Statement, Product line*) which were of interest to the national news agency; this use-case dictated also adding or removal of some frame elements (arguments) – the resulting frames are shown in Fig. 4.

Although we refer to this FrameNet subset as a "Latvian FrameNet", the information extraction approach described in this paper is equally applicable also to the English FrameNet subset of the same 26 frames.

3   Knowledge Representation in FN-CNL

FrameNet itself does not define any AKR paradigm – it is merely a lexicographic annotation framework. To define an AKR framework FrameNet needs to be combined with an entity identification framework, often regarded as Named Entity Linking (NEL) to create a usable AKR framework or ontology shown in Fig. 4 (this is OWLGrEd[3] visualization of the actual OWL ontology[4] used for knowledge representation in Latvian FN-CNL). Optionally, this AKR framework can further be empowered by adding an explicit time dimension as described at the end of this section.

The novelty behind the AKR framework in Fig. 4 is explicit separation of classes denoting real-world entities (light boxes) and classes denoting temporal situations captured by FrameNet frames (dark boxes). This allows AKR framework in Fig. 4 to bridge the gap between the natural language and the traditional database schemas or OWL ontologies used in information systems. From the traditional database or OWL/RDF viewpoint our AKR ontology in Fig. 4 is "non-traditional", because natural language predicates there are encoded as n-ary relations by the dark FrameNet classes, rather than by binary object-properties typical for simplistic RDF subject-predicate-object triples. As an example of n-ary predicate occurring in natural language see in Fig. 2 predicate "stint" with three arguments: duration, position, and employer.

A simplification made in the AKR framework in Fig. 4 is that only Persons and Organizations have their own dedicated light-color classes – all other frame elements are encoded by OWL data-properties of string type. This was done by purpose, because the national news agency was interested only in profiles of persons and organizations, meaning that only individuals of these classes need to be mapped to the real-world entities (which is a difficult task, discussed in Section 4). The rest of frame element fillers remain identified by the text strings as they appear in the source text.

It shall be noted that the AKR framework in Fig. 4 does not define any constraints (such as cardinality constraints – e.g., a person can have only one mother). This observation means that there is an additional conversion and constraint-checking step necessary, if the data from the AKR framework in Fig. 4 needs to be used in a more traditional database enforcing constraints on the valid data sets.

Although not yet implemented in a practical information extraction system for Latvian FrameNet, there is a further refinement possible [6] for the above described AKR framework – adding the time dimension (see Fig. 5). Note that *Time* is the dominant frame element inherited in almost all frames (see Fig. 4). For most frames extracted from the newswire texts the time of their occurrence is either explicitly specified in the text and can be retrieved by frame-semantic parser as frame element *Time* or approximate time can be retrieved from the metadata of the newswire article publication date.

---

[3] http://owlgred.lumii.lv
[4] http://www.ltn.lv/~guntis/FrameNetLV.owl

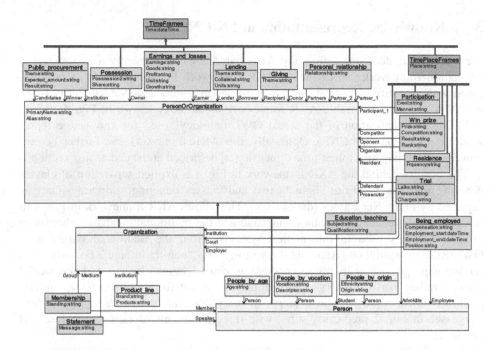

Fig. 4. OWLGrEd diagram of Latvian FrameNet frames (dark boxes) and Named Entity categories for frame element filler types (light boxes)

Having time associated with all extracted frames opens a possibility for avoiding seemingly contradictory facts in AKR database (e.g. *"F. Hollande is the president of France"* and *"N. Sarkozy is the president of France"*). Instead we can create a sequence of AKR database instances (e.g., one per every day of history) with each instance containing only the facts which were true on that particular day and thus make these AKR database instances internally non-contradictory (e.g. *"N. Sarkozy is the president of France"* (in DB instances for 2010) and *"F. Hollande is the president of France"* (in DB instances for 2013)). Inserting frames extracted from the text by the frame-semantic parser into the proper AKR database instance (or sequence of instances) is not an easy task [6, 10], as some frames describe an instantaneous event (e.g. frame *Attack*) while other frames describe a state which is true over prolonged period of time (e.g. frame *Being employed*). Nevertheless, resolving the time dimension (and for some sorts of tasks – also spatial movement dimension, see slides[5] from [6]) would extend the FN-CNL AKR capability to cover more of newswire text content.

---

[5] Animation on Slide 22 at http://www.semti-kamols.lv/doc_upl/polysemy.pdf

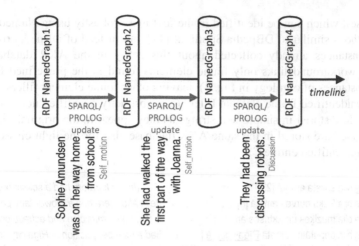

Fig. 5. Implementation of explicit time dimension as a sequence of AKR database copies representing the state of the world at the sequential time moments. The timeline example refers to the story illustrated in Fig. 7.

Implementation of the time dimension in the AKR framework resolves the ontology (database) versioning problem – a typical problem in simplistic ontologies or information systems loosing historic data when up-to-date information is entered (e.g. entering *"F. Hollande is the president of France"* deletes historic data *"N. Sarkozy is the president of France"*). Cross Document Coreference resolution systems (CDC, discussed in Section 4) are a good example where such historic data is useful for disambiguating entities in the documents from different time periods.

4   Information Extraction with FN-CNL

The increasing accuracy of frame-semantic parsing (discussed in Section 2.1) enables streamlining of information extraction task from natural language texts, such as newswire articles. Essentially the goal of such information extraction is populating the AKR ontology shown in Fig.4 with instance data retrieved from the source text. To this goal, frame-semantic parser (producing instances for the blue boxes in Fig. 4) has to be combined with Cross Document Coreference (CDC) techniques [13] to automatically determine which mentions in the text refer to the same real-world entity (instances for the yellow boxes in Fig. 4).

We have implemented such integrated information extraction system and populated it with data from approximately 1 million newswire articles. From the practical standpoint it turned out that the bottleneck of the approach is Named Entity discovery and linking accuracy – even at estimated 80% CDC accuracy it too often merged together different real-world entities with similar names or did not link together alternative spellings for the same entity, making the overall results unusable. To mitigate the problem, we deflected to the use of a predefined list of manually disambiguated well-known person and organization entities with their canonical names and commonly used aliases, which can be identified in the text more robustly using Named Entity Linking methods similar to DBpedia Spotlight [12], but instead of DBpedia rooted in the frame instances already collected about this entity in the AKR database. Of course, this workaround links only frame elements found in the predefined list (the light class instances of ontology in Fig. 4), leaving other frame element fillers unidentified. The unidentified frame element fillers (e.g. abstractly quantified nouns or plurals) are therefore stored in simple text strings as they appear in the original sentences (technically they are stored in the same AKR database also for the light classes, only tagged as "unidentified entities").

leva Akuratere bija solista amatā [23]   (leva Akuratere had a soloist position)
leva Akuratere bija Puķu burves amatā [8]   (leva Akuratere had a Flower fairy position)
leva Akuratere bija mūziķes un aktrises amatā [5]   (... had a musician and actress position)
leva Akuratere bija deputātes amatā Rīgas domē [(... had a member position in Riga city council)
leva Akuratere bija solista amatā Koncertuzvedumā [4]   (... had a soloist position in a Concert)
leva Akuratere bija dziedātājas amatā [3]   (... had a singer position)
leva Akuratere bija triju Zvaigžņu ordeņa virsnieka amatā Latvijā [3] (...had an Honor position in Latvia)

Fig. 6. A fragment of the automatically generated person profile (FN-CNL verbalization of *Being employed* frame). Linked Named Entities are underlined and the counts of found duplicates [in brackets] indicate the confidence level.

This mixed approach allows for creating a convenient user interface, where instance data from the AKR database in Fig. 4 is verbalized in FN-CNL using a light version of [11] producing simple FN-CNL sentences as illustrated in Fig. 6 which further can be arranged in the Curriculum Vitae like document.

5   FrameNet Controlled Natural Language (FN-CNL)

FN-CNL was inspired by PAO-CNL described in [6]. As illustrated in Fig. 1, FN-CNL is a verbalization of the knowledge representation database content (all or partial) by means of some FrameNet verbalization framework, such as [11].

We have implemented FN-CNL verbalization for AKR of 26 frames in Latvian FrameNet and also tested that frame-semantic parsing on this FN-CNL output achieves close to 100% accuracy (which can further be improved by hand-editing human-editable C6.0 generated frame-semantic parsing rules illustrated in Fig. 3). FN-CNL verbalization examples can potentially be used for learning unambiguous FN-CNL by human writers.

In general FN-CNL is not restricted to 26 frames of Latvian FrameNet – FN-CNL can be based on any set of frames of interest in the particular application domain thus making it adaptable to cover other linguistic or semantic domains like those currently addressed by ACE or other CNLs.   Fig. 7 illustrates FN-CNL on the example of first sentences from the J.Gaardner's novel "Sophie's World" which is often used in multilingual NLP research[6]. On left is shown information extraction from the natural language resulting into AKR in the columns labeled "Object" and "FN Events". The columns on the right illustrate multilingual FN-CNL verbalization of the AKR in English and in Latvian (effectively a more formal paraphrase of the original natural language text). The paraphrase highlights the time dimension present in this example, which can be captured[7] in the knowledge representation approach illustrated in Fig. 5.

NL text	Objects	FN Events	EN Paraphrase	LV Paraphrase
Sophie Amundsen was on her way home from school.	X1:Sophie Amundsen; X72:home; X73:school; X3:way;	E1:Self_motion(self_mover:X1; source:X73; goal:X72; path:X3)	E1:Sophie Amundsen moved from school to home.	E1:Sofija Amundsena pārvietojās no skolas uz mājām
She had walked the first part of the way with Joanna.	X4: the first part of X3; X5:Joanna;	E2: Self_motion(self_mover:X1; path:X4; co_theme:X5; time:during E1)	E2:During E1 the first part of the way Sophie Amundsen walked with Joanna.	E2: E1 laikā ceļa pirmo pusi Sofija Amundsena gāja kopā ar Jūrunu.
They had been discussing robots.	X6: robots;	E3: Discussion(interlocutors: X1,X5; topic:X6; time:during E2)	E3:During E2 Sophie Amundsen and Joanna discussed robots.	E3: E2 laikā Sofija Amundsena un Jūruna apsprieda robotus.
Joanna thought		E4:Opinion(cognizer:X5; opinion:E5; time:during E3)	E4:During E3 Joanna stated E5.	E4: E3 laikā Jūruna apgalvoja E5.
the human brain was like an advanced computer.	X7:the human brain; X8: an advanced computer;	E5: Similarity(entity1:X7; entity2:X8)	E5:The human brain is similar to an advanced computer.	E5: Cilvēka smadzenes ir līdzīgas sarežģītam datoram.

Fig. 7. A FN-CNL information extraction example on the left and FN-CNL verbalization examples in English and in Latvian on the right. The columns in the middle illustrate the abstract knowledge representation.

6   Conclusions

We have illustrated the mutually enriching relationship between the information extraction and CNL domains and described a complete natural language information extraction framework based on FN-CNL and AKR. The framework is implemented in a news agency in Latvia where it automatically extracts the profiles of public figures and organizations from newswire articles archive. As for future research we are looking into possibilities to go beyond the information extraction from the natural lan-

---

[6] http://www.language-archives.org/item/oai:tekstlab.uio.no:N10394
[7] See full example in http://attempto.ifi.uzh.ch/site/cnl2012/slides/gruzitisetal_framenet.pdf

guage texts and abstract knowledge representation (AKR) towards extracting the abstract meaning representation (AMR) [17] of the entire natural language sentences.

It is interesting to note that when the information extraction frame-semantic parser is used by the national news agency, it inevitably becomes a "national parser", because the news agency uses it to evaluate the quality of articles – how high or low information extraction scores the writing of the particular journalist achieves. This stimulates editors to avoid highly ambiguous phrases in their writing and thus might be one of the first cases where a CNL starts affecting the written natural language use on the national scale.

Acknowledgement. This research was partially supported by the Project Nr.2DP/2.1.1.1.0/13/APIA/VIAA/014 (ERAF) "Identification of relations in newswire texts and graph visualization of the extracted relation database" under contract Nr. 1/5-2013, LU MII Nr. 3-27.3-5-2013.

References

1. Fillmore, C.J., Johnson, C.R., Petruck, M.R.L.: Background to FrameNet. International Journal of Lexicography 16, 235–250 (2003)
2. Baker, C., Ellsworth, M., Erk, K.: SemEval-2007 task 19: Frame semantic structure extraction. In: Proceedings of SemEval-2007: 4th International Workshop on Semantic Evaluations, Prague, pp. 99–104 (2007)
3. Johansson, R., Nugues, P.: LTH: semantic structure extraction using nonprojective dependency trees. In: Proceedings of SemEval-2007: 4th International Workshop on Semantic Evaluations, Prague, pp. 227–230 (2007)
4. Fuchs, N.E., Kaljurand, K., Kuhn, T.: Attempto Controlled English for Knowledge Representation. In: Baroglio, C., Bonatti, P.A., Małuszyński, J., Marchiori, M., Polleres, A., Schaffert, S. (eds.) Reasoning Web. LNCS, vol. 5224, pp. 104–124. Springer, Heidelberg (2008)
5. Burchardt, A., et al.: Using FrameNet for the semantic analysis of German: Annotation, representation, and automation. In: Boas, H.C. (ed.) Multilingual FrameNets in Computational Lexicography: Methods and Applications. Mouton de Gruyter, Berlin (2009)
6. Gruzitis, N., Barzdins, G.: Polysemy in Controlled Natural Language Texts. In: Fuchs, N.E. (ed.) CNL 2009 Workshop. LNCS (LNAI), vol. 5972, pp. 102–120. Springer, Heidelberg (2010)
7. Wyner, A., et al.: On Controlled Natural Languages: Properties and Prospects. In: Fuchs, N.E. (ed.) CNL 2009 Workshop. LNCS (LNAI), vol. 5972, pp. 281–289. Springer, Heidelberg (2010)
8. Angelov, K., Ranta, A.: Implementing controlled languages in GF. In: Fuchs, N.E. (ed.) CNL 2009 Workshop. LNCS (LNAI), vol. 5972, pp. 82–101. Springer, Heidelberg (2010)
9. Dannells, D.: Applying semantic frame theory to automate natural language template generation from ontology statements. In: Proceedings of the 6th International Natural Language Generation Conference, pp. 179–183. ACM (2010)
10. Murray, W., Singliar, T.: Spatiotemporal Extensions to a Controlled Natural Language. In: Kuhn, T., Fuchs, N.E. (eds.) CNL 2012 Workshop. LNCS (LNAI), vol. 7427, pp. 61–78. Springer, Heidelberg (2012)

11. Gruzitis, N., Paikens, P., Barzdins, G.: FrameNet Resource Grammar Library for GF. In: Kuhn, T., Fuchs, N.E. (eds.) CNL 2012 Workshop. LNCS (LNAI), vol. 7427, pp. 121–137. Springer, Heidelberg (2012)
12. Daiber, J., Jakob, M., Hokamp, C., Mendes, P.N.: Improving efficiency and accuracy in multilingual entity extraction. In: Proceedings of the 9th International Conference on Semantic Systems, pp. 121–124. ACM (2013)
13. Wick, M., Singh, S., Pandya, H., McCallum, A.: A Joint Model for Discovering and Linking Entities. In: Proceedings of the 2013 Workshop on Automated Knowledge Base Construction, pp. 67–72. ACM (2013)
14. Das, D., Chen, D., Martins, A.F.T., Schneider, N., Smith, N.A.: Frame-Semantic Parsing. Computational Linguistics 40(1), 9–56 (2014)
15. Barzdins, G., Gosko, D., Rituma, L., Paikens, P.: Using C5.0 and Exhaustive Search for Boosting Frame-Semantic Parsing Accuracy. In: Proceedings of the 9th Language Resources and Evaluation Conference (LREC), Reykjavik, pp. 4476–4482 (2014)
16. Quinlan, J.R.: C4.5: Programs for Machine Learning. Morgan Kaufmann Publishers (1993)
17. Banarescu, L., Bonial, C., Cai, S., Georgescu, M., Griffitt, K., Hermjakob, U., Knight, K., Koehn, P., Palmer, M., Schneider, N.: Abstract Meaning Representation for Sembanking. In: Proc. Linguistic Annotation Workshop (2013)

INAUT, a Controlled Language for the French Coast Pilot Books *Instructions nautiques*

Yannis Haralambous, Julie Sauvage-Vincent, and John Puentes

Institut Mines-Télécom, Télécom Bretagne & UMR CNRS 6285 Lab-STICC
Technopôle Brest Iroise CS 83818, 29238 Brest Cedex 3, France

Abstract. We describe INAUT, a controlled natural language dedicated to collaborative update of a knowledge base on maritime navigation and to automatic generation of coast pilot books (*Instructions nautiques*) of the French National Hydrographic and Oceanographic Service SHOM. INAUT is based on French language and abundantly uses georeferenced entities. After describing the structure of the overall system, giving details on the language and on its generation, and discussing the three major applications of INAUT (document production, interaction with ENCs and collaborative updates of the knowledge base), we conclude with future extensions and open problems.

Introduction

Instructions nautiques is the name of a nautical book series [5] published by the French Marine Hydrographic and Oceanographic Service (SHOM). They are the French counterpart of the *United States Coast Pilot* [3], published by the United States National Oceanic and Atmospheric Administration's Office of Coast Survey, and of the British Admiralty Sailing Directions [7] published by the United Kingdom Hydrographic Office.

These publications aim to supplement charts (both paper ones and ENCs = Electronic Nautical Charts), in the sense that they provide the mariner with supplemental information not in the chart.

Information for the *Instructions nautiques* is provided by survey vessels, port officers, maritime officers and mariners in general. In some cases, it may require immediate update, for example to notify a shipwreck or some important change of the navigation conditions.

The SHOM is building a knowledge base that will cover both ENCs and nautical instructions. This knowledge base will communicate with ENCs and navigation equipment and, since updates can be frequent, the *Instructions nautiques* will have to be generated on-the-fly by the knowledge base.

To summarize, we have two constraints:

1. the information contained in the knowledge base, has to be easily updatable by people not necessarily proficient in the ontology formalism;
2. the *Instructions nautiques*, or at least part of them, have to be automatically generated out of the knowledge base.

B. Davis et al. (Eds.): CNL 2014, LNAI 8625, pp. 102–111, 2014.

To fulfill constraint 1, we have built INAUT, a controlled language based on French natural language, and dedicated to the population and update of the SHOM knowledge base. Contraint 2 is fulfilled by generation of texts in INAUT out of the knowledge base. In fact, the texts generated will be in a more "literary" and concise version of the language, called LitINAUT (= Literary INAUT, §4) that will bring them closer to legacy human author production.

To our knowledge, INAUT is the first maritime CNL[1].

In the following, we present our model of the *Instructions nautiques* (§1), the SHOM knowledge base (§2), the controlled language (§3) and its generation (§4), the main operations (interaction with ENCs (§5) and collaborative updates of the knowledge base (§6)) as well as future extensions and open problems (§7).

1   Modelling the *Instructions nautiques*

We model the *Instructions nautiques* as a set of three graphs $(\mathbf{S}, \mathbf{G}, \mathbf{K})$: the *hierarchical structure of the document* $\mathbf{S}$, the *geographic areas graph* $\mathbf{G}$ and the *SHOM knowledge base* $\mathbf{K}$ (see §2). Between these graphs we have two functions: g which maps some nodes of $\mathbf{S}$ and of $\mathbf{K}$ (those that are goereferenced) to nodes of $\mathbf{G}$, and κ that maps leaf nodes of $\mathbf{S}$ to subgraphs of $\mathbf{K}$. Furthermore, we have a set $\mathbf{T}$ of *titles of hierarchical subdivisions*, a set $\mathbf{A}$ of *geopolygons*, and functions τ and α mapping nodes of $\mathbf{S}$ (resp. $\mathbf{G}$) to $\mathbf{T}$ (resp. $\mathbf{A}$). Finally, there is a set $\mathbf{M}$ of functions $\{\mu\}$ defined both as $\mathbf{T} \to \mathbf{T}$ and as $\mathbf{A} \to \mathbf{A}$, called *modifiers*. Here are the details:

- graph $\mathbf{S}$ represents the hierarchical structure of a given volume. $\mathbf{S}$ is rooted, oriented and ordered. Let $V(\mathbf{S})$ be the vertices and $E(\mathbf{S})$ the edges of $\mathbf{S}$;
- the five first levels of $V(\mathbf{S})$ represent hierarchical subdivisions. Let us denote ℓ the level function. The root n_0 represents the entire document;
- function $\tau \colon V(\mathbf{S}) \to \mathbf{T}$ maps every node n to a title $\tau(n)$,
- $V(\mathbf{S})$ can be written as[2] $V(\mathbf{S}) = V_G \sqcup V_{\neg G}$ (V_G are the *georeferenced nodes*) where we have a function $g \colon V_G \to \mathbf{G}$ that maps every georeferenced node to a node in $\mathbf{G}$, which again is mapped to a geopolygon in $\mathbf{A}$ by α;
- when generating a volume of the *Instruction nautiques*, the leafs of $\mathbf{S}$ are mapped to subgraphs of $\mathbf{K}$ through function κ. These subgraphs are then converted to text paragraphs in LitINAUT language;
- edges $E(\mathbf{G})$ of $\mathbf{G}$ represent *partial inclusion* $\dot{\subset}$ in $\mathbf{A}$, in the sense that we have $G'G \in E(\mathbf{G})$ (or $a(G')\dot{\subset}a(G)$) if and only if $\mathrm{Area}(a(G') \cap a(G)) > 0.8\,\mathrm{Area}(a(G'))$;
- the barycenters of $\mathrm{Im}\,\alpha \circ g$ when restricted to $V_G \cup \ell^{-1}(i)$ for $i \in \{1, 2, 3\}$ follow a path on the map, which corresponds to an itinerary along the coasts

---

[1] With the exception of Seaspeak [6], a CNL defined in 1985 by the International Maritime Lecturers Association. In 2001 it evolved into SMCP (Standard Marine Communication Phrases [2]) which is still used today. These CNLs, dedicated to oral communication between ships, are "human-only".

[2] We denote by $\sqcup$ the disjoint union: $C = A \sqcup B \iff (C = A \cup B) \wedge (A \cap B = \varnothing)$.

of France. The extremities of this itinerary for a given volume are given in $t(n_0)$ where n_0 is the root of **S**. We call this path, the *guiding path* of the volume.

- modifiers μ serve to describe locations relatively to other locations. For example, the modifier "au nord de X" (= to the North of X), applied to location "[cap Cerbère]" will produce "au nord de [cap Cerbère]" which is a new geographic entity, the polygon of which is calculated automatically out of $\alpha(g([\text{cap Cerbère}]))$. Some modifiers are shown in Fig. 1.

au Nord de X   aux abords de X   aux abords N de X   au fond de X   à l'entrée de X

Fig. 1. The main modifiers: solid polygon represents the original area A, dashed polygon the modified one $\mu(A)$

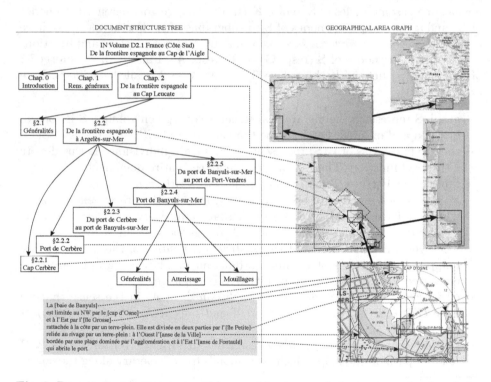

Fig. 2. Document structure tree and geographic area graph for an example taken from Vol. D2.1 of the *Instructions nautiques*

On Fig. 2 the reader can see an example of *Instructions nautiques* data in our model: on the left, the document structure tree, on the right, the geographical area graph. The gray box contains the LitINAUT text generated from section *Généralités* of §2.2.4. In the text, geographical entities are marked up by brackets. Dashed arrows between the two graphs represent function g.

2   The SHOM Knowledge Base

Let us define (extending Cimiano [1]) a knowledge base **K** as being a 16-tuple

$$(\mathfrak{C}, \leqslant_C, \mathfrak{A}, \mathfrak{R}_S, \mathfrak{R}_C, \mathfrak{T}, \mathfrak{I}, \mathfrak{V}, L_{\mathfrak{C}}, L_{\mathfrak{A}}, L_{\mathfrak{R}_S}, L_{\mathfrak{R}_C}, L_{\mathfrak{I}}, \sigma, \iota, \lambda)$$

where $\mathfrak{C}, \mathfrak{A}, \mathfrak{R}_S, \mathfrak{R}_C, \mathfrak{T}, \mathfrak{I}, \mathfrak{V}$ are sets of concepts, attributes, simple relations, complex relations, types, instances and values, $\leqslant_C$ is a hierarchy of concepts, $L_{\mathfrak{C}}, L_{\mathfrak{A}}, L_{\mathfrak{R}_S}, L_{\mathfrak{R}_C}, L_{\mathfrak{I}}$ are sets of names of concepts, attributes, simple relations, relations and instances, and σ, ι, λ denote signature, instantiation, lexicalization, as follows:

1. $\iota \colon \mathfrak{C} \to 2^{\mathfrak{I}}$;
2. the signature of an attribute is $\sigma \colon \mathfrak{A} \to \mathfrak{C} \times \mathfrak{T}$ and its instances $\iota \colon \mathfrak{A} \to 2^{\mathfrak{I} \times \mathfrak{V}}$;
3. simple relations are relations between exactly two instances, without relation attributes. Hence we have $\sigma \colon \mathfrak{R}_S \to \mathfrak{C} \times \mathfrak{C}$ and $\iota \colon \mathfrak{R}_S \to 2^{\mathfrak{I} \times \mathfrak{I}}$;
4. complex relations are relations between n instances ($n \geqslant 2$) which can also have relation attributes. Hence we have: $\sigma \colon \mathfrak{R}_C \to \times^n \mathfrak{C} \times \times^m \mathfrak{T}$ (where $\times^n$ denotes n-fold product) and $\iota \colon \mathbf{R} \to 2^{\times^n \mathfrak{I} \times \times^m \mathfrak{V}}$, with $n \geqslant 2$, $m \geqslant 0$;
5. an noteworthy difference between complex relations and simple relations, is lexicalization. Indeed, we have: $\lambda \colon \mathfrak{C} \to L_{\mathfrak{C}}$, $\lambda \colon \mathfrak{I} \to L_{\mathfrak{I}}$, $\lambda \colon \mathfrak{A} \to L_{\mathfrak{A}}$, $\lambda \colon \mathfrak{R}_S \to L_{\mathfrak{R}_S}$ as expected, but $\lambda \colon \mathfrak{R}_C \to L_{\mathfrak{R}_C} \times \times^n L_{\mathfrak{R}_S} \times \times^m L_{\mathfrak{A}}$, i.e., a relation has its own name, but requires also names for all instances involved in the relation as well as all relation attributes.

The concepts $\mathfrak{C}$ of the SHOM knowledge base **K**, belong to the domain of maritime navigation: ports, capes, sea currents, ships, etc.

As for **S** nodes, instances $\mathfrak{I}$ are of two types $\mathfrak{I} = \mathfrak{I}_G \sqcup \mathfrak{I}_{\neg G}$: $\mathfrak{I}_G$ are georeferenced entities: "[baie de Banyuls]", "[cap d'Osne]", etc., in the sense that there is a map g between **I** and the graph **G**; $\mathfrak{I}_{\neg G}$ are non-georeferenced instances, such as "agglomération", "port," etc. They don't need to be located on the map, and their purpose is purely descriptive of the environment.

Notice that the names of $\mathfrak{I}_G$ instances often contain a hint to the predominant concept to which they belong ("baie", "cap", "port", etc.), while in the case of $\mathfrak{I}_{\neg G}$ instances, their names are often names of predominant concepts *per se*.

Simple relations $\mathfrak{R}_S$ represent verbs in passive or active voice "est abrité par", "est possible", etc. Notice that most relations representing a passive verb have a symmetric relation representing the corresponding active verb: "A est abrité par B" has the symmetric relation "B abrite A";

LitINAUT:
La [baie de Banyuls] est limitée au NW par le [cap d'Osne] et à l'Est par l'[île Grosse] rattachée à la côte par un terre-plein. Elle est divisée en deux parties par l'[île Petite] reliée au rivage par un terre-plein : à l'Ouest l'[anse de la Ville] bordée par une plage dominée par l'agglomération et à l'Est l'[anse de Fontaulé] qui abrite le port.

INAUT:
La [baie de Banyuls] est limitée au NW par le [cap d'Osne]. La [baie de Banyuls] est limitée à l'Est par l'[île Grosse]. L'[île Grosse] est rattachée à la côte par un terre-plein. La [baie de Banyuls] est divisée en deux parties par l'[île Petite] : à l'Ouest l'[anse de la Ville] et à l'Est l'[anse de Fontaulé]. L'[île Petite] est reliée au rivage par un terre-plein. L'[anse de la Ville] est bordée par une plage. La plage est dominée par l'agglomération. L'[anse de Fontaulé] abrite le port.

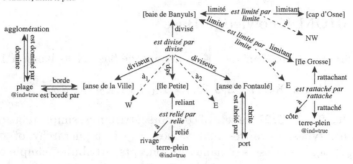

Fig. 3. A paragraph in INAUT, LitINAUT, and represented in the knowledge base

Complex relations are n-ary ($n \geqslant 2$) and can have attributes: for example "est limité par" has attribute "direction." In this case, lexicalization requires names for all instances or attributes participating in the relation. In the case of "est limité par" the members of the relation are instances "limitant", "limité" and attribute "à."

As an example, the reader can see on Fig. 3 the sentence of Fig. 2, represented in LitINAUT, INAUT and as a subgraph of **K**. Instances "[baie de Banyuls]", "[cap d'Osne]", etc. belong to $\mathfrak{I}_G$. Instances "côte", "plage", "port", "rivage", belong to $\mathfrak{I}_{\neg G}$. Complex relations are reified as nodes. Attributes of instances have been included underneath, marked by character @.

3   The Controlled Languages INAUT and LitINAUT

INAUT is a controlled language with a rather large vocabulary (based on the existing *Instructions nautiques* corpus) but with a simple syntax, given by the following grammar:

$$S \rightarrow NP\ VP$$
$$NP \rightarrow \text{MODIF DET NN} \mid \text{DET NN} \mid \text{NN}$$
$$NN \rightarrow \text{ADJ NN} \mid \text{NN ADJ NOUN}$$
$$VP \rightarrow \text{VERB NP} \mid \text{VERB NP PP}$$
$$PP \rightarrow \text{PREP DET NN} \mid \text{PREP NN}$$

where symbols in small caps are terminal, all NOUNs belong to $L_{\mathfrak{I}}$ (the set of lexical references for instances of **K**) and to $\mathfrak{V}$ (the set of values of attributes of **K**), all VERBs belong to $L_{\mathfrak{R}_S} \cup L_{\mathfrak{R}_C}$, all ADJectives belong to $\mathfrak{V}$, and MODIFiers, DETerminants and PREPositions belong to a closed list.

The VERB, always in 3rd person or in the infinitive, can be active or passive. In most cases it is possible to change the voice of the verb, which implies a permutation of the NPs in SUBJECT and OBJECT position, leaving the PPs intact:

La [baie de Banyuls] est limitée par le [cap d'Osne] au NW.
Le [cap d'Osne] limite la [baie de Banyuls] au NW.

Definite articles are used for all instances in **G** the names of which start with the name of a concept to which belongs the instance: for example, the name "baie de Banyuls" starts with "baie" (= bay) which is the name of a concept in $\mathfrak{C}$, hence in INAUT the definite article is used: "la [baie de Banyuls]".
Otherwise, no article is used:

[Notre-Dame de la Salette] est un amer remarquable à l'WSW du port.

Instances in $\mathfrak{I}_{\neg G}$ are, by default, used with definite articles. When an indefinite article is required, the information is stored in a dedicated attribute. Indefinite articles are used in OBJECT position only:

L'[anse de la Ville] est bordée par une plage. La plage est dominée par l'agglomération.

Modifiers are represented by (a closed set of) expressions outside the brackets of the geographic entity: in "au fond de l'[anse de la Ville]", we have modifier "au fond de" and entity "[anse de la Ville]." In **K** there is a *modifier relation* whenever a modifier is used. This relation does not produce INAUT text but serves to connect subgraphs in **K** during content determination (§4).

In the following sections we will discuss the three main operations of controlled languages INAUT and LitINAUT: generation (§ 4), interaction with ENCs (§ 5), collaborative updates of the knowledge base (§ 6).

4   Controlled Language Generation

One of the design goals of our system is to be able to produce automatically a large part of the *Instructions nautiques*, so that after collaborative updates new versions of the entire document can automatically be produced.

We have divided the task into two stages: (1) produce INAUT text corresponding to a given leaf node of **S**; (2) convert INAUT language into LitINAUT.

Suppose given a leaf node S of **S**. Producing the corresponding INAUT text is typically a Natural Language Generation problem.

Reiter & Dale [4, § 3.3] divide the language generation task into seven subtasks: content determination, document structuring, lexicalisation, aggregation, referring expression generation, linguistic realisation and structure realisation.

Content determination. Using Algorithm 1, we find the subgraph K of **K** which is geographically the most relevant to S. We apply tags to its connected components using a rule-based decision system: for example, when a connected component contains the instance "mouillage" then it is tagged as belonging to a leaf node of type "Mouillages." If after applying the rules no tag has been affected, then the component belongs to a leaf node of default type "Généralités."

Input: S, G, K and a leaf node $S \in \mathbf{S}$
Result: The subgraph $K \subset \mathbf{K}$ which represents the text corresponding to S

$G_S \leftarrow g(S)$;
$K \leftarrow \varnothing$;
for $G \in \mathbf{G}$ **do**
   if $G \dot{\subset} G_S$ *and* $g^{-1}(G) \in \mathfrak{I}_G$ **then**
      | $K \leftarrow K \cup g^{-1}(G)$;
   end
end
for $k \in K$ **do**
   if $\exists k'$ *such that* $kk' \in \mathrm{Undirected}(\mathbf{K})$ *and* $kk' \notin K$ **then**
      if $k' \in \mathfrak{I}_{\neg G}$ *or* $k' \in \mathfrak{V}$ *or* $(k' \in \mathfrak{I}_G$ *and* $g(k') \dot{\subset} G_S)$ **then**
         | $K \leftarrow K \cup kk'$;
      end
      if $k' \in \mathfrak{R}_C$ *and* $\exists k''$ *member of* k' *such that* $g(k'') \dot{\subset} G_S$ **then**
         $K \leftarrow K \cup kk'$;
         for m *member of* k' **do**
            | $K \leftarrow K \cup k'm$;
         end
      end
   end
end

Algorithm 1. Content determination algorithm

Document structuring. This is the most difficult phase since it deals with the order in which sentences are written. Let K bet the subgraph of $\mathbf{K}$ to be converted into INAUT.

We subdivide the task in four subtasks:

1. sort connected components K_i of K;
2. for each component find a starting node s;
3. find the order in which the relations of each component will be converted into INAUT, starting from s;
4. convert relations into INAUT in the order given by 1 and 3.

For subtask 1, we will sort components. The sorting criteria are: (a) if there is a significant difference in size between the cumulated geographic areas of two components, the larger one will precede the smaller one, (b) otherwise, calculate the barycenters of cumulated geographic areas of components; the path defined by their barycenters should be roughly parallel to the guiding path of the volume. For example, on Fig. 2 the areas of nodes §2.2.1–§2.2.5 follow a SE to NW direction, this direction can be chosen for the order of connected components.

To accomplish steps 2 and 3 we define weights w on nodes and relations. Calculation of these weights is based on criteria we will describe below, as well as on training using machine learning algorithms on the existing *Instructions nautiques* corpus.

Notice that we use undirected graphs since every edge can be inverted by changing voice.

The first and most obvious criterion is the relation between nodes in K_i and the parent of the leaf node of $\mathbf{S}$ that established the connection with $\mathbf{K}$ (i.e., $\kappa^{-1}(K)$). If among the nodes there is one whose geographic area and/or name matches as closely as possible the one of the parent of the leaf node, it is a good choice. For example, in our case, node §2.2.4 of **S** is "Port de Banyuls-sur-Mer" which is much closer to "baie de Banyuls" than to "cap d'Osne", both in terms of geographic area than simply of string comparison of names.

The second criterion for choosing the starting node is its position in the **G** lattice. Let $k_m = g^{-1}(\max_{\mathbf{G}} g(K_i))$. If $k_m \in K_i$ then it is an obvious choice. Otherwise we take local maxima in **G** and proceed with weighting.

Finally, another criterion is of semantic nature, the one of "interest" for the navigator: an order can be established between concepts to which instances of K_i belong, for example a port instance will be more interesting than a beach instance. This weight is inherited by neighboring nodes: for instance, a bay containing a port is more interesting than a bay containing a beach, etc.

The "semantic weight" of instances can be calculated by machine learning.

Once the starting point has been established, we proceed to subtask 3. We will use a variant of DFS (depth-first search) to search K_i.

Subtask 4 is the simplest one: from relations in **K** we build INAUT sentences, by applying rules, for example choosing the verb's voice according to the direction of the search in K_i, adding articles matching nouns, etc. There still remains a difficulty: finding the right order of prepositional phrases, as in:

La [baie de Banyuls] est limitée par le [cap d'Osne] au NW.
La [baie de Banyuls] est limitée au NW par le [cap d'Osne].

When the difference may be purely stylistic (as above), the order can be obtained by machine learning. In other cases, such as in "est divisé par" of Fig. 2, it is mandatory to group some relations: the text representing "à_i" must immediately follow the one representing "diviseur$_i$" since indices disappear in the textual realization and only proximity allows to distinguish the divisors of the entity.

Another important phenomenon is text added by default: for example, to realize relation "est divisé par" we need to add the number of divisors, this is done by counting the members of the relation of type "diviseur" and generate "en deux parties" (= in two parts).

Aggregation and referring expressions generation: LitINAUT language. At this stage, generation of INAUT has been completed. The result, as it can be seen in Fig. 3, is not very eloquent, but remains closely related to the structure of **K**, so that it is easier for contributors to supply modifications and additions written in INAUT. To produce a human readable text as part of automatically generated *Instructions nautiques* document, we need two extra steps: aggregation of several sentences into a single one, and generation or referring expressions. The result of these two operations is called LitINAUT language.

By the fact of using DFS to search K_i, often the object of a sentence is the subject of the following one. Aggregation merges them into a single sentence:

L'[anse de la Ville] est bordée par une plage.
La plage est dominée par l'agglomération.
→ L'[anse de la Ville] est bordée par une plage, dominée par l'agglomération.

In other cases, consecutive sentences have the same object and the same verb; in that case we use conjunction:

La [baie de Banyuls] est limitée au NW par le [cap d'Osne].
La [baie de Banyuls] est limitée à l'Est par l'[île Grosse].
→ La [baie de Banyuls] est limitée au NW par le [cap d'Osne] et à l'Est par l'[île Grosse].

When we have object identity but with different verbs, referring expressions are generated:

La [baie de Banyuls] est divisée en deux parties par... → Elle est divisée en deux parties par...

In some cases, text is omitted from the realization because it is obtained from the context: for example, in realizing the text corresponding to a subdivision of type "Mouillages" (= mooring), we will systematically omit the part "Le mouillage est autorisé à" since it is implied by the subdivision title.

These are just some examples of mechanisms used to convert INAUT into LitINAUT. Work is in progress to enhance the result and bring it closer to legacy (human authored) text.

5   Interaction with ENCs

As said in the introduction, *Instructions nautiques* are defined as a complement to charts, and, in particular, to ENCs. Therefore it is important to define interactions between **K** and ENCs, via INAUT. By specifying, for example, an area of interest on an ENC (for example, by drawing a zone on a touchscreen) the user may receive LitINAUT text in return. Generating this text automatically has the advantage of being (a) limited to the zone of interest given by the user; (b) conform to local conditions, for example time of the day (some relations or attributes in **K** may be time-dependent) or meteorological conditions, or parameters of the user's vessel (size, tonnage, etc.); (c) up-to-date, since other users may constantly provide new information.

To provide adaptive LitINAUT text, we first position the area U given by the user in **A**, and hence in **G**. Knowing the subgraph of **G** that matches as closely as possible U in **A**, we find the relevant nodes in **K** by going through g^{-1}. These nodes form a subgraph of **K** and we apply the techniques described in 4 to generate the corresponding text in LitINAUT.

Additional structure can be added to the text sent to the ENC device, so that the user can filter the text and display only specific types of information, as for example information on mooring, landing, etc.

6   Collaborative Updates of the Knowledge Base

It is important for the SHOM knowledge base to be kept constantly up-to-date. To achieve this goal, INAUT will be used as a tool for collaborative update.

Indeed, INAUT has been designed as the optimal compromise between easiness of use (since contributors have a priori no KM proficiency) and formality (as the knowledge base will be fed directly by the incoming data).

To make the system more robust, we validate on two levels. First, the lexical and syntactic level: a Web interface analyzes segments written in INAUT and validates them. In case of errors it provides correction hints. Second, the semantic level: a human controller monitors incoming INAUT data which, depending on the contributors trust level are automatically fed into the knowledge base (with the possibility of making the modification retroactive) or are stored in a waiting list until manual validation.

7   Conclusion and Future Work

We have described the controlled natural language INAUT (and its variant LitINAUT) which is used for the update of the SHOM maritime knowledge base, for automatic generation of *Instructions nautiques* documents and for interaction with ENCs.

Among our plans is the extension of INAUT into a QA system. This requires extension of INAUT to interrogative sentences and increased use of the concept hierarchy. Another extension deals with the issue of *dangerosity*. Indeed, one of goals of *Instructions nautiques* is to alert the navigator on possible dangers. Ideally, the ENC should automatically send queries about dangerosity to the knowledge base involving the current position of the vessel and various external conditions, and in case of a positive answer, alert the navigator by all means possible. Special NLG techniques can then be used, since the communicative goal will not be simply to inform, but to alert.

References

1. Cimiano, P.: Ontology Learning and Population from Text. Algorithms, Evaluation and Applications. Springer (2008)
2. IMO: IMO Standard Marine Communication Phrases, with pronunciation. International Maritime Organization (2005)
3. NOAA: United States Coast pilot,
   http://www.nauticalcharts.noaa.gov/nsd/cpdownload.htm
4. Reiter, E., Dale, R.: Building Natural Language Generation Systems. Cambridge University Press (2000)
5. SHOM: Instructions nautiques,
   http://www.shom.fr/les-produits/produits-nautiques/ouvrages-nautiques/instructions-nautiques/
6. Strevens, P., Johnson, E.: SEASPEAK: a project in applied linguistics, language engineering, and eventually ESP for sailors. The ESP Journal 2(2), 123–129 (1983),
   http://www.sciencedirect.com/science/article/pii/0272238093900020
7. UKHO: Admiralty sailing directions,
   https://www.ukho.gov.uk/PRODUCTSANDSERVICES/PAPERPUBLICATIONS/Pages/NauticalPubs.aspx

Are Style Guides Controlled Languages?
The Case of Koenig & Bauer AG

Karolina Suchowolec*

University of Hildesheim, Germany
karolina.suchowolec@uni-hildesheim.de

Abstract. Controlled languages for industrial application are often regarded as a response to the challenges of translation and multilingual communication [3, pp. 52–53], [5, p. 212], [2, pp. i–iii]. This paper presents a quite different approach taken by Koenig & Bauer AG, where the main goal was the improvement of the authoring process for technical documentation. Most importantly, this paper explores the notion of a controlled language and demonstrates how style guides can emerge from non-linguistic considerations. Moreover, it shows the transition from loose language recommendations into precise and prescriptive rules and investigates whether such rules can be regarded as a full-fledged controlled language.

1 Introduction

A considerable amount of research on controlled languages deals with English. In this paper, I examine an approach for an industrial application of a controlled language in German at the printing press manufacturer Koenig & Bauer AG (KBA).[1] In comparison to well-known industrial examples such as CFE/CTE or ASD-STE100 [2], [13], [cf. 3], KBA did not create an independent project on a controlled language. Instead, the company's main goal was to redefine the authoring process for technical documentation. Language standardization was needed to support this goal. I will explain this background in the first section. The following section will give a closer look at the results of different projects that originated different language rules. These rules and style guides will illustrate how KBA unintentionally laid the foundations for a de facto controlled language. After showing some future directions for the project, I will discuss its results within the current theoretical frameworks.

Although this paper derives from a case study, its main goal is to explore the notion of a controlled language and to demonstrate how style guides can

---

* I would like to thank Koenig & Bauer AG for the permission to publish this paper, in particular Elmar Tober, who has been supervising the projects, and Sabine Lobach for providing up-to-date data. In addition, I would like to thank Klaus Schubert, Wolfgang Ziegler, and the anonymous reviewers for their critical comments.
[1] The author was employed at the company and implemented the terminology management as well as advised other projects on linguistic matters.

B. Davis et al. (Eds.): CNL 2014, LNAI 8625, pp. 112–122, 2014.

emerge from non-linguistic considerations. Moreover, this paper shows the transition from loose language recommendations to precise and prescriptive rules. It also investigates whether such rules can be regarded as a full-fledged controlled language.

2   Background

Koenig & Bauer AG is one of the leading printing press manufacturers, operating from Würzburg, Germany, employing around 6,200 (2012) people worldwide. The variety of products covers a. o. web offset, sheetfed offset, and security printing. The annual reports[2] indicate that over 80 % of the products are exported, which makes translation of documentation and localization of the press software an important step in the production process. Further, the web printing presses are unique custom-made production plants rather than standard models. In consequence, every operating manual is a unique document, describing specific features and the configuration of the press for a given customer. Such a document can be up to 800 pages long. It is translated into one language (national or regional language of the customer) and some customers require an additional English translation. In short it means: one press – one manual in the source language (German) – one manual in the target language. There are certainly some core parts of the press and some partial configurations recurring for many customers. In order to make the authoring process for technical documentation more efficient, it was, therefore, important to facilitate identifying, indexing, storing, retrieving, and combining the recurring information units. This task had to be accomplished before addressing any issues of translation. In other words: the company was mainly interested in increasing the reuse of the content.

In order to redefine standard procedures for technical documentation, the company launched six projects in 2007. These projects contribute to the overarching goal of improving the reuse as follows [14], [21]:

1. CMS: Project aiming at the implementation of a content management system for editing, storing, retrieving and managing modularized content.
   TIM-RS® by Fischer Computertechnik[3] was chosen as the CMS with the PI-Mod[4] as a data model for authoring. PI-Mod allows semantic as well as topic-based XML markup for text chunks and modular reusable information. This project provides the technology foundation for the reuse.
2. Writers' manual: In this project, meta documentation of the CMS project was developed. The manual describes allowed XML elements: their content, dependencies, and, where necessary, their linguistic form. Moreover, it provides general recommendations on orthography and style for the technical documentation.

---

[2] http://www.kba.com/investor-relations/berichte
[3] http://www.fct.de/de/loesungen/technische-dokumentation.html
[4] http://www.pi-mod.de

3. Terminology management: A project on standardization of the specialized vocabulary. The goals were here to define standard procedures for the terminology management, to model the terminology database in SDL MultiTerm,[5] and to develop linguistic rules for evaluation and selection of preferred terms.
4. Translation: Most documents at KBA are written in German and the company does not have in-house translators; therefore the project defines general conditions for the translation services. In the context of this paper, the most important decisions are the prescribed use of Translation Memories, development of and adherence to the foreign-language equivalents to the provided German terminology as well as development of and adherence to general style guides for each foreign language as needed.
5. Graphics: Due to the variability of the products, a full reuse of graphics in operating manuals is impossible. This project should nonetheless define common standards regarding the exporting of graphics from CAD systems, further processing and managing in the CMS environment.
6. Parts catalog: In contrast to the above, this project focuses not on reuse, but on making the editing and publishing of the parts catalog more simple and transparent.

As we see, there was no particular project for developing a controlled language as such. Yet, relevant issues and requirements concerning language use are scattered across all projects.

3 Language Constraints at KBA

KBA chose a modular approach towards development of technical documentation, which means that the documents are built up by combining different text modules and chunks. These chunks can already be stored in a database; however, they could be written by different writers at a different time and for different products. The reuse principle requires not only homogeneous layout and typography, but also explicit linguistic rules for all writers involved in order to keep or achieve consistent language. Not only does consistent language make the manuals more readable for the target (human) audience, but at the same time it also supports the implementation of the reuse technology; for instance: the vocabulary is used to index modules and chunks. Therefore, consistent terminology improves the (machine-aided) retrieval.

In conclusion, it was the variability of the products as well as the desire to make the process of the technical writing more efficient that led to the development of the style/syntax and lexical rules. In addition, improving the readability and translatability was an important aspect of standardizing the vocabulary.

In the following section, I will elaborate on the linguistic results of the projects 1–4 described above dividing them into issues concerning lexicon and syntax/style. By giving some examples of the rules and by describing the rule-formation process, I would like to draw attention to some aspects that will be

---

[5] http://www.sdl.com/products/sdl-multiterm/desktop.html

subsequently crucial to the understanding of a controlled language. First, KBA went beyond the regular terminology management by developing a rule-based selection of preferred terms. Second, some imprecise style guides emerged from non-linguistic considerations. Thanks to human and later machine-aided editing, the rules have become more explicit and prescriptive. The following sections will illustrate this transition.

3.1 Lexical Level

KBA imposed two constraints to the standardization of the specialized vocabulary.[6] The first constraint limited the in-house standardization to the German terms only. The second one restricted the scope of standardization to the specific printing vocabulary, leaving out the more general technical terms or terms used in other domains such as economics. Importantly, KBA required the selection of preferred terms to be reproducible and transparent to the writers. Therefore, linguistic criteria were developed for evaluating existing terms, which can be applied for coining new terms as well. Using a corpus of company's vocabulary, semantic and morphological aspects of the word formation patterns were identified and evaluated. An essential part was to identify the patterns leading to ambiguity and synonymy, for instance:

- Ambiguity: Nominalization using the suffix *-ung* can both indicate a process or a device performing the process: *wenden* (*to turn a sheet for perfecting*) → *Wendung* (*the process of perfecting or a perfecting unit*).
- Synonymy:
  - A process can be expressed through nominalization with suffix *-ung* (see above) or conversion of the infinite verb form: *wenden* → *Wendung* vs. *Wenden*.
  - Different features of a concept can be stressed in synonymous terms: **Chrom**walze (*chrome roller*, focus on material) vs. **Feuchtreib**walze (*dampener distributor roller*, focus on function).
  - The hypernymy can be explicitly stated using the hypernym in compound nouns, or this relation can be stated implicitly: *Farbreib***walze** (*oscillating ink roller*) vs. *Farbreiber* (**ink oscillator*).

One of the goals in developing the linguistic criteria/rules was to achieve a one-to-one relation between the word formation pattern and the semantic class of the objects. In other words, the *signifiant* should indicate the class of the *signifié*, as illustrated by the following rules:

- Use conversion to indicate the process: *Wenden*.
- Use the nominalization with *-ung* or *-or/-er* to indicate a (complex) device: *Wendung*, *Längsschneider* (*slitter*).[7]

---

[6] This section is based on [21].

[7] The corpus indicates a complementary distribution of both patterns with only few exceptions.

- Use hypernym for composition of (less complex) parts: *Farbreibwalze*, *Schneidmesser* (*cutting knife*).
- Use the following ranking of features to be included in the term: 1) function 2) object 3) working principle 4) shape 5) material 6) temporal, graduate, internal features [cf. 18, p. 14].
- Do not use more than 4 lexical morphemes in a compound noun, 3 morphemes are preferred.

These criteria are intended to be an assistance rather than absolute rules for selecting the preferred terms. In case they lead to the selection of extremely unusual forms, established terms are preferred.

These rules, steps and roles in the terminology management process as well as the definition of the data structure for the terminology database were fixed in a terminology manual. Only after this definition task was completed, the actual standardization of the lexicon began. Contrary to the manual, which recommended management similar to model B of ISO 15188 [10], the initial standardization followed rather model D. The first terminology draft was proposed by the terminologist and consulted with the technical writers. The final form was released only after consulting with the constructing engineers, who gave their feedback on every term in the draft.

Applying the theoretical principles of terminology management by Wüster [22], [cf. 1], the standardization process was concept-driven. Manually extracted terms were first arranged into concept systems (multiple arrangement of one term was allowed) and then given a definition. Only after both the concept systems and the definition were specified, the preferred term was chosen according to the rules described above.

SDL MultiTerm was used from the very beginning. In addition, the initial management employed MS PowerPoint (concept systems) and MS Excel (definitions and synonyms), in order to facilitate the feedback by the engineers. Moreover, the workflow software quickTerm by Kaleidoscope[8] is now being implemented, which will help to shift back to the originally intended management as in the model B.

Currently, the database contains 614 concepts (1689 terms), covering almost entirely the printing specific vocabulary for the operating manuals. Roughly 30 % of the German terms have an approved foreign-language equivalent in one or more of the following languages: English, French, Dutch, Russian, Swedish, and Spanish. The equivalents are provided by the translation services based on the given German terminology and are not double-checked by KBA before final release. However, quickTerm allows users to send their feedback on all languages.

3.2 Syntactic and Stylistic Level

Unlike the lexical level, where an effort was put in the linguistic evaluation of the corpus data and development of systematic rules for word formation,

---

[8] http://www.kaleidoscope.at/Deutsch/Software/QuickTerm/quickterm.php

the development of the stylistic and syntactic rules was a byproduct of the implementation of PI-Mod.

PI-Mod uses XML elements to mark up information in a text according to its semantics, for instance as <step>, <descriptive>, <precondition>, <cause>, or <solution>. After agreeing on the elements needed for operating manuals, the standardization of syntax and style for some elements began. This standardization was necessary for a similar reason as the lexical one: competing syntactic patterns were in use, for instance, imperative verb form vs. infinite verb form used as imperative in <step> (in <action>), full sentence vs. ellipsis in <cause> etc.

There is no record of the decision-making process for these rules, as the focus of the CMS project was on the technical rather than linguistic specification [14]. However, the original writers' manual and personal communication indicate that the prescribed style patterns were a combination of so-called good practice for technical documentation, implicit or explicit but merely oral arrangements among the writers, and the standard examples used in the general PI-Mod specification.

The rules can be divided into general and element specific rules. Here are some examples of the original recommendations developed during the CMS project:

– Avoid Passive Voice.
– Structure information logically, for instance if – then, or condition – step.
– Element <step> (as child element of <action>):
  Use the formal imperative verb form ('Sie').
– Element <symptom>:
  Write from user's perspective, do not use questions.
  Example: *Mastarm fährt nicht richtig hoch.* [sentence with a finite verb][9]
– Element <cause> (as child element of <safetyadvice>):
  Name the cause of the hazard with one word or in a short and expressive sentence. Use an exclamation point.
  Example 1: *Verbrühungsgefahr durch herausspritzendes Öl!* [ellipsis, no finite verb]
  Example 2: *Öldruck in Arbeitshydraulik kann Manometer zerstören!* [sentence with a finite verb]
– Element <cause> (as child element of <errordescription>):
  Describe the cause of an error in one word or in a short and expressive sentence.
  Example 1: *Kein Kraftstoff im Tank.* [ellipsis, no finite verb]
  Example 2: *Pumpe hat zu wenig Leistung.* [sentence with a finite verb]

Initially, the syntactic and stylistic rules were enforced by human editing within the department. Already at that point it became clear that some rules remained ambiguous. As demonstrated in the examples above, some rules were linguistically imprecise, some lacked an explicit form, some depended on (sometimes contradicting) examples and did not indicate whether they were recommendations or prescriptions. The room for interpretation lowered the consistency

---

[9] Information in brackets was not indicated in the manual.

of the texts and in consequence – the reuse. Therefore, the rules and examples in the writers' manual have been gradually replaced by more precise ones, for instance:

- Element <cause> (as child element of <safetyadvice>):
  Use ellipsis (construction with no finite verb). Do not use full sentences with verbs. Name the cause of the hazard with one word (*Verbrührungsgefahr, Verbrennungsgefahr*). Use an exclamation point.
  Positive example: *Maschinenschaden durch liegengebliebenes Werkzeug!*
  Negative example: *Liegengebliebenes Werkzeug führt zu Maschinenschaden.*
- Element <cause> (as child element of <errordescription>):
  Use a full sentence with a verb. Do not use ellipsis. Use a period at the end of the sentence.
  Positive example: *Kein Kraftstoff ist im Tank.*
  Negative example: *Kein Kraftstoff im Tank.*

Further specification of the rules has been reinforced by the implementation of a controlled language checker (CLC, Acrolinx[10]), since the rules had to be easily transformed into a machine-readable form. Hence, the syntactic/stylistic level is being further consolidated.

Although not used from the beginning, a CLC was considered a medium-term goal. At this time, the system is being implemented to fit into the already existing linguistic environment. With respect to style and syntax, KBA rules are being mapped to the standard Acrolinx set of rules and the system is being checked in a test environment. Practical application is expected not earlier than in the summer 2014. Despite offering solutions for terminology management, Acrolinx will solely be used for proofreading. SDL MultiTerm will remain the primary source for the lexical level of the language.

4 Prospects

The four crucial projects resulting in the linguistic rules – CMS, terminology, writers' manual and translation – are completed. Yet, the maintenance and further development of the rules is an on-going process. Other tasks like the productive use of a CLC are still to be accomplished. More importantly, described development is normative only to the department of technical documentation; however other departments can obviously benefit from the use of language restrictions as well. Some applications might regard CAD models, ERM (mainly terminology), and press software (both terminology and syntax/style). Although some ways of implementing a controlled language to these applications have already been explored, they still remain a challenge for the future.

Overall the main goal of modular approach and reuse still has to be evaluated. KBA is going to track the reuse applying the REx method [16]. Resulting data could then be used for further interpretation of the linguistic contribution to the (improved) reuse.[11]

---

[10] http://www.acrolinx.com
[11] Wolfgang Ziegler, email communication (February 20, 2014).

5   Discussion

Before any specific issues concerning language at KBA can be discussed, it needs to be determined whether the rules and developments described above constitute a controlled language.

The term *controlled language* is not used in any internal documents to describe the lexical or syntactic rules for technical documentation. Rather, there is an issue of terminology and writing rules (*Schreibregeln*) – both being treated separately. The constraints on the language are put into an overarching context of standardization, just like XML markup, modular editing or data indexing in the CMS. This might be the result of the distribution of the linguistic decisions over the four projects. In consequence, an explicit notion of a *controlled language* has not yet emerged.

From the theoretical point of view, however, the linguistic constraints at KBA satisfy all of the criteria by Kuhn [12, p. 123]: They are based on just one language and restrict its system on the orthographic, morphological, lexical, syntactic and textual level, combining both prescriptive and proscriptive rules [5, p. 228]. Although no empirical studies are available, we can assume that the output is easily recognizable as German to an expert familiar with the sublanguage of printing. And finally, although the already established forms that had developed in an unsystematic way were preferred, the codification of the forms in manuals was a deliberate and, to a certain extent, systematic process. Therefore, we can regard these linguistic constraints as a controlled language.

Having clarified the status of the linguistic constraints at KBA as controlled language, we can try to determine its type.

We can apply to it the categories human-oriented and machine-oriented as proposed by Huijsen [9]. The development of the controlled language at KBA indicates an expansion of originally predominant human-oriented language to a language that comprises both human- and machine-relevant features, but a clear determination is difficult. Both categories seem to be tendencies rather than a dichotomy, which supports the main view in the literature [9, p. 2], [cf. 12, p. 125].

Moreover, we can examine further motives for this controlled language. There are three main groups of motives discussed in the literature: 1) to improve the communication among humans, 2) to improve the translation, and 3) to represent formal notations [12, p. 125], [cf. 9, p. 1], [cf. 19, p. 225], [cf. 20, p. 134], leading Kuhn to postulate three main types of controlled languages [12, p. 125]. As demonstrated above, these motives were not of primary concern for the style rules at KBA, where the increase of reuse was the main goal. The reuse issue of a controlled language is not a new topic in the literature. It has been discussed in several case studies (CTE: [6, p. 422], [13, p. 194]). It is also mentioned in some general overviews on controlled languages, but it rarely seems to be the major aspect discussed (in detail: [5, pp. 206–207], briefly: [8, p. 11], [15, p. 248], [17, p. 62], left out: [2, pp. i–iii], [3]). Clearly, the reuse motive is missing in the classification by Kuhn. This might suggest the fourth type of a controlled language – to improve (the efficiency of) the authoring process for technical documentation – an issue which seems to be underrepresented in the literature.

Certainly, a legitimate question may arise whether a controlled language for the content reuse serves solely the purpose of ensuring the readability of the text for the target audience. As such, it could be subsumed under the first type of controlled languages. As we saw, controlled language at KBA, in particular the vocabulary, ensures not only the consistency of a text, but also the retrieval of modules, and, hence, contributes to the reuse in various ways. It is not to say that KBA was unaware that the improved clarity and precision of a controlled language have impact on the readability for the target audience, as well as improve (human and machine-aided) translatability and help control company's liability in case of damage to persons or facilities [14], [21], [cf. 11, p. 443], [cf. 19, pp. 225–230]. These secondary motives were certainly important for the support of the projects at different management levels in the company [cf. 4, Modul 1]. Yet these general considerations only became tangible once the modular editing for improving the reuse started to be implemented, since, in an obvious way, the modular approach jeopardizes the consistency with all the consequences.

What is more, the aspect of human understanding can also be found in controlled languages for translation – a controlled language ensures a.o. a correct and readable output of (human, machine-aided or machine) translation. Nonetheless, controlled languages for translation constitute their own type. Altogether, taken the classification by Kuhn as a starting point, it seems, by analogy to the controlled languages for translation, reasonable to add the fourth type of controlled languages mentioned above to the classification.

Another matter to discuss is the use of CLC and a general acceptance of a controlled language. Based on observation, the need for the application of language rules is generally understood and accepted by the technical writers. First tests of CLC seem to conform this. However, ambiguous terms lower the precision of the CLC, which is consistent with the difficulties mentioned in the literature [9, p. 8], [15, p. 252]. Splitting the vocabulary into domains, as suggested by the software provider and by some authors [15, p. 276] seems to lack of a good splitting criterion that would not cause too much term overlap between the domains, requiring some essential changes in the database definition and a reconsideration of the concept-driven terminology management. Currently, different models for software feedback and score in case of ambiguity are being tested. Overall, the problem remains unsolved. The main question concerning this type of feedback is whether it will have an impact on the effectiveness and on general acceptance of a CLC by the writers.

Looking from a broader perspective, the case of KBA sheds some light on the more general issue of the acceptance of a controlled language by the writers. Godden reports on the difficulties with the editor-centered model for CASL at General Motors, where the writers not previously trained in the rules were reluctant to accepting the changes proposed by the editor. Some better results were achieved by a hybrid model, requiring prior training of the writers [7], [cf. 5, pp. 215–216], [cf. 8, pp. 107–112]. We do not have similar data concerning machine editing at KBA yet, but the experience with the human editing shows a promising degree of acceptance of the language rules and proposed changes in case of a clear violation of the rules. I presume that there is a link between cooperative approach to the definition of the rules, resulting on the one hand in a 'sense of community' and on the other in a better comprehension of the rules, leading altogether to an increase of acceptance. There has already been an awareness of this phenomenon, particularly in the literature on terminology management [5, p. 166], [cf. 17, p. 63] but empirical studies are still needed.

6 Concluding Remarks

The case of KBA shows that the notion of a controlled language needs to be reexamined. It can emerge as a result of deliberate decisions that are not necessarily labeled and conceived as a design of a controlled language. The distinction between controlled languages and style guides is indeed vague [12, p. 124] and needs to be examined on a case by case basis, and perhaps only at a given point in time. This also suggests that there might be more companies having language regulations that do not see themselves as being concerned by the discourse of controlled languages. Furthermore, a new type of a controlled language – to improve the authoring process for technical documentation – needs to be considered.

From the practical point of view, the case of KBA shows that the development in technology has made a controlled language more attainable. There is no longer a need for custom-built software solutions to implement the specifications of a controlled language. There is an array of standard software that can be customized to fit specific needs, which makes a controlled language easier and more affordable to develop and implement, opening the field to medium-size companies.

References

1. Arntz, R., Picht, H., Schmitz, K.D.: Einführung in die Terminologiearbeit, 7th edn. Olms, Hildesheim (2014)
2. ASD Industries Association of Europe: Simplified Technical English. Specification ASD-STE100. International specification for preparation of maintenance documentation in a controlled language (6) (January 2013)
3. Crabbe, S.: Controlled languages for technical writing and translation. In: Conference Proceedings of the Ninth Portsmouth Translation Conference of the Translator as Writer, Portsmouth, pp. 48–62 (2009)
4. Deutscher Terminologie-Tag e.V., Deutsches Institut für Terminologie e.V.: Terminologiearbeit – Best Practices 2.0 (Ordner) (2014)
5. Drewer, P., Ziegler, W.: Technische Dokumentation. Übersetzungsgerechte Texterstellung und Content-Management. Vogel Verlag, Würzburg (2011)
6. Gallup, S.: Caterpillar Technical English and automatic machine translation. In: STC Proceedings, pp. 421–424 (1993)
7. Godden, K.: The evolution of CASL controlled authoring at General Motors. In: Proceedings of the Third International Workshop on Controlled Language Applications, CLAW 2000, pp. 14–19 (2000)

8. Hebling, U.: Controlled Language am Beispiel des Controlled English. Diplomarbeit, Universität Heidelberg (2002)
9. Huijsen, W.O.: Controlled language – an introduction. In: Proceedings of the Second International Workshop on Controlled Language Applications, CLAW 1998, pp. 1–15 (1998)
10. International Organization for Standardization: ISO 15188:2001(E): Project management guidelines for terminology standardization (2001)
11. Kittredge, R.I.: Sublanguages and controlled languages. In: Mitkov, R. (ed.) The Oxford Handbook of Computational Linguistics, pp. 430–447. Oxford University Press, Oxford (2003)
12. Kuhn, T.: A survey and classification of controlled natural languages. Computational Linguistics 40(1), 121–170 (2014), http://www.mitpressjournals.org/doi/abs/10.1162/COLI_a_00168
13. Lockwood, R.: Machine translation and controlled authoring at Caterpillar. In: Sprung, R.C. (ed.) Translating into Success. Cutting-edge Strategies for Going Multilingual in a Global Age. American Translators Association Scholarly Monograph Series, vol. XI, pp. 187–202. John Benjamins Publishing Company, Amsterdam/Philadelphia (2000)
14. Messaoudi, N.: Content Engineering zur Einführung eines Redaktionssystems bei der Koenig & Bauer AG – Informationsmodellierung, Modularisierung und automatisierte Publikation. Diplomarbeit, Hochschule Karlsruhe – Technik und Wirtschaft (2009) (undisclosed)
15. Nyberg, E., Mitamura, T., Huijsen, W.O.: Controlled language for authoring and translation. In: Somers, H. (ed.) Computers and Translation. A translator's Guide, Benjamins Translation Library, vol. 35, pp. 245–281. John Benjamins Publishing Company, Amsterdam/Philadelphia (2003)
16. Oberle, C., Ziegler, W.: Content Intelligence für Redaktionssysteme. CMS-Kennzahlen mit der REx-Methode. Technische Kommunikation (6), 48–54 (2012)
17. Ramírez Polo, L.: Use and evaluation of controlled languages in industrial environments and feasibility study for the implementation of machine translation. Ph.D. thesis, Universidad de Valencia (2012)
18. Reinhardt, W., Köhler, C., Neubert, G.: Deutsche Fachsprache der Technik. Olms, Hildesheim (1992)
19. Schubert, K.: Gestaltete Sprache. Plansprachen und die regulierten Sprachen der internationalen Fachkommunikation. In: Schubert, K. (ed.) Planned Languages: From Concept to Reality, pp. 223–257. Hogeschool voor Wetenschap & Kunst, Brussel (2001)
20. Schubert, K.: Kommunikationsoptimierung. Vorüberlegungen zu einem fachkommunikativen Forschungsfeld. trans-kom 2(1), 109–150 (2009), http://www.trans-kom.eu/bd02nr01/trans-kom_02_01_06_Schubert_Kommunikationsoptimierung.20090721.pdf
21. Suchowolec, K.: Terminologiearbeit im Unternehmen. Einführung eines Gesamtkonzeptes. Magisterarbeit, Technische Universität Dresden (2009) (undisclosed)
22. Wüster, E.: Einführung in die allgemeine Terminologielehre und terminologische Lexikographie. Romanistischer Verlag, Bonn (1991)

Lexpresso: A Controlled Natural Language

Adam Saulwick

Defence Science & Technology Organisation, Australia

Abstract. This paper presents an overview of 'Lexpresso', a Controlled Natural Language developed at the Defence Science & Technology Organisation as a bidirectional natural language interface to a high-level information fusion system. The paper describes Lexpresso's main features including lexical coverage, expressiveness and range of linguistic syntactic and semantic structures. It also touches on its tight integration with a formal semantic formalism and tentatively classifies it against the PENS system.

Keywords: Controlled Natural Language, Formal Semantics, Linguistic structures, Human–Computer Interaction, High-level Information Fusion.

1 Introduction

'Lexpresso' is a Controlled Natural Language (CNL) developed at the Defence Science & Technology Organisation as a bidirectional natural language interface to a high-level, agent-based, information fusion system called Consensus. This paper is the first published description of Lexpresso's broad features, including lexical coverage, and range of syntactic and semantic structures. It also describes the tight integration with DSTO's bespoke formal semantic formalism, Mephisto, initially conceived by Lambert & Nowak [1]. Lexpresso was first developed in 2008 and is under active development.[1]

The Consensus system performs high-level information fusion of heterogeneous data for Situation Awareness. In our current demonstration system, synthesised input data types include maritime and aviation tracks[2], natural English texts, emails and spoken English statements. In general terms the Consensus system is designed to demonstrate a working solution to problems of high-level information fusion by the 'semiautomation of [some of] the functionalities of

---

[1] Some previous work in natural language interfaces at DSTO focussed on automated speech-to-text recognition linked to template rules. From June 2007 to July 2008 a DSTO initiated collaborative research program into situation awareness was conducted between DSTO and NICTA, see [2]. Among other things, this research involved the development of a CNL which was based on, or inspired by, PENG [3, 4]. Subsequent to these activities Lexpresso was built from scratch by DSTO.

[2] Synthesised tracks are currently processed at circa 100 per second and contain fields for source, temporal offset, track ID, time, coordinates, direction, speed, class, type, allegiance and nationality.

B. Davis et al. (Eds.): CNL 2014, LNAI 8625, pp. 123–134, 2014.

sensation, perception, cognition, comprehension, and projection that [are] otherwise performed by people for situation awareness' [5]. Among other functions Consensus does this by automatically transforming diverse information sources into a canonical semantic machine-readable form called Mephisto which facilitates computational reasoning. A problem however is that Mephisto is only interpretable by machines or by a few human experts (and then slowly) and so, human interaction with Consensus would be very difficult, if not impossible, even for specialists, without a natural interface. Lexpresso is that interface. It bridges the natural-language/formal-language gulf and thus it permits relatively natural interaction with a formal semantic reasoning system via spoken and written controlled natural English.[3]

Lexpresso's bidirectionality means that it has both input and generation capabilities. Further, because Lexpresso is tightly coupled with Consensus's formal semantic knowledge representation and reasoning system whose primary function is automated inferencing over real-time track data and texts for enhanced situation awareness, it provides human users with the enhanced ability to query the nature of current and historical real-world and potentially far-flung events. Answers are given in the form of situation reports. These reports may concern the transit or spatiotemporal interaction of observed maritime, land &/or air-based platforms and even the social relationships between people inferred from certain text descriptions.

While these capability descriptions are accurate, they are not intended to obfuscate Lexpresso's limitations. Its breadth and degree of coupling with Mephisto are the subject of ongoing research and development. Consensus is a prototype system and, subject to space constraints, some limitations will be mentioned in Section 4.

The remainder of this paper is structured as follows. Section 2 describes the system architecture and the main CNL modules. Sections 3 and 4 exemplify the main syntactic and semantic structures respectively. Section 5 proposes a classification of Lexpresso based on the PENS system. Section 6 concludes with a summary.

2   System Architecture and Module Functions

Echoing the traditional transformational grammar distinction [6, 7], language processing in Lexpresso is conceived on a spatial metaphor of depth in which 'surface CNL' refers to observed spoken or written forms of language and 'deep CNL' refers to an underlying abstraction with certain linguistic features. Input processing takes surface language and transforms it into deep linguistic structures. After further processing to remove ambiguities, these are converted into our universal semantic representations called Mephisto structures. Reasoning and inferencing is primarily performed on Mephisto structures. Output processing takes Mephisto structures and uses the same core syntactic parser to validate and generate surface CNL for consumption by users.

---

[3] Consensus also utilises other interfaces such as a 3-dimensional geospatial display and a virtual adviser avatar. These are not discussed here.

Lexpresso is designed as a modular system to facilitate integration of new features as required. Depending on how one counts them, it consists of around 17 modules, see Figure 1. Due to space constraints not all components are described.

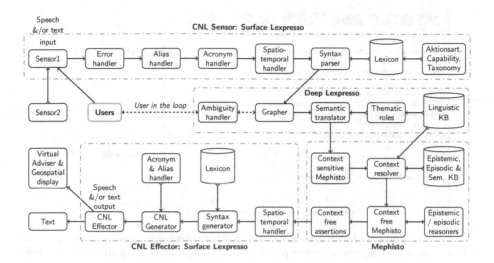

Fig. 1. Lexpresso system architecture

CNL Sensor. This is the users' primary input screen. It contains a text panel for typing controlled natural English. Spoken English also appears in this panel via the Automated Speech Recogniser. Sentences can be automatically or manually inserted. Manual insertion is an interactive process and thus permits error correction prior to further processing. Once inserted the input appears in the CNL Sensor log window accompanied by the name of the 'teller' and a status message. Each line is also timestamped, displayed directly above it, see Figure 2.[4]

Error handler. During manual insertion, a pre-parser checker notifies the user of unknown or undefined words or out-of-grammar expressions. This provides dynamic feedback on lexical coverage and grammaticality of surface input to inform the user of input status.

Alias handler. This module converts particular multi-word expressions into atomic terms for manipulation at the deep linguistic level, e.g. `'Becker'`, `'Bender'`, `air, force, base` becomes `becker_bender_AFB`. It is also used to handle contractions, e.g. 'can't' becomes 'cannot'. It is also used for mapping fixed idiomatic forms to a single lexical correspondence. Although the functionality of the aliasing module is currently used for simple surface level structures, it is also capable of handling metonymy.

---

[4] The 'sensor' & 'effector' terminology is adopted from the Attitude Too cognitive model [8].

Acronym handler. This module expands acronyms and titles into multi-word expressions. It also constrains their syntactic position (e.g. pre-/post-nominal) based on their part-of-speech.

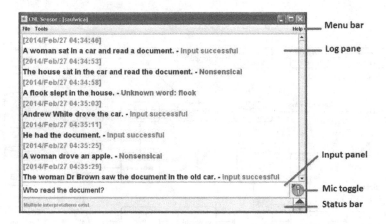

Fig. 2. CNL Sensor: showing sample text (with timestamps, proper names, person title & anaphoric resolution), input panel (with possible query), colour-coded feedback messages in log pane, microphone toggle button (on) for speech input & status message

Spatiotemporal handler. This module converts date and time information into universal standard timestamps, accepting a broad range of natural language expressions such as time-formatted numerals (e.g. 13:59:59 or Zulu time, and a variety of time points in natural language, e.g. 1 PM, one o'clock). Each time is calculated against Coordinated Universal Time (UTC). Our system is designed to allow the sensor, effector and cognition modules to be in different spatiotemporal locations, hence the generation of temporal phrases is calculated on an off-set to UTC.

Temporal intervals are also handled. Surface level forms include the template 'from TIME to TIME', and a range of temporal words, including 'today', days of the week, months of the year, decades, and centuries, etc. Where required by natural English, these phrases can be further modified with prepositions, such as 'from 12:00 to 13:00', 'in January', 'for a week', and with temporal grounding to specific times, such as 'last week', 'yesterday', 'in one month'. Inferencing with these temporal expressions as reference points is done in the cognition using Allen interval algebra [9], not discussed further here.

Lexpresso pays careful attention to the subtleties of the English tense system. For instance the relationship between the time of user interaction and the tense of the assertion or query is captured and stored as temporal information relevant to each entity. To achieve this, each input is internally labelled with utterance type and time. The latter becomes the reference time for every CNL interaction.

For instance, in (1),[5] via a `tells` predicate, the system registers that it has perceived a CNL Sensor interaction at a certain time and from a certain teller; here the author.

(1)   Mon Jun 02 10:33:48 CST 2014 [SENSOR : INTERACTION]
         perceive(cnl_sensor,tells(teller(@(skc1,invl
         (timestamp(2014,6,2,1,3,48),timestamp(2014,6,2,1,3,48)),s_5),
         Adam_Saulwick),...)),

Example (2) demonstrates how the system stores spatiotemporal information about entities.[6] Given the simple past tense of the surface input sentence in (2a), the time of 'standing' is encoded at the deep Mephisto cognitive level (2b) to have taken place *before* the time of the assertion registered in (1).

(2)   a. I: The woman stood in the house.
       b. C: animate(@(skc2,t_4,s_2)),female(@(skc2,t_4,s_2)),
              before(t_4,invl(timestamp(2014,6,2,1,3,48),
              timestamp(2014,6,2,1,3,48))),
              location_in([stands(@(skc2,t_4,s_2))],@(skc3,t_4,s_3)),
              woman(@(skc2,t_4,s_2),[animate,definite,singular,...]),
              house(@(skc3,t_4,s_3),[definite,singular,prep(in)]),
              stands[@(skc2,t_4,s_2)],[past,...])).
       c. O:The woman stood in the house before Monday the 2nd of June
           2014 at 10:33:48 AM.

For explicitness by default the time before which the event is asserted to have occurred is rendered visible to the user in the CNL Effector window, as in (2c).[7]

The location of the 'standing' event in (2) is encoded via a `location_in` predicate which is formed on the fly from a combination of surface language and automatically identified semantic roles (see *Thematic roles* below). (2b) shows this binary predicate with manner and referenced arguments, each encoding

---

[5] Our notation uses a ternary @-predicate—adopted from the Mephisto conceptualisation with a perdurantist philosophy which 'holds that an identity is formed from different things at different times, that an identity is a process, an assembly of different temporal parts'—representing @(label, time, space). (Space constraints prohibit discussion of this, but see [1].) The first argument is the entity's identifier (here a Skolem constant), the second is a temporal point, interval or even a sum of temporal intervals, and the third is the space it occupies. See [10] for further details.

[6] Abbreviations to the examples indicate representations at Input (I), Cognition (C), and Output (O) levels. Skolem constant numbers have been simplified for expository purposes but numbers are automatically assigned at input. Further, information not germane has been omitted and replaced by ellipses. Space limits a full description of the contents of C here.

[7] A number of the other underlying linguistic features of the surface input are also sent to the cognition—namely animacy, gender, part-of-speech, number, and definiteness—as exemplified for the intransitive simple past phrase in (2). These are used for various internal purposes, such as anaphoric resolution, predicate argument typing and grammatical agreement.

their skolem identifiers, space and time. As with all Mephisto structures, this deep predicate can be utilised by Mephisto reasoners for logical inference. The formation of a variety of other spatial predicates follows this principle.

Syntax parser. This module defines and selects hand-crafted grammatically valid syntactic forms to ensure compliance with Lexpresso's controlled English syntax. Selected syntactic structures are described further in Section 3.

Lexicon. This module is used by the parser to instantiate leaf nodes. The lexicon covers core and domain specific terminology. It includes all major parts of speech containing over 20,000 unique word-forms comprised of a core of circa 12,130 high frequency English tokens plus non-high frequency general and domain specific terms. The class of nouns is comprised of circa 6,900 common nouns, circa 1,000 proper names and 62 forms of pronouns. Nouns are categorised according to certain features: mass/count, number, gender, alienability, and possible syntactic dependencies.

The class of verbs is comprised of main verbs, auxiliaries and modal auxiliaries. There are circa 8,380 main verbs classified according to a number of features, including semantic type, agreement, tense, aspect and mood inflection, syntactic and semantic frames, e.g. [11, 12, 13].

The class of adjectives is comprised of circa 2,644 forms and categorised into attributive, predicative, comparative and superlative types. Adjectives and other modifiers are further categorised according to the following primarily semantic types: age, amplifier, century, colour, compass, denominal, evaluative, girth, height, noun, objective, ordinal, participle, provenance, religion, shape, size, subjective, weak. This classification is used to stipulate the order adjectives in noun phrases.

Other classes of words consist of articles, cardinal and ordinal numerals, prepositions and other forms such as conjunctions, *wh*-words and directionals. Finally, there is a special sub-lexicon of domain specific expanded acronyms containing over 41,000 entries.

The Lexicon and Parser draw on syntactic and semantic knowledge (including *Aktionsart* [14], entity functional capability, and taxonomic relations) to constrain possible interpretations and reduce over-generation of deep CNL structures.

At this point in the system architecture linguistic content moves from surface to deep Lexpresso modules.

Grapher & Ambiguity handler. The Grapher transmutes parser outputs into graph structures so associations and semantic structures can be more easily reviewed than with parser output. In cases of multiple interpretations, e.g. (3b), a separate module identifies user defined interpretation preferences. This selects top ranked interpretations in a given context. Where multiple interpretations are equally ranked a separate graph structure is generated for each. The user can compare and select the desired interpretation to ensure each semantic form passed to the reasoner is unambiguous. Evaluation of this potentially burdensome method is required.

Semantic translator & Thematic roles. The graph structure is then converted into our universal semantic constructs for use by automated inferencing modules, not discussed here. Thematic roles and other linguistic information are identified by combining lexical and constructional semantics from the Syntax parser, Lexicon and Aktionsart modules with the Linguistic Knowledge Base. The results of this process ensure deep structures contain the requisite richness of linguistic semantic information for both inferencing and language generation. The Thematic roles module associates possible semantic roles with generic entities at the highest possible level in the Taxonomy. Subsumed entities will inherit the role associated with their genus.

Context resolver. Lexical semantic features associated with nouns (such as gender, animacy, cognitive or other capability) are identified via a relatively shallow hierarchy and used to resolve anaphoric pronouns and *wh*-forms. Types of NP anaphors include personal, reflexive, reciprocal and indefinite pronouns, as well as demonstratives. The only current VP anaphor is forms of the generic verb 'do'. A number of rules (not discussed here) determine how anaphors are resolved.

Where possible the CNL Effector (see Figure 1) makes use of existing Lexpresso modules as already described (such as the lexicon and parser and associated semantic knowledge) to handle the generation of surface language from deep Mephisto semantic constructs. Space constraints prohibit further explanation here.

3 Syntactic Structures

This section exemplifies selected basic syntactic structures permitted by the parser. Space constraints prohibit a comprehensive exposition of all of Lexpresso's syntax. The expository emphasis is on giving a sense of Lexpresso's expressiveness.

Sentence Types. These include declaratives, interrogatives, directives and indirect speech acts.

Declaratives. These sentence types include basic intransitives (3a), transitives (3b) and ditransitives (3c) with and without adjuncts.

(3) a. The boy slept on Monday.

   b. The woman in the car read the message on the sign.

   c. The woman gave the man the document.

Interrogatives. These can query for a range of syntactic elements: the subject (4a), object (4b) or predicate, such as generic 'do', (4c) of the basic sentences, as well as temporal information (4d) and locational adjuncts (4e). Indefinite pronouns can be used to query for any argument; (4f) demonstrates its use in a yes/no query.

(4)   a. Who gave the document to the boy?
      b. What did the woman read?
      c. What did the boy do?
      d. When did she read it?
      e. What region is she in?
      f. Did anyone see the woman?

Directives. These are currently limited to commands to the system to generate situation reports on specified tracks monitored by a track sensor module (not discussed here), e.g. 'Show merchant ship situation report on MR41_PAN-EAV' and 'Show commercial aircraft situation report on NAT57_FL310'. The range of useful commands to the system will to a certain extent dictate development of other directives. Directives are queries expressed in the imperative mood.

Indirect speech. These cover statements with embedded speech act verbs, such as 'say' and 'tell', e.g. 'Michael said that the woman read the document.' and 'Michael told Kerry that the woman read the document.' Subclauses introduced by 'that' are also permitted in other sentence types, not exemplified here.

Noun Phrases. These can be highly complex with multiple layers of embedding and recursion. The tree structures in (5) cover two primary basic types of noun phrase: (5a) specifies nouns with pre and post modifiers, whereas (5b) specifies conjoined noun phrases. Note its recursion.

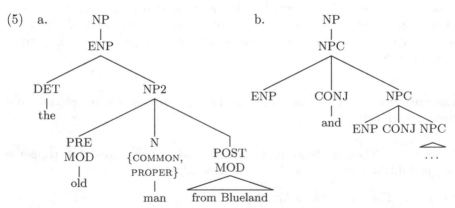

The modifier node is itself internally complex and permits modification by complements and adjuncts, as in (6). Justifications are not given here.

(6)   a.   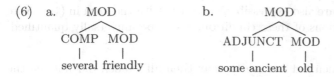   b.

Finally, the trees in (7) exemplify permitted noun phrases with genetive-*s*. Again note the recursion in (7a).

(7)   a.   b.

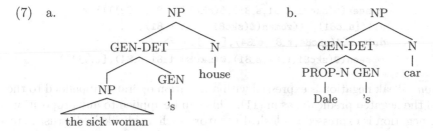

4   Semantic Structures

Kuhn [15] identified some five expressiveness features of Controlled Natural Languages (see a–e in *Fairly high expressiveness* in Section 5 below). I briefly exemplify these with I and C forms for each semantic type.

Universal quantification over individuals. Instances of universally quantified entities without an article (8a) are rendered with an `all` predicate (8b) referencing its universally quantified Skolem constant together with the list of relevant linguistic features. Numerals are converted into set operations and can quantify all argument positions and predicates, e.g. 'Three men read four documents twice'.

(8)   a.   I: Women stand.
       b.   C: `all([skc2],woman(@(skc2,t_3,s_2),[female,plural,...])`
                `=> stands(@(skc2,t_3,s_2),[general_habitual,...]))`.

Binary or higher relations. In principle Lexpresso does not place a restriction on the arity of relations (`reads(x,y)` in (9b) exemplifies a binary predicate). However, our ability to reason with higher arity relations is determined by the reasoners used, not discussed here. Our reasoner does not restrict arity either and indeed allows atomic propositions to occur as relation arguments.

General rule structures. Multiple universal quantification can target all argument positions of relations, as in (9).

(9)   a.   I: All women always read all documents.
       b.   C: `all([skc81,skc82,t_81],((woman(@(skc81,t_81,s_81),[...])&`
                `document(@(skc82,t_81,s_82),[...]))`
                `=> reads(@(skc81,t_81,s_81),@(skc82,t_81,s_82),[...])))`.

If–then conditionals are also expressible, currently with the form in (10). Note that all argument positions of these conditionals can be universally quantified, as in (10) with 'all'.

(10)   a. I: If all women did not see the car then all women did not see the driver.

        b. C: `all([skc81],((woman(@(skc81,t_81,s_81),[...]) &`
            `car(@(skc82,t_81,s_82),[...]))  =>`
            `¬ sees(@(skc81,t_81,s_81),@(skc82,t_81,s_82)))) =>`
            `all([skc81], ((woman(@(skc81,t_81,s_81),[...]) &`
            `driver(@(skc84,t_81,s_84),[...]))  =>`
            `¬ sees(@(skc81,t_81,s_81),@(skc84,t_81,s_84),[...]))).`

Negation. Weak negation is expressed with a negation operator appended to the front of the negated predicate, as in (11). This can be applied to any proposition. Strong negation is expressed via lexical negators such as 'dislike', 'distrust', etc.

(11)   a. I: The woman did not read the document.

        b. C: `woman(@(skc81,t_22,s_81),[definite,...]),`
            `document(@(skc07,t_22,s_07),[definite,...]),`
            `¬reads(@(skc81,t_22,s_81),@(skc07,t_22,s_07),[past,...]).`

Second-order universal quantification. This was exemplified in (9) in which the predicate 'read' is universally quantified by 'always' and rendered as an operator over the time of the predicate.

Other features articulated by Kuhn as determinants of expressiveness were existential quantification, as in (2), equality, as in (12), and types of speech acts (not exemplified due to space constraints but mentioned in Section 3).

(12)   a. I: Andrew White is the Prime Minister.

        b. C: `Andrew_White(@(skc6,t_10,s_6),[...]),`
            `prime_minister(@(skc7,t_10,s_7),[...]),`
            `identical[@(skc6,t_10,s_6),@(skc7,t_10,s_7)].`

Discourse structures. The paragraph is taken as the basic unit of discourse. For the purpose of anaphoric resolution, a new paragraph signifies a new discourse context. A single sentence can constitute a paragraph. Anaphora occurs within a discourse unit.

5   Classification of Lexpresso

Kuhn [15] presented a classification scheme for CNLs labelled with the acronym PENS. This classifies a CNL according to a five-tier ranking (with 5 for maximal) for each of four orthogonal categories of Precision, Expressiveness, Naturalness and Simplicity. Based on my assessment of Lexpresso against Kuhn's 'PENS' scheme, I tentatively classify it as P^{3-4} E^4 N^{4-5} S^3 as evidenced by the following paragraphs.

Precision—reliably & semi-deterministically interpretable. P^{3-4} Although it is not currently possible for any natural English language text to be deterministically transformed by Lexpresso into a formal logic representation, the syntax is heavily restricted enough to make automatic interpretation reliable. In cases where the natural language syntax is ambiguous and not automatically disambiguated, multiple interpretations are presented. The user is then consulted to select the desired interpretation. Once done, controlled natural language is deterministically translated into formal structures. There is also a well established, conceptually broad, underlying formalism.

Fairly high expressiveness. E^4 The range of propositions that Lexpresso can express includes all those articulated by Kuhn: (a) universal quantification over individuals; (b) relations of arity greater than 1; (c) general rule structures (if-then conditionals with multiple universal quantification that can target all argument positions of relations; (d) negation (strong negation or negation as failure); (e) general second-order universal quantification over concepts and relations; (f) existential quantification; (g) equality; and (h) types of speech acts including declarative, interrogative, directive and indirect. See Section 3 for examples.

Fair degree of naturalness. N^{4-5} While large scale texts have not been written in the language, small fairly natural texts and spoken interactions with internal interdependencies are parsable.

Simplicity. S^3 Lexpresso can be exactly, comprehensively defined with accepted grammatical and logical notations but it is likely to require more than ten pages to describe all its syntactic and semantic properties.[8]

6   Conclusion

This brief introduction to the Controlled Natural Language—Lexpresso—has presented the system architecture, and exemplified its main syntactic and semantic features. These features have been compared to Kuhn's [15] PENS classification system. Against this comparison I have tentatively classified Lexpresso as a P^{3-4} E^4 N^{4-5} S^3 CNL. According to this classification Lexpresso is a reliably or perhaps deterministically interpretable language, with high expressiveness, considerable naturalness and would require a lengthy treatment to cover its syntax and semantics. Given the page limit, this paper has not in any detail discussed Lexpresso's limitations nor the tight integration with the knowledge representation and reasoning capabilities which constitutes a significant component of our high-level information fusion system for which Lexpresso functions as a natural language interface.

---

[8] The description of Lexpresso's features presented here is not considered comprehensive and therefore does not qualify as an indicator of its simplicity score.

Acknowledgements. I thank Dale Lambert, Kerry Trentelman, Andrew Zschorn and Takeshi Matsumoto for discussions on issues raised in this paper and the first two named plus Nathalie Colineau and three anonymous reviewers for valuable comments on an earlier version. Both Andrew Zschorn and Takeshi Matsumoto have contributed to the development of Lexpresso.

References

1. Lambert, D., Nowak, C.: The mephisto conceptual framework. Technical Report DSTO-TR-2162, Defence Science and Technology Organisation (2008)
2. Baader, F., et al.: A novel architecture for situation awareness systems. In: Giese, M., Waaler, A. (eds.) TABLEAUX 2009. LNCS, vol. 5607, pp. 77–92. Springer, Heidelberg (2009)
3. Schwitter, R., Tilbrook, M.: Dynamic semantics at work. In: Proceedings of the International Workshop on Logic and Engineering of Natural Language Semantics (in conjunction with the 18th Annual Conference of the Japanese Society for Artificial Intelligence), Kanazawa, Japan, pp. 49–60 (2004)
4. Schwitter, R., Tilbrook, M.: Processable english (2007)
5. Lambert, D., Blasch, E., Bossé., E.: Introduction. In: Blasch, E., Bossé, E., Lambert, D. (eds.) High-Level Information Fusion Management and Systems Design, pp. 173–190. Artech House (2012)
6. Chomsky, N.: Syntactic Structures. Mouton & Co., 's-Gravenhage (1957)
7. Chomsky, N.: Aspects of the theory of syntax. MIT Press (1965)
8. Lambert, D., Lambert, A.: The legal agreement protocol. In: Blasch, E., Bossé, E., Lambert, D. (eds.) High-Level Information Fusion Management and Systems Design, pp. 173–190. Artech House (2012)
9. Allen, J.: Maintaining knowledge about temporal intervals. Commun. ACM 26, 832–843 (1983)
10. Saulwick, A.: Spatiotemporal reasoning over natural language. In: CoSLI-3 3rd Workshop on Computational Models of Spatial Language Interpretation and Generation (2013)
11. Fillmore, C.: Frame semantics and the nature of language. In: Annals of the New York Academy of Sciences: Conference on the Origin and Development of Language and Speech, vol. 280, pp. 20–32 (1976)
12. Ruppenhofer, J., Ellsworth, M., Petruck, M., Johnson, C., Scheffczyk, J.: FrameNet II: Extended Theory and Practice. International Computer Science Institute, Berkeley, California (2006) (Distributed with the FrameNet data)
13. Fillmore, C., Lee-Goldman, R., Rhomieux, R.: The framenet constructicon. In: Boas, H., Sag, I. (eds.) Sign-Based Construction Grammar. CSLI Lecture Notes (2012)
14. Vendler, Z.: Verbs and times. In: Linguistics in Philosophy. Cornell University Press, Ithaca (1967)
15. Kuhn, T.: A survey and classification of controlled natural languages. Computational Linguistics, 121–170 (2013)

A CNL for Contract-Oriented Diagrams

John J. Camilleri, Gabriele Paganelli, and Gerardo Schneider

Department of Computer Science and Engineering,
Chalmers University of Technology and the University of Gothenburg, Sweden
{john.j.camilleri,gerardo}@cse.gu.se, gabpag@chalmers.se

Abstract. We present a first step towards a framework for defining and manipulating normative documents or contracts described as *Contract-Oriented (C-O) Diagrams*. These diagrams provide a visual representation for such texts, giving the possibility to express a signatory's obligations, permissions and prohibitions, with or without timing constraints, as well as the penalties resulting from the non-fulfilment of a contract. This work presents a CNL for verbalising *C-O Diagrams*, a web-based tool allowing editing in this CNL, and another for visualising and manipulating the diagrams interactively. We then show how these proof-of-concept tools can be used by applying them to a small example.

Keywords: normative texts, electronic contracts, c-o diagrams, controlled natural language, grammatical framework.

1 Introduction and Background

Formally modelling normative texts such as legal contracts and regulations is not new. But the separation between logical representations and the original natural language texts is still great. CNLs can be particularly useful for specific domains where the coverage of full language is not needed, or at least when it is possible to abstract away from some irrelevant aspects.

In this work we take the *C-O Diagram* formalism for normative documents [1], which specifies a visual representation and logical syntax for the formalism, together with a translation into timed automata. This allows model checking to be performed on the modelled contracts. Our concern here is how to ease the process of writing and working with such models, which we do by defining a CNL which can translate unambiguously into a *C-O Diagram*. Concretely, the contributions of our paper are the following:

1. Syntactical extensions to *C-O Diagrams* concerning executed actions and cross-references (section 2.3);
2. A CNL for *C-O Diagrams* implemented using the Grammatical Framework (GF), precisely mapping to the formal grammar of the diagrams (section 3).
3. Tools for visualising and manipulating *C-O Diagrams* (section 2):
   (a) A web-based visual editor for *C-O Diagrams*;
   (b) A web-based CNL editor with real-time validation;
   (c) An XML format COML used as a storage and interchange format.

B. Davis et al. (Eds.): CNL 2014, LNAI 8625, pp. 135–146, 2014.

$$C := (agent, name, g, tr, O(C_2), R)$$
$$| \ (agent, name, g, tr, P(C_2), \epsilon)$$
$$| \ (agent, name, g, tr, F(C_2), R)$$
$$| \ (\epsilon, name, g, tr, C_1, \epsilon)$$
$$C_1 := C \ (And \ C)^+ \ | \ C \ (Or \ C)^+ \ | \ C \ (Seq \ C)^+ \ | \ Rep(C)$$
$$C_2 := a \ | \ C_3 \ (And \ C_3)^+ \ | \ C_3 \ (Or \ C_3)^+ \ | \ C_3 \ (Seq \ C_3)^+$$
$$C_3 := (\epsilon, name, \epsilon, \epsilon, C_2, \epsilon)$$
$$R := C \ | \ \epsilon$$

Fig. 1. Formal syntax of *C-O Diagrams* [1]

We also present a small example to show our CNL in practice (section 4) and an an initial evaluation of the CNL (section 5). In what follows we provide some background for *C-O Diagrams* and GF.

1.1 *C-O Diagrams*

Introduced by Martínez et al. [2], *C-O Diagrams* provide a means for visualising normative texts containing the modalities of obligation, permission and prohibition. They allow the representation of complex clauses describing these norms for different signatories, as well as *reparations* describing what happens when obligations and prohibitions are not fulfilled.

The basic element is the *box* (see Fig. 4), representing a basic contract clause. A box has four components: i) *guards* specify the conditions for enacting the clause; ii) *time restrictions* restrict the time frame during which the contract clause must be satisfied; iii) the *propositional content* of a box specifies a modality applied over actions, and/or the actions themselves; iv) a *reparation*, if specified, is a reference to another contract that must be satisfied in case the main norm is not. Each box also has an *agent* indicating the performer of the action, and a unique *name* used for referencing purposes. Boxes can be expanded by using three kinds of refinement: *conjunction, choice,* and *sequencing.*

The diagrams have a formal definition given by the syntax shown in Fig. 1. For an example of a *C-O Diagram*, see Fig. 5 (this example will be explained in more detail in section 4).

1.2 Grammatical Framework

GF [3] is both a language for multilingual grammar development and a type-theoretical logical framework, which provides a mechanism for mapping abstract logical expressions to a concrete language. With GF, the language-independent structure of a domain can be encoded in the abstract syntax, while language-specific features can be defined in potentially multiple concrete languages.

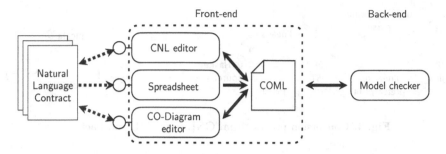

Fig. 2. The contract processing framework. Dashed arrows represent manual interaction, solid ones automated interaction.

Since GF provides both a *parser* and *lineariser* between concrete and abstract languages, multi-lingual translation can be achieved using the abstract syntax as an interlingua.

GF also comes with a standard library called the *Resource Grammar Library* (RGL) [4]. Sharing a common abstract syntax, this library contains implementations of over 30 natural languages. Each resource grammar deals with low-level language-specific details such as word order and agreement. The general linguistic descriptions in the RGL can be accessed by using a common language-independent API. This work uses the English resource grammar, simplifying development and making it easier to port the system to other languages.

2   Implementation

2.1   Architecture

The contract processing framework presented in this work is depicted in Fig. 2. There is a *front-end* concerned with the modelling of contracts in a formal representation, and a *back-end* which uses formal methods to detect conflicts, verify properties, and process queries about the modelled contract. The back-end of our system is still under development, and involves the automatic translation of contracts into timed automata which can be processed using the UPPAAL tool [5].

The front-end, which is the focus of this paper, is a collection of web tools that communicate using our XML format named COML.[1] This format closely resembles the *C-O Diagram* syntax (Fig. 1). The tools in our system allow a contract to be expressed as a CNL text, spreadsheet, and *C-O Diagram*. Any modification in the diagram is automatically verbalised in CNL and vice versa. A properly formatted spreadsheet may be converted to a COML file readable by the other editors. These tools use HTML5 [6] local storage for exchanging data.

---

[1] An example of the format, together with an XSD schema defining the structure, is available online at http://remu.grammaticalframework.org/contracts

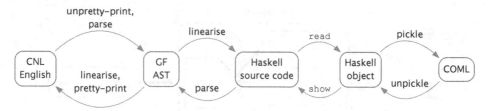

Fig. 3. Conversion process from CNL to COML and back

Translation Process. The host language for all our tools is Haskell, which allows us to define a central data type precisely reflecting the formal *C-O Diagram* grammar (Fig. 1). We also define an abstract syntax in GF which closely matches this data type, and translate between CNL and Haskell source code via two concrete syntaxes. As an additional processing step after linearisation with GF, the generated output is passed through a pretty-printer, adding newlines and indentations as necessary (section 3.2). The Haskell source code generated by GF can be converted to and from actual objects by deriving the standard Show and Read type classes. Conversion to the COML format is then handled by the HXT library, which generates both a parser and generator from a single *pickler* function. The entire process is summarised in Fig. 3.

2.2   Editing Tools

The visual editor allows users to visually construct and edit *C-O Diagrams* of the type seen in section 4. It makes use of the mxGraph JavaScript library providing the components of the visual language and several facilities such as converting and sending the diagram to the CNL editor, validation of the diagram, conversion to PDF and PNG format.

The editor for CNL texts uses the ACE JavaScript library to provide a text-editing interface within the browser. The user can verify that their CNL input is valid with respect to grammar, by calling the GF web service. Errors in the CNL are highlighted to the user. A valid text can then be translated into COML with the push of a button.

2.3   Syntactic Extensions to *C-O Diagrams*

This work also contributes two extensions to *C-O Diagram* formalism:
1. To the grammar of guards, we have add a new condition on whether an action a has been performed ($done(a)$);
2. We add also a new kind of box for cross-references. This enhances *C-O Diagrams* with the possibility to have a more modular way to "jump" to other clauses. This is useful for instance when referring to *reparations*, and to allow more general cases of "repetition".

Our tool framework also includes some additional features for facilitating the manipulation of *C-O Diagrams*. The most relevant to the current work is the automatic generation of clocks for each action. This is done by implicitly creating a clock `t_name` for each box `name`. When the action or sub-contract `name` is completed, the clock `t_name` is reset, allowing the user to refer to the time elapsed since the completion of a particular box.

3   CNL

This section describes some of the notable design features of our CNL. Examples of the CNL can be found in the example in section 4.

3.1   Grammar

The GF abstract syntax matches closely the Haskell data type designed for *C-O Diagrams*, with changes only made to accommodate GF's particular limitations. Optional arguments such as guards are modelled with a category `MaybeGuard` having two constructors `noGuard` and `justGuard`, where the latter is a function taking a list of guards, `[Guard]`. The same solution applies to timing constraints. Since GF does not have type polymorphism, it is not possible to have a generalised `Maybe` type as in Haskell. To avoid ambiguity, lists themselves cannot be empty; the base constructor is for a singleton list.

In addition to this core abstract syntax covering the *C-O Diagram* syntax, the GF grammar also imports phrase-building functions from the RGL, as well as the large-scale English dictionary `DictEng` containing over 64,000 entries.

3.2   Language Features

Contract Clauses. A simple contract verbalisation consists of an **agent**, **modality**, and an **action**, corresponding to the standard subject, verb and object of predication. The modalities of obligation, permission and prohibition are respectively indicated by the keywords `required`, `may` (or `allowed` when referring to complex actions) and `mustn't` (or `forbidden`).

Agents are noun phrases (NP), while actions are formed from either an intransitive verb (V), or a transitive verb (V2) with an NP representing the object. This means that every agent and action must be a grammatically-correct NP/VP, built from lexical entries found in the dictionary and phrase-level functions in the RGL. This allows us to correctly inflect the modal verb according to the agent (subject) of the clause:

```
1 : Mary is required to pay
2 : Mary and John are required to pay
```

Constraints. The arithmetic in the *C-O Diagram* grammar covering guards and timing restrictions is very general, allowing the usual comparison operators between variable or clock names and values, combined with operators for negation and conjunction. Their linearisation can be seen in line 9 of Fig. 6.

Each contract clause in a *C-O Diagram* has an implicit timer associated with it called t_name, which is reset when the contract it refers to is completed. These can be referred to in any timing restriction, effectively achieving relative timing constraints by referring to the time elapsed since the completion of another contract.

Conjunction. Multiple contracts can be combined by conjunction, choice and sequencing. GF abstract syntax supports lists, but linearising them into CNL requires special attention. Lists of length greater than two must be bulleted and indented, with the entire block prefixed with a corresponding keyword:

```
1 : all of
  - 1a : Mary may eat a bagel
  - 1b : John is required to pay
```

When unpretty-printed prior to parsing, this is converted to:

```
1 : all of { - 1a : Mary ... bagel - 1b : John ... pay }
```

For a combination of exactly two contracts, the user has the choice to use the bulleted syntax above, or inline the clauses directly using the appropriate combinator, e.g. **or** for choice. This applies to combination of contracts, actions and even guards and timing restrictions.

In the case of actions the syntax is slightly different since there is a single modality applied to multiple actions. Here, the actions appear in the infinitive form and the combination operator appears at the end of each line (except the final one):

```
2 : Mary is allowed
  - 2a : to pay , or
  - 2b : to eat a bagel
```

This list syntax allows for nesting to an arbitrary depth.

Names. The *C-O Diagram* grammar dictates that all contract clauses should have a name (*label*). These provide modularity by allowing referencing of other clauses by label, e.g. in reparations and relative timing constraints. Since the CNL cannot be lossy with respect to the COML, these labels appear in the CNL linearisation too (see Fig. 6). Clause names are free strings, but must not contain any spaces. This avoids the need for double quotes in the CNL. These labels do reduce naturalness somewhat, but we believe that this inconvenience can be minimised with the right editing tool.

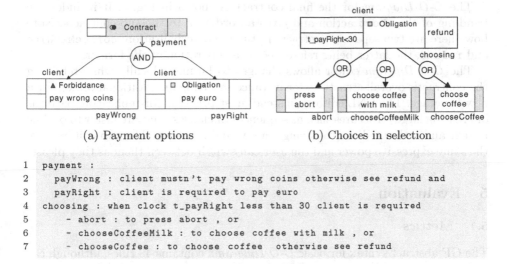

(a) Payment options   (b) Choices in selection

```
1  payment :
2     payWrong : client mustn't pay wrong coins otherwise see refund and
3     payRight : client is required to pay euro
4  choosing : when clock t_payRight less than 30 client is required
5     - abort : to press abort , or
6     - chooseCoffeeMilk : to choose coffee with milk , or
7     - chooseCoffee : to choose coffee  otherwise see refund
```

Fig. 4. Different kinds of complex contracts and their verbalisation

4 Coffee Machine Example

A user Eva must analyse the following description of the operation of a coffee machine, and construct a formal model for it. She will do this interactively, switching between editing the CNL and the visual representation.

> To order a drink the client inputs money and selects a drink. Coffee can be chosen either with or without milk. The machine proceeds to pour the selected drink, provided the money paid covers its price, returning any change. The client is notified if more money is needed; they may then add more coins or cancel the order. If the order is cancelled or nothing happens after 30 seconds, the money is returned. The machine only accepts euro coins.

Eva first needs to identify: i) the *actors* (client and machine), ii) the *actions* (pay, accept, select, pour, refund), iii) and the *objects* (beverage, money, timer). The first sentence suggests that to obtain a drink the client *must* insert coins. Eva therefore drops an `obligation` box in the diagram editor and fills the name, agent and action fields. Only accepting euro is modelled as a prohibition to the client using a `forbiddance` box. The two boxes are linked using a `contract` box as shown in Fig. 4a.

Eva now wants to model the choice of beverage, and the possibility the aborting of the process. She creates an `obligation` box named `choosing`, adding the timed constraint `t_payRight < 30` to model the 30 second timeout. She then appends two action boxes using the `or` refinement, corresponding to the choice of drinks (see Fig. 4b). Eva translates the diagram to CNL and modifies the text, adding the action `abort : to press abort` as a refinement of `choosing`. The result is shown in line 4 of Fig. 6.

The *C-O Diagram* for the final contract is shown in Fig. 5. It includes the handling of the `abort` action and gives an ordering to the sub-contracts. Note how there are two separate contracts in the CNL verbalisation: `coffeeMachine` and `refund`, the latter being referenced as a reparation of the former.

The *C-O Diagram* editor allows changes to be made locally while retaining the contract's overall structure, for instance inserting an additional option for a new beverage. The CNL editor is instead most practical for replicating patterns or creating large structures such as sequences of clauses, that are faster to outline in text and rather tedious to arrange in a visual language. The two editors have the same expressive power and the user can switch between them as they please.

5 Evaluation

5.1 Metrics

The GF abstract syntax for basic *C-O Diagrams* contains 48 rules, although the inclusion of large parts of the RGL for phrase formation pushes this number up to 251. Including the large-scale English dictionary inflates the grammar to 65,174 rules. As a comparison, a previous similar work on a CNL for the contract logic $\mathcal{CL}$ [7] had a GF grammar of 27 rules, or 2,987 when including a small verb lexicon.

5.2 Classification

Kuhn suggests the PENS scheme for the classification of CNLs [8]. We would classify the CNL presented in the current work as $P^5E^1N^{2\text{-}3}S^4$, F W D A. P (precision) is high since we are implementing a formal grammar; E (expressivity) is low since the CNL is restricted to the expressivity of the formalism; N (naturalness) is low as the overall structure is dominated with clause labels and bullets; S (simplicity) is high because the language can be concisely described as a GF grammar. In terms of CNL properties, this is a written (W) language for formal representation (F), originating from academia (A) for use in a specific domain (D).

The P, E and S scores are in line with the problem of verbalising a formal system. The low N score of between 2–3 is however the greatest concern with this CNL. This is attributable to a sentence structure is not entirely natural, somewhat idiosyncratic punctuation, and a bulleted structure that could restrict readability. While these features threaten the naturalness of the CNL in raw form, we believe that sufficiently developed editing tools have a large part to play in dealing with the structural restrictions of this language. Concretely, the ability to hide clause labels and fold away bulleted items can significantly make this CNL easier to read and work with.

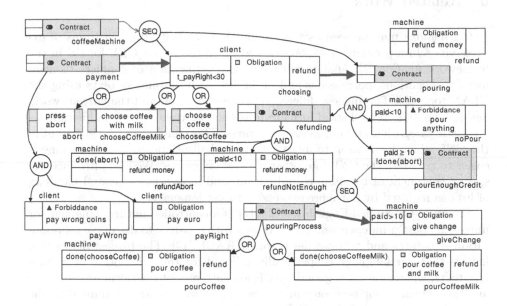

Fig. 5. The complete *C-O Diagram* for the coffee machine example

```
1   coffeeMachine : the following, in order
2    - payment : payWrong : client mustn't pay wrong coins otherwise
3        see refund and payRight : client is required to pay euro
4    - choosing : when clock t_payRight less than 30 client is required
5      - abort : to press abort , or
6      - chooseCoffeeMilk : to choose coffee with milk , or
7      - chooseCoffee : to choose coffee  otherwise see refund
8    - pouring : all of
9      - pourEnoughCredit : when abort is not done and variable paid
10        not less than 10 first pouringProcess : pourCoffee : if
11        chooseCoffee is done machine is required to pour coffee
12        otherwise see refund or pourCoffeeMilk : if chooseCoffeeMilk
13        is done machine is required to pour coffee and milk
14        otherwise see refund , then giveChange : if variable paid
15        greater than 10 machine is required to give change
16      - noPour : if variable paid less than 10 machine mustn't pour
             anything
17      - refunding : refundNotEnough : if variable paid less than 10
18        machine is required to refund money and refundAbort : if
19        abort is done machine is required to refund money
20   refund : machine is required to refund money
```

Fig. 6. The final verbalisation for the coffee machine example

6   Related Work

C-O Diagrams may be seen as a generalisation of $\mathcal{CL}$ [9,10,11] in terms of expressivity.[2] In a previous work, Angelov et al. introduced a CNL for $\mathcal{CL}$ in the framework AnaCon [7]. AnaCon allows for the verification of conflicts (contradictory obligations, permissions and prohibitions) in normative texts using the CLAN tool [12]. The biggest difference between AnaCon and the current work, besides the underlying logical formalism, is that we treat agents and actions as linguistic categories, and not as simple strings. This enables better agreement in the CNL which lends itself to more natural verbalisations, as well as making it easier to translate the CNL into other natural languages. We also introduce the special treatment of two-item co-ordination, and have a more general handling of lists as required by our more expressive target language.

Attempto Controlled English (ACE) [13] is a controlled natural language for universal domain-independent use. It comes with a parser to discourse representation structures and a first-order reasoner RACE [14]. The biggest distinction here is that our language is specifically tailored for the description of normative texts, whereas ACE is generic. ACE also attempts to perform full sentence analysis, which is not necessary in our case since we are strictly limited to the semantic expressivity of the *C-O Diagram* formalism.

Our CNL editor tool currently only has a basic user interface (UI). As already noted however, it is clear that UI plays a huge role in the effectiveness of a CNL. While our initial prototypes have only limited features in this regard, we point to the ACE Editor, AceRules and AceWiki tools described in [15] as excellent examples of how UI design can help towards solving the problems of writability with CNLs.

7   Conclusion

This work describes the first version of a CNL for the *C-O Diagram* formalism, together with web-based tools for building models of real-world contracts.

The spreadsheet format mentioned in Fig. 2 was not covered in this paper, but we aim to make it another entry point into our system. This format shows the mapping between original text and formal model by splitting the relevant information about modality, agent, object and constraints into separate columns. As an initial step, the input text can be separated into one sentence per row, and for each row the remaining cells can be semi-automatically filled-in using machine learning techniques. This will help the first part of the modelling process by generating a skeleton contract which the user can begin with.

We plan to extend the CNL and *C-O Diagram* editors with better user interfaces for easing the task of learning to use the respective representations and helping with the debugging of model errors. We expect to have more integration

---

[2] On the other hand, $\mathcal{CL}$ has three different formal semantics: an encoding into the μ-calculus, a trace semantics, and a Kripke-semantics.

between the two applications, in particular the ability to focus on smaller subsections of a contract and see both views in parallel. While the CNL editor already has basic input completion, it must be improvemed such that completion of functional keywords and content words are handled separately. Syntax highlighting for indicating the different constituents in a clause will also be implemented.

We currently use the RGL *as is* for parsing agents and actions without writing any specific constructors for them, which creates the potential for ambiguity. While this does not effect the conversion process, ambiguity is still an undesirable feature to have in a CNL. Future versions of the grammar will contain a more precise selection of functions for phrase construction, in order to minimise ambiguity.

Finally, it is already clear from the shallow evaluation in section 5 that the CNL presented here suffers from some unnaturalness. This can to some extent be improved by simple techniques, such as adding variants for keywords and phrase construction. Other features of the *C-O Diagram* formalism however are harder to linearise naturally, in particular mandatory clause labels and arbitrarily nested lists of constraints and actions. We see this CNL as only the first step in a larger framework for working with electronic contracts, which must eventually be more rigorously evaluated through a controlled usability study.

Acknowledgements. The authors wish to thank the Swedish Research Council for financial support under grant nr. 2012-5746. We are also very grateful to the anonymous reviewers for their suggestions, in particular with regards to CNL evaluation and classification using the PENS scheme.

References

1. Díaz, G., Cambronero, M.E., Martínez, E., Schneider, G.: Specification and Verification of Normative texts using C-O Diagrams. IEEE Transactions on Software Engineering (2013)
2. Martínez, E., Cambronero, E., Diaz, G., Schneider, G.: A Model for Visual Specification of e-Contracts. In: IEEE SCC 2010, pp. 1–8. IEEE Computer Society (2010)
3. Ranta, A.: Grammatical Framework: Programming with Multilingual Grammars. CSLI Publications, Stanford (2011)
4. Ranta, A.: The GF Resource Grammar Library. Linguistic Issues in Language Technology 2(2) (2009)
5. Larsen, K.G., Pettersson, P., Yi, W.: Uppaal in a nutshell. International Journal on Software Tools for Technology Transfer 1(1-2), 134–152 (2014)
6. Navara, E.D., Pfeiffer, S., Berjon, R., Faulkner, S., Leithead, T., O'Connor, E.: HTML5. Candidate recommendation, W3C (2014), http://www.w3.org/TR/2014/CR-html5-20140204/
7. Angelov, K., Camilleri, J.J., Schneider, G.: A Framework for Conflict Analysis of Normative Texts Written in Controlled Natural Language. Journal of Logic and Algebraic Programming 82(5-7), 216–240 (2013)
8. Kuhn, T.: A Survey and Classification of Controlled Natural Languages. Computational Linguistics 40(1) (2014)

9. Prisacariu, C., Schneider, G.: A Formal Language for Electronic Contracts. In: Bonsangue, M.M., Johnsen, E.B. (eds.) FMOODS 2007. LNCS, vol. 4468, pp. 174–189. Springer, Heidelberg (2007)
10. Prisacariu, C., Schneider, G.: $\mathcal{CL}$: An Action-Based Logic for Reasoning about Contracts. In: Ono, H., Kanazawa, M., de Queiroz, R. (eds.) WoLLIC 2009. LNCS, vol. 5514, pp. 335–349. Springer, Heidelberg (2009)
11. Prisacariu, C., Schneider, G.: A dynamic deontic logic for complex contracts. Journal of Logic and Algebraic Programming 81(4), 458–490 (2012)
12. Fenech, S., Pace, G.J., Schneider, G.: CLAN: A Tool for Contract Analysis and Conflict Discovery. In: Liu, Z., Ravn, A.P. (eds.) ATVA 2009. LNCS, vol. 5799, pp. 90–96. Springer, Heidelberg (2009)
13. Fuchs, N.E., Schwertel, U., Schwitter, R.: Attempto Controlled English (ACE) Language Manual, Version 3.0. Technical Report 99.03, Department of Computer Science, University of Zurich (1999)
14. Fuchs, N.E.: First-Order Reasoning for Attempto Controlled English. In: Rosner, M., Fuchs, N.E. (eds.) CNL 2010. LNCS, vol. 7175, pp. 73–94. Springer, Heidelberg (2012)
15. Kuhn, T.: Controlled English for Knowledge Representation. Doctoral thesis, University of Zurich (2010)

Handling Non-compositionality in Multilingual CNLs

Ramona Enache, Inari Listenmaa, and Prasanth Kolachina

University of Gothenburg, Sweden
{ramona.enache, inari.listenmaa, prasanth.kolachina}@cse.gu.se

Abstract. In this paper, we describe methods for handling *multilingual* non-compositional constructions in the framework of GF. We specifically look at methods to detect and extract non-compositional phrases from parallel texts and propose methods to handle such constructions in GF grammars. We expect that the methods to handle non-compositional constructions will enrich CNLs by providing more flexibility in the design of controlled languages. We look at two specific use cases of non-compositional constructions: a general-purpose method to detect and extract multilingual multiword expressions and a procedure to identify nominal compounds in German. We evaluate our procedure for multiword expressions by performing a qualitative analysis of the results. For the experiments on nominal compounds, we incorporate the detected compounds in a full SMT pipeline and evaluate the impact of our method in machine translation process.

1   Introduction

The work describes a series of methods used to enrich multilingual CNLs written in the grammar formalism GF (Grammatical Framework)[20] with multilingual multiword expressions (MMWEs). This aims to give a better separation between compositional and non-compositional constructions in GF applications and a better understanding on representing MMWEs in GF. We present two new GF modules: one for constructions in a multilingual setting, and one specifically for German compound nouns.

We are targeting cases where translation equivalents have different syntactic structure: this covers pairs such as English–French (*apple juice, jus de pommes* 'juice of apples') and English–Finnish (*kick the bucket, heittää henkensä* 'throw one's life'). Only the latter pair contains a monolingually non-compositional structure, i.e. having an interpretation that cannot be inferred from the components, but we consider both of them as MMWEs, due to the non-compositionality of translation.

We propose a solution to this, that relies on prior analysis of the domain, since GF applications are normally developed starting from positive examples covering the domain [22]. We start from a parallel corpus describing the scope of the grammar and identify MMWEs in order to add them to the grammar as special constructions.

A special case of MMWEs, which we treat separately is that of nominal compounds in German. The need for a multilingual lexicon of such compounds and their translations originated from the use of GF in machine translation [10], [11]. This use case is of particular interest, since it is easier to evaluate—both in terms of precision and recall of the method, and in terms of impact on the machine translation process.

B. Davis et al. (Eds.): CNL 2014, LNAI 8625, pp. 147–154, 2014.

This paper is structured as follows: Section 2 describes the background and related work; Section 3 describes the implementation of the general MWE detection and compound detection methods; Section 4 describes a preliminary evaluation, and finally Section 5 describes future work.

2   Background and Related Work

2.1   Grammatical Framework

GF (Grammatical Framework) is a grammar formalism particularly fit for multilingual natural language applications. In the recent years, it has been used extensively for developing (multilingual) CNLs, such as the in-house implementation of Attempto Controlled English [21], domain-specific applications for mathematical exercises [25], [27], [26], speech-based user interfaces [14], tourist phrases [23], business models [8] and cultural heritage artifacts [6], [7].

Applications written in GF are represented by their *abstract syntax*, which models the semantics of the domain in a language-independent fashion, and a number of *concrete syntaxes*, mapping the semantics to a number of target languages, most commonly natural languages.

The difficulty when dealing with compositional and non-compositional constructs in GF arises, in fact, from the multilingual character of the applications. It is of particular difficulty to design the abstract syntax in a way that accommodates all the concrete syntaxes, without the need for further change. As a potential solution to this, there has been work done on deriving the abstract syntax from an existing ontology [2] or FrameNet [13], [12]. However, such resources are not always available.

2.2   Multiword Expressions

There is a significant body of research on MWEs, ranging from classification [4], linguistic analysis [24] to methods to detect MWEs (for both monolingual [15], [18] and multilingual settings [29], [5], [28]) and evaluation measures for these methods [19].

Following the MWE taxonomy from [4] into fixed, semi-fixed and syntactically flexible expressions, we note that applying the same scale to MMWEs, it is the semi-fixed and syntactically flexible constructions that are most effectively representable in GF. The reason is that GF allows for generalisations in terms of arguments (for relational MWEs, such as transitive verb phrases), declension forms and topicalisation in the sentence.

3   Methods for MMWE Extraction

3.1   General MMWE Candidate Extraction

The algorithm for general MMWE extraction parses a pair of sentences (X, Y) with a wide-coverage GF grammar, often resulting in multiple parse trees for each sentence. Then it compares all pairs of trees $\{(x, y) \mid x \in parse(X), y \in parse(Y)\}$, and if no identical trees are found, the phrases are candidates for containing BMWEs.

```
weather_adjCl : AP -> Cl ;          -- it is warm / il fait chaud (Fre)
n_units_AP    : Card -> CN -> A -> AP ; -- x inches long
glass_of_CN   : NP -> CN ;          -- glass of water / lasillinen vettä (Fin)
where_go_QCl  : NP -> QCl ;         -- where did X go / vart gick X (Swe)
```

Fig. 1. Example of constructions

Part of the test material was not parsed by the regular GF grammar. To add robustness, we used a new chunking grammar[1] for the language pair English–Swedish. French and German didn't have the chunking grammar implemented, so for pairs including them, we used robust parsing in GF [1], [3]. With the chunking grammar, the trees kept their local structure better, whereas the robust parser resulted in flatter structure, making the distance to any well-formed tree high. Thus these sentences were always reported as BMWE candidates. For our small test set, this wasn't a problem, but for future work, a fallback for partial trees should be considered, e.g. one that translates the sentences both ways and calculates the word error rate.

We used material from two sources. First, we took 246 sentences from the Wikitravel phrase collection[2] in English, German, French and Swedish. The material consists of sentences such as asking for direction or expressing needs, in various language pairs of which other is English. For another type of text, we took the 61–sentence short story "Where is James?", from the website UniLang[3], which contains free material for language learning. In total our test set was 307 sentences, functioning mostly as a proof of concept.

After running the experiments, we found various MMWE candidates in all language pairs. We added relevant new findings to the GF multilingual dictionary, some replacing the old translations, some as new lexical items. However, the majority of the candidates were predicates that span over a larger structure, and couldn't be covered just by lexicon—instead, we added them to a new module, called *Construction* (see Figure 1).

The module is, in the spirit of construction grammar, between syntax and lexicon. Instead of applying to categories in general, most of the functions in the module are about particular predicates which are found to work differently in different languages. The purpose of the module is hence not so much to widen the scope of string recognition, but to provide trees that are abstract enough to yield correct translations. It is being developed incrementally, but we envision being able to develop the module in a more systematic manner by employing data-driven methods, such as extracting constructions from a treebank.

3.2 GF Lexicon of Compound Words

A substantial part of the work on MWEs involved the detection and representation of compound words in GF. The motivation for this lies in the need to improve GF-

---

[1] https://github.com/GrammaticalFramework/GF/blob/master/lib/
   src/experimental/Chunk.gf
[2] http://wikitravel.org/en/List_of_phrasebooks
[3] http://www.unilang.org/

```
fun ConsNomCN : N -> CN -> CN ;
fun Cons_sCN : N -> CN -> CN ;
fun Cons_enCN : N -> CN -> CN ;
```

Fig. 2. Example of compounds

driven machine translation from English into German, especially in the bio-medical domain [9].

The goal is to extract pairs consisting of German compound words and their English translations from parallel corpus, to syntactically analyse the compound and to build a GF representation of the pair, which will be added to a compound lexicon. Because the most frequent such compound words are nominals [4], we consider them as the use case of our method.

The method relies on a GF resource describing rules for nominal compounding. The following rules describe three types of compounding: first one with the modifier in nominative, second one with the morpheme 's' in the end (*Lebensmittel* 'life-s-means') and third one with the ending 'en' (*Krankenwagen* 'sick-en-vehicle').

The basic procedure is the following:

- we extract candidate pairs, which fulfil the following criteria:
  - their probability is above a confidence threshold
  - the English part parses as an NP in GF
  - the German part is composed of one word
- we employ a greedy algorithm to split the German word into a number of lexical items from the German monolingual dictionary from GF (based on Wiktionary), based on the German compound grammar described above; we select the split which employs the least number of tokens
- we add the pair of GF trees to a lexical resource for compounds

In our experiments, phrase translations extracted from a English-German parallel corpus [17] are used to detect possible nominal compounds in German. For practical reasons, we restrict the set of possible phrase translations to phrases determined to be *constituents* in the parse tree for the English sentence by a constituency parser [16]. This restricts the amount of noise in the translation memories, where *noise* is defined as a pair of random sequence of words in English and German that are seen together in the translations. Furthermore, we restrict our interest to entries that are labelled as noun phrases by the parser.

4   Evaluation

4.1   Evaluation of General MMWE Extraction

As a tentative evaluation for the general MMWE extraction method, we used the results of the language pair English–Swedish and did qualitative analysis of the findings. We chose Swedish, because it had the best grammar coverage out of the languages we tested; the results for French and German were poorer, due to the flat structure of trees from robust parsing. The chunking grammar made it possible to compare trees even when one has a complete parse and other not, since the well-formed sentence can also be expressed as chunks.

Table 1. General MMWE extraction

Not MWE candidates	92
MWE candidates	215
False positives	44
Lexical MWEs	29
Predicates	142
All sentences	**307**

Table 1 shows the results of the analysis. Of the 307 sentences in English and Swedish, we found 215 candidates, of which 44 were considered false positives, due to parsing problems. For the algorithm to recognise two sentences as identical, it needs to have parsed them properly, so we did not get false negatives.

Out of the remaining 171 candidates, we classified 29 to be lexical MWEs, such as English *locker* vs. Swedish *låsbart skåp* 'lockable closet', or *hide from* vs. *gömma sig för* 'hide REFL for'. Not all of them were one-to-many; in 11 cases it was just a question of similar words, such as *little* and *small* used in the parallel sentences.

142 candidates were predicates that span over a larger structure. The expressions could be classified to the following subcategories: a) greetings; b) weather expressions; c) time expressions; d) money; e) units of measurement, containers; f) spatial deixis.

These expressions are non-compositional due to different factors: e.g. greetings and weather expressions are highly idiomatic, fixed phrases. Other cases, such as units, are less rigid: a certain semantic class of words appears in structures like *glass of NP*, which work differently in different languages. For example, Swedish uses no preposition, Finnish uses a special form *glassful*. Since adding a general rule for *NP of NP* would be overgenerating, we added these constructions separately for each container word (e.g. *glass, bottle, cup, bucket*).

An example of spatial deixis is the correspondence of direction adverbs between languages: e.g. the word *where* in the sentence *where did X go* should be translated in German to *wohin* 'where to' instead of *wo* 'where in'; same with *here* and *there*. We added these constructions as combinations of a motion verb and a direction adverb.

Finally, a number of the 142 phrases were correctly recognised as containing a differing subtree, but we judged the difference not to be general enough to be added as a construction. For example, sentence (1) from the short story has the auxiliary verb *can* in the English version and not in the Swedish, and the adverb *tydligt* means 'clearly, distinctly'. While not general enough for the construction module, results like this could still be useful for some kind of application grammar; the method correctly recognises them, as long as the sentences are fully parsed.

(1) Hon hör   det tydligt nu   (Swe)
     'she hears it   clearly now'
     She can hear it well now (Eng)

4.2 Evaluation of German Nominal Compounds

We evaluated the German nominal compounds detected by our algorithm based on their utility in the task of machine translation. In this experiment, we provided the detected nominals as possible dictionary items to an SMT pipeline and extracted a translation memory from a news domain corpora augmented with the nominal compounds. We evaluated the improvements in translation quality after augmenting the translation memories with these nominal compounds. Translation quality is evaluated in terms of BLEU score, a standard metric used in evaluating performance of MT systems. Table 2 shows the BLEU scores obtained from two different SMT systems, a baseline system and the same system using the translation memory augmented with nominal compounds. The BLEU scores are reported on standard test datasets used in the evaluation of SMT systems.[4]

The improvement gained by using this simple method suggests that a proper handling of MWEs could improve the BLEU scores in an even more significant manner, by taking advantage of the full power of the GF representations, mainly by aligning all declension forms of MWEs and adding them to the translation memories.

Table 2. BLEU scores obtained from the SMT systems

SMT system	newstest2011	newstest2012
Baseline	11.71	11.64
+Compounds	11.83	11.96

5 Future Work

As GF has proven to be a reliable environment for writing multilingual CNLs and compositionality is a known problem of such applications, our method to isolate non-compositional constructions would be a great aid for the development of GF grammars, if it were applied on more domains and language sets. In this manner, one could also asses the generality of the method, both in terms of languages and types of constructions, more clearly.

For the purpose of aiding the development of GF domain grammars, we are also considering a combination between our method and the related efforts of constructing multilingual FrameNet-based grammars [13], [12].

---

[4] The datasets can be found at
http://www.statmt.org/wmt14/translation-task.html. We use the newstest2011 and newstest2012 datasets in our experiments.

Regarding the use of MWE in machine translation, one can consider integrating the GF resources in a more meaningful manner, by not just aligning the basic forms, but also the declension forms. The MWE resources could also be helped to improve the existing GF-driven hybrid translation systems [9].

Last, but not least, as our initial experiments have shown a rather large number of false positives, we aim to develop specific pre-processing methods to address this issue. A boost in accuracy would lead to a decrease in the size of the initial resources that are automatically created and reduce the effort for evaluation. A possible solution would be comparing the shape of the parse trees, in order to asses differences in the constructions.

In conclusion, our work represents the first step in handling non-compositional constructions in multilingual GF applications. The methods are still under development, but they still highlight the significant advantages that the feature brings, both to general CNLs written in GF and to large translation systems.

Acknowledgements. The authors would like to thank Koen Claessen and Aarne Ranta for their input on both the methods developed and this paper. Moreover, we would like to thank Víctor Sánchez-Cartagena for the fruitful discussion on a previous version of the MWE detection algorithm and the ideas on how to implement it for parallel free text.

We also want to thank the Swedish Research Council for financial support under grant nr. 2012-5746 (Reliable Multilingual Digital Communication: Methods and Applications).

References

1. Angelov, K.: The Mechanics of the Grammatical Framework. PhD thesis, Chalmers University of Technology (2011)
2. Angelov, K., Enache, R.: Typeful Ontologies with Direct Multilingual Verbalization. In: Rosner, M., Fuchs, N.E. (eds.) CNL 2010. LNCS, vol. 7175, pp. 1–20. Springer, Heidelberg (2012)
3. Angelov, K., Ljunglöf, P.: fast statistical parsing with parallel multiple context-free grammars. In: European Chapter of the Association for Computational Linguistics, Gothenburg (2014)
4. Baldwin, T., Kim, S.N.: Multiword expressions. In: Handbook of Natural Language Processing, 2nd edn. (2010)
5. Bouamor, D., Semmar, N., Zweigenbaum, P.: Identifying bilingual multi-word expressions for statistical machine translation. In: Calzolari, N., Choukri, K., Declerck, T., Doan, M.U., Maegaard, B., Mariani, J., Moreno, A., Odijk, J., Piperidis, S. (eds.) Proceedings of the Eight International Conference on Language Resources and Evaluation (LREC 2012), Istanbul, Turkey, European Language Resources Association (ELRA) (May 2012)
6. Dannélls, D., Damova, M., Enache, R., Chechev, M.: A framework for improved access to museum databases in the semantic web. In: Recent Advances in Natural Language Processing (RANLP) (2011)
7. Dannélls, D., Enache, R., Damova, M., Chechev, M.: Multilingual online generation from semantic web ontologies. In: WWW 2012, EU projects track (2012)
8. Davis, B., Enache, R., van Grondelle, J., Pretorius, L.: Multilingual Verbalisation of Modular Ontologies using GF and Lemon. In: Kuhn, T., Fuchs, N.E. (eds.) CNL 2012. LNCS, vol. 7427, pp. 167–184. Springer, Heidelberg (2012)

9. Enache, R.: Frontiers of Multilingual Grammar Development. PhD thesis, University of Gothenburg (2013)
10. Enache, R., España-Bonet, C., Ranta, A., Màrquez, L.: A hybrid system for patent translation. In: Proceedings of the 16th Annual Conference of the European Association for Machine Translation (EAMT 2012), Trento, Italy, pp. 269–276 (2012)
11. España-Bonet, C., Enache, R., Angelov, K., Virk, S., Galgóczy, E., Gonzàlez, M., Ranta, A., Màrquez, L.: WP5 final report: Statistical and robust machine translation (D 5.3) (2013)
12. Grūzītis, N., Dannélls, D.: Extracting a bilingual semantic grammar from FrameNet-annotated corpora (2014)
13. Gruzitis, N., Paikens, P., Barzdins, G.: FrameNet Resource Grammar Library for GF. In: Kuhn, T., Fuchs, N.E. (eds.) CNL 2012. LNCS, vol. 7427, pp. 121–137. Springer, Heidelberg (2012)
14. Kaljurand, K., Alumäe, T.: Controlled natural language in speech recognition based user interfaces. In: Kuhn, T., Fuchs, N.E. (eds.) CNL 2012. LNCS, vol. 7427, pp. 79–94. Springer, Heidelberg (2012)
15. Kiela, D., Clark, S.: Detecting compositionality of multi-word expressions using nearest neighbours in vector space models. In: EMNLP, pp. 1427–1432. ACL (2013)
16. Klein, D., Manning, C.D.: Accurate Unlexicalized Parsing. In: Proceedings of ACL (2003)
17. Koehn, P.: Europarl: A Parallel Corpus for Statistical Machine Translation. In: Proceedings of the 10th Machine Translation Summit (2005)
18. Korkontzelos, I.: Unsupervised Learning of Multiword Expressions. PhD thesis, University of York (2010)
19. Ramisch, C., De Araujo, V., Villavicencio, A.: A broad evaluation of techniques for automatic acquisition of multiword expressions. In: Proceedings of ACL 2012 Student Research Workshop, ACL 2012, Stroudsburg, PA, USA, pp. 1–6. Association for Computational Linguistics (2012)
20. Ranta, A.: Grammatical Framework: Programming with Multilingual Grammars. CSLI Publications (2011)
21. Angelov, K., Ranta, A.: Implementing Controlled Languages in GF. In: Fuchs, N.E. (ed.) CNL 2009. LNCS, vol. 5972, pp. 82–101. Springer, Heidelberg (2010)
22. Ranta, A., Camilleri, J., Détrez, G., Enache, R., Hallgren, T.: Grammar tool manual and best practices (D 2.3) (2012)
23. Ranta, A., Enache, R., Détrez, G.: Controlled language for everyday use: The MOLTO phrasebook. In: Rosner, M., Fuchs, N.E. (eds.) CNL 2010. LNCS, vol. 7175, pp. 115–136. Springer, Heidelberg (2012)
24. Sag, I.A., Baldwin, T., Bond, F., Copestake, A., Flickinger, D.: Multiword expressions: A pain in the neck for NLP. In: Gelbukh, A. (ed.) CICLing 2002. LNCS, vol. 2276, pp. 1–15. Springer, Heidelberg (2002)
25. Saludes, J., Xambó, S., The, G.F.: Mathematics Library. In: Proceedings of First Workshop on CTP Components for Educational Software, THedu 2011 (2011)
26. Saludes, J., Xambó, S.: Proceedings of EACA 2012, TODO (2012)
27. Saludes, J., Xambó, S.: Multilingual Sage. Tbilisi Mathematical Journal (2012)
28. Tsvetkov, Y., Wintner, S.: Extraction of multi-word expressions from small parallel corpora. In: Huang, C.-R., Jurafsky, D. (eds.) COLING (Posters), pp. 1256–1264. Chinese Information Processing Society of China (2010)
29. Villada Moirón, B., Tiedemann, J.: Identifying idiomatic expressions using automatic word alignment. In: Proceedings of the EACL 2006 Workshop on Multiword Expressions (2006)

Controlled Natural Language Generation from a Multilingual FrameNet-Based Grammar

Dana Dannélls and Normunds Gruzitis

Språkbanken, University of Gothenburg, Sweden
Department of Computer Science and Engineering, University of Gothenburg, Sweden
dana.dannells@svenska.gu.se, normunds.gruzitis@cse.gu.se

Abstract. This paper presents a currently bilingual but potentially multilingual FrameNet-based grammar library implemented in Grammatical Framework. The contribution of this paper is two-fold. First, it offers a methodological approach to automatically generate the grammar based on semantico-syntactic valence patterns extracted from FrameNet-annotated corpora. Second, it provides a proof of concept for two use cases illustrating how the acquired multilingual grammar can be exploited in different CNL applications in the domains of arts and tourism.

Keywords: Controlled Natural Language, FrameNet, Natural Language Generation, Multilinguality, Grammatical Framework.

1 Introduction

Two years ago, at CNL 2012, a conception of a general-purpose semantic grammar based on FrameNet (FN) was proposed [1] to facilitate the development of multilingual controlled natural language (CNL) applications in Grammatical Framework (GF). GF [2], a type-theoretical grammar formalism and a toolkit, provides a wide-coverage resource grammar library (RGL) for nearly 30 languages that implement a shared syntactic API [3]. The idea behind the FN-based grammar is to provide a frame semantic abstraction layer, a shared semantic API, over the syntactic RGL.

Following this proposal, a shared abstract syntax of wide-coverage English and Swedish semantic grammars has been recently extracted from FN-annotated corpora [4]. In this work, we take this approach one step further, and the contribution of this paper is two-fold. First, we offer a methodological approach to automatically generate concrete syntaxes based on the extracted abstract syntax. Second, we provide a proof of concept for two use cases illustrating how the acquired multilingual grammar can be exploited in different CNL applications in the domains of arts and tourism. Although we focus on English and Swedish, the same approach is intended to be applicable to other languages as well.

The future potential of our work is to provide a means for multilingual verbalization of FN-annotated databases that have been populated in information extraction processes by FN-based semantic parsers and that potentially can be mapped with the FN-based API automatically [5].

B. Davis et al. (Eds.): CNL 2014, LNAI 8625, pp. 155–166, 2014.

2 Background

2.1 FrameNet (FN)

FrameNet is a lexico-semantic resource based on the theory of frame semantics [6]. According to this theory, a semantic *frame* representing a cognitive scenario is characterized in terms of *frame elements* (FE) and is evoked by target words called *lexical units* (LU). An LU entry carries semantic and syntactic valence information about the possible realizations of FEs. The syntactic and semantic valence patterns are derived from FN-annotated corpora. FEs are classified in *core* and *non-core* FEs. A set of core FEs uniquely characterize the frame and syntactically correspond to verb arguments, in contrast to non-core FEs (adjuncts) which can be instantiated in many other frames. In this paper, we consider only those frames for which there is at least one corpus example where the frame is evoked by a verb. The frame-based grammar currently covers only core FEs.

The FrameNet approach provides a benchmark for representing large amounts of word senses and word usage patterns through the linguistic annotation of corpus examples, therefore the exploitation of FN-like resources has been appealing for a range of advanced NLP applications such as semantic parsing [7], information extraction [8] and natural language generation [9]. There are available computationally oriented FNs for German, Japanese, Spanish [10] and Swedish [11]. More initiatives exist for other languages. In this paper, we consider two FNs: the original Berkeley FrameNet (BFN) [6] and the Swedish FrameNet (SweFN) [11].

BFN version 1.5 defines more than 1,000 frames,[1] of which 556 are evoked by around 3,200 verb LUs in more than 68,500 annotated sentences [4]. Although BFN has been developed for English, its inventory of frames and FEs is being reused for many other FNs [10]. Hence, the abstract semantic layer of BFN can be seen as an interlingua for linking different FNs.

SweFN mostly uses the BFN frame inventory, however, around 50 additional frames have been introduced in SweFN, and around 15 BFN frames have been modified (in terms of FEs). The SweFN development version contains more than 900 frames of which 638 are evoked by around 2,300 verb LUs in more than 3,700 annotated sentences [4].[2]

2.2 Grammatical Framework (GF)

The presented grammar is implemented in GF, a categorial grammar formalism specialized for multilingual (parallel) grammars [2]. One of the key features of GF grammars is the separation between an abstract syntax and concrete syntaxes. The abstract syntax defines the language-independent structure, the semantics of a domain-specific application grammar or a general-purpose grammar library, while the concrete syntaxes define the language-specific syntactic and lexical realization of the abstract syntax.

---

[1] https://framenet.icsi.berkeley.edu/

[2] http://spraakbanken.gu.se/swefn/ (a snapshot taken in February 2014)

Remarkably, GF is not only a grammar formalism or programming language. It also provides a general-purpose resource grammar library (RGL) for nearly 30 languages that implement the same abstract syntax, a shared syntactic API [3]. The use of the shared syntactic types and functions allows for rapid and rather flexible development of multilingual application grammars without the need of specifying low-level details like inflectional paradigms and syntactic agreement.

3   FrameNet-Based Grammar

The language-independent conceptual layer of FrameNet, i.e. frames and FEs, is defined in the abstract syntax of the multilingual FN-based grammar, while the language-specific lexical layers, i.e. the surface realization of frames and LUs, are defined in concrete syntaxes.[3] The syntactic API of RGL is used for generalizing and unifying the syntactic types and constructions used in different FNs, which facilitates porting the implementation to other languages. The FN-based grammar, in turn, provides a frame semantic abstraction layer to RGL, so that the application grammar developer can primarily manipulate with plain semantic constructors in combination with some simple syntactic constructors instead of comparatively complex syntactic constructors for building verb phrases (VP). Moreover, the frame constructors can be typically specified for all languages at once in the shared concrete syntax (functor) of an application grammar.

3.1   Abstract Syntax

Following a recently proposed approach [4], we have extracted a set of shared semantico-syntactic frame valence patterns from the annotated sentences in BFN and SweFN. For instance, the shared valence patterns for the frame Desiring are:

Desiring/V_{Act} Experiencer/NP_{Subj} Focal_participant/Adv
Desiring/$V2_{Act}$ Experiencer/NP_{Subj} Focal_participant/NP_{DObj}
Desiring/VV_{Act} Event/VP Experiencer/NP_{Subj}

which correspond, for instance, to these annotated examples in BFN:[4]

[Dexter]$_{Experiencer/NP}$ [YEARNED]$_V$ [for a cigarette]$_{Focal\_participant/Adv}$
[she]$_{Experiencer/NP}$ [WANTS]$_{V2}$ [a protector]$_{Focal\_participant/NP}$
[I]$_{Experiencer/NP}$ would n't [WANT]$_{VV}$ [to know]$_{Event/VP}$

In contrast to the previous experiment [4], where the focus was on the abstract grammar, here we generate the concrete syntaxes taking the syntactic roles for FEs of type NP into account: subject (Subj), direct object (DObj) and indirect object (IObj). Thus, we also consider the grammatical voice (Act/Pass) in the pattern comparison, as well as the target verb type deduced from the syntactic types and roles of involved FEs. Additionally, we handle FEs of common types of

---

[3] http://www.grammaticalframework.org/framenet/
[4] The actual BFN phrase types are generalized by RGL types.

subclauses (generalized to S, embedded sentences), as well as finite and gerundive VPs, and PPs where the preposition governs a wh-clause or a gerundive VP, so that the fraction of skipped BFN examples is reduced form 14% to 4%, and no SweFN examples are skipped.

The extracted sets of valence patterns usually vary across languages depending on corpora. For multilingual applications we are primarily interested in valence patterns whose implementation can be generated for all considered languages. Thus, we focus on valence patterns that are shared between FNs. The multilingual criteria also help in reducing the number of incorrect patterns due to annotation errors introduced by the automatic POS tagging and syntactic parsing. However, patterns that are not verified across FNs could be separated into FN-specific extra modules of the grammar.

To find a representative yet condensed set of shared valence patterns, we compare the extracted patterns by subsumption instead of exact match [4]. Pattern A subsumes pattern B if A.frame = B.frame, A.verbType = B.verbType, A.voice = B.voice, and B.FEs $\subseteq$ A.FEs (taking into account the syntactic types and roles). If a pattern of FN_1 is subsumed by a pattern of FN_2, it is added to the shared set (and vice versa). In the final set, patterns which are subsumed by other shared patterns are removed. To reduce the propagation of annotation errors even more, we filter out once used BFN valence patterns before performing the cross-FN pattern comparison.[5]

In the result, from around 66,800 annotated sentences in BFN and around 4,100 annotated sentences in SweFN, we have extracted a set of 717 shared semantico-syntactic valence patterns covering 423 frames.

Frame valence patterns are declared in the grammar as functions (henceforth called frame functions) that take one or more core FEs and one verb as arguments. For each frame, the set of core FEs is often split into several alternative functions according to the corpus evidence.[6] Different subsets of core FEs may require different types of target verbs. We also differentiate between functions that return clauses in the passive voice from functions that return active voice clauses because the subject and object FEs swap their syntactic roles and/or the order (which otherwise is not reflected in the abstract syntax). If the verb type and voice suffixes are not sufficient to make the function name unique, a discriminative number is added as well. For instance, consider the following abstract functions derived from the above given valence patterns:[7]

> *fun* Desiring_V : Experiencer_NP $\rightarrow$ Focal_participant_Adv $\rightarrow$ V $\rightarrow$ Clause
> *fun* Desiring_V2_Act : Experiencer_NP $\rightarrow$ Focal_participant_NP $\rightarrow$ V2 $\rightarrow$ Clause
> *fun* Desiring_V2_Pass : Experiencer_NP $\rightarrow$ Focal_participant_NP $\rightarrow$ V2 $\rightarrow$ Clause
> *fun* Desiring_VV : Event_VP $\rightarrow$ Experiencer_NP $\rightarrow$ VV $\rightarrow$ Clause

---

[5] A similar pre-filtering is currently not reasonable for SweFN due to its small size.

[6] It is often unlikely that all core FEs can be used in the same sentence.

[7] Note that Desiring_V2_Pass is not directly acquired from a shared pattern; missing passive voice patterns could be derived from the corresponding active voice patterns. Also note that the syntactic roles are not reflected in the abstract syntax; they are used to generate the implementation of frame functions in the concrete syntaxes.

In GF, constituents and features of phrases are stored in objects of record types, and functions are applied to such objects to construct phrase trees. In the abstract syntax, both argument types and the value type of a function are separated by right associative arrows, i.e. all functions are curried. Arguments of a frame function are combined into an object of type Clause that differs form the RGL type Cl. A Clause whose linearization type is {np : NP; vp : VP} comprises two constituents of RGL types. It is a deconstructed Cl where the subject NP is separated from the rest of the clause. The motivation for this is to allow for nested frames (see Section 4.1) and for adding non-core FEs before combining the NP and VP parts into a clause (see Section 4.2).

In the FN-based grammar, FEs are declared as semantic categories (types) that are subcategorized by RGL types, and these discriminators are also encoded by suffixes in FE names to keep the names unique, for instance:

   cat Experiencer_NP

Note that the FE Focal_participant is typically realized as a noun phrase (NP), but some intransitive verbs require it as a prepositional phrase (PP), hence this FE is subcategorized using the RGL types NP and Adv (adverbial modifier). In GF, the type Adv covers both adverbs and PPs, and there is no separate type for PPs. Also note that the word order is not specified in the abstract syntax (FEs in the function type signatures are given alphabetically), and all FE arguments are specified in concrete syntaxes as optional, i.e. any FE can be an empty phrase if it is not expressed in the sentence.

The frame-evoking target verb, either intransitive (V), transitive (V2) or di-transitive (V3), is always given as the last, mandatory argument. We additionally differentiate two special cases of transitive verbs: verb-phrase-complement verbs (VV) and sentence-complement verbs (VS), as well as a special case for each of them allowing also for an indirect object (V2V and V2S respectively).

LUs are represented as functions that take no arguments. To distinguish be-tween different senses and types of LUs, the verb type and the frame name is added to lexical function names, for instance:

   (Eng) *fun* want_VV_Desiring : VV
   (Swe) *fun* vilja_VV_Desiring : VV

However, LUs between BFN and SweFN are not directly aligned, therefore an FN-specific lexicon is generated for each language containing more than 3,300 entries for English and more than 1,100 entries for Swedish. The domain-specific translation equivalents can be aligned in application grammars.

We assume that verbs of the same type evoking the same frame share a set of generalized syntactic valence patterns. Patterns requiring, for instance, a tran-sitive verb cannot be evoked by an intransitive verb. Otherwise, the current approach does not limit the set of verbs that can evoke a frame, and the set of prepositions that can be used for an FE if it is realized as a PP. We expect that appropriate verbs and prepositions are specified by the application gram-mar that uses the FN-based grammar as an API. Hence, this approach allows to evoke a frame by a metaphor, i.e. an LU that normally evokes another frame.

3.2 Concrete Syntaxes

The exact behaviour of the types and functions declared in the abstract syntax is defined in the concrete syntax for each language.

The mapping from the semantic FN types to the syntactic RGL types is straightforward and is shared for all languages in a functor, for instance:

    lincat Focal_participant_NP = Maybe NP
    lincat Focal_participant_Adv = Maybe Adv

To allow for optional FEs (verb arguments that might not be expressed in the sentence), all linearization types are of type Maybe whose behaviour is similar to the analogous type in Haskell: a value of type Maybe x either contains a value of type x (represented as Just x), or it is empty (represented as Nothing).

To implement the frame functions, particularly to fill the VP part of Clause objects, RGL constructors are applied to the arguments depending on their RGL types and syntactic roles. The implementation of functions declared in the previous section is systematically generated for English and Swedish as follows:

    lin Desiring_V experiencer focal_participant v = {
        np = fromMaybe NP experiencer ;
        vp = mkVP (mkVP v) (fromMaybe Adv focal_participant) }

    lin Desiring_V2_Act experiencer focal_participant v2 = {
        np = fromMaybe NP experiencer ;
        vp = mkVP v2 (fromMaybe NP focal_participant) }

    lin Desiring_V2_Pass experiencer focal_participant v2 = {
        np = fromMaybe NP focal_participant ;
        vp=mkVP (passiveVP v2) (mkAdv by8agent_Prep (fromMaybe NP experiencer))
    }

    lin Desiring_VV event experiencer vv = {
        np = fromMaybe NP experiencer ;
        vp = mkVP (mkVV vv) (fromMaybe VP event) }

Apart from RGL constructors (mkVP, mkVV, passiveVP, mkAdv, etc.[8]), a helper function fromMaybe is used to handle the potentially optional FEs. This function takes a Maybe value and returns an empty phrase of the specified type if the Maybe value is empty (Nothing); otherwise it returns the Maybe value.

The RGL-based code templates used to implement the above functions can be reused for many other frame functions. Given the 717 extracted shared semantico-syntactic valence patterns, there are only 25 syntactic valence patterns that match all 717 patterns if we consider only the syntactic types and roles of FEs, and the grammatical voice the roles depend on. These patterns (except 5 once used) are listed in Table 1 that shows that the syntactic patterns underlying functions Desiring_V, Desiring_V2_Act, Desiring_V2_Pass and Desiring_VV already cover 55% of all shared patterns. For the same verb types, similar syntactic patterns (RGL-based code templates) cover another 39% of frame functions. The similar templates can be derived in several (incl. combined) ways:

---

[8] http://www.grammaticalframework.org/lib/doc/synopsis.html

- more adverbial modifiers can be added by recursive calls of the respective mkVP constructor, or modifiers can be removed at all;
- the NP part of the return values can be fixed to an empty NP if no FE is expected to fill the subject role (e.g. due to examples in the imperative mood; however, a missing subject FE could be often automatically added);
- in the passive voice, the direct object can be possibly fixed to an empty NP.

Table 1. Syntactic valence patterns matching the shared semantico-syntactic patterns

Verb	Voice	FE types and roles	Freq.	Verb	Voice	FE types and roles	Freq.
V2	Act	NP_{DObj} NP_{Subj}	238	V	Act	Adv	8
V	Act	Adv NP_{Subj}	138	V2	Act	Adv NP_{DObj}	8
V2	Pass	NP_{Subj}	70	V2V	Act	NP_{IObj} NP_{Subj} VP	5
V	Act	NP_{Subj}	65	VS	Pass	S	3
V2	Act	Adv NP_{DObj} NP_{Subj}	62	V	Act	Adv Adv Adv NP_{Subj}	2
V2	Pass	Adv NP_{Subj}	31	V2	Act	Adv Adv NP_{DObj} NP_{Subj}	2
VS	Act	NP_{Subj} S	26	V2	Pass	Adv	2
VV	Act	NP_{Subj} VP	18	V2	Pass	Adv Adv NP_{Subj}	2
V	Act	Adv Adv NP_{Subj}	14	V3	Act	NP_{IObj} NP_{Subj}	2
V2	Act	NP_{DObj}	14	VS	Act	Adv NP_{Subj} S	2

The remaining 6% of the shared patterns represent the use of other verb types: V3, V2V, VS and V2S. Basic code templates that are reused to implement the corresponding frame functions (VP parts) are illustrated by these examples:

mkVP v3 (fromMaybe NP recipient) (fromMaybe NP theme)
-- Giving: $[she]_{Donor/NP}$ $[handed]_{V3}$ $[him]_{Recipient/NP}$ $[the\ ring]_{Theme/NP}$

mkVP vs (fromMaybe S message)
-- Hear: $[we]_{Hearer/NP}$ $[heard]_{VS}$ $[it\ was\ a\ good\ school]_{Message/S}$

mkVP v2v (fromMaybe NP addressee) (fromMaybe VP message)
-- Request: $[UK]_{Speaker/NP}$ $[urges]_{V2V}$ $[Savimbi]_{Addressee/NP}$ $[to\ keep\ the\ peace]_{Message/VP}$

mkVP v2s (fromMaybe NP addressee) (fromMaybe S content)
-- Suasion: $[he]_{Speaker/NP}$ $[persuaded]_{V2S}$ $[himself]_{Addressee/NP}$ $[that\ they\ helped]_{Content/S}$

Note that the RGL type S, embedded declarative sentence, is used only if the subclause can be verbalized using the subjunction *that*; otherwise such FEs are subcategorized as Adv, and the application grammar developer has to specify the subjunction by applying the RGL constructor mkAdv : Subj $\rightarrow$ S $\rightarrow$ Adv. Also note that FEs of type VP or S, or Adv encapsulating an S represent nested frames. We use the type S instead of Cl to allow for specifying sentence level parameters like tense, anteriority and polarity of the nested frames.

The implementation of frame functions, although currently kept separate for each language, mostly could be shared due to the syntactic abstraction provided by RGL. In general, however, the order of Adv FEs can differ across languages.

4   Case Studies

We illustrate the use of the FrameNet-based API to GF RGL by re-engineering two existing multilingual GF application grammars: one for translating standard tourist phrases [12] and another for generating descriptions of paintings [13], both developed in the MOLTO project.[9] In both cases, we preserve the original functionality, and we do not make any changes in the application abstract syntax. Changes affect only the concrete syntaxes of English and Swedish.

4.1   Phrasebook

Although the Phrasebook grammar covers many idiomatic expressions that cannot be translated using the same frame or for which the FN-based approach would not be suitable at all, it includes around 20 complex clause-building functions that can be handled by the FN-based grammar. To illustrate the use of the semantic API, we re-implement the following Phrasebook functions:

```
ALive   : Person -> Country -> Action  -- e.g. 'we live in Sweden'
AWant   : Person -> Object -> Action   -- e.g. 'I want a pizza'
AWantGo : Person -> Place -> Action    -- e.g. 'I want to go to a museum'
```

by applying the frame functions Desiring_V2_Act and Desiring_VV introduced in Section 3, and some additional functions:

```
Motion_V_2    : Goal_Adv -> Source_Adv -> Theme_NP -> Clause
Possession_V2 : Owner_NP -> Possession_NP -> Clause
Residence_V   : Location_Adv -> Resident_NP -> Clause
```

By using RGL constructors, ALive is implemented for English, Swedish and other languages in the same way, except that different verbs are used:

```
ALive p co = mkCl p.name (mkVP (mkVP (mkV "live")) (mkAdv in_Prep co))
ALive p co = mkCl p.name (mkVP (mkVP (mkV "bo")) (mkAdv in_Prep co))
```

First, the language-specific verbs can be factored out by introducing a shared abstract verb in the domain lexicon (e.g. live_V that links live_V_Residence and bo_V_Residence). Second, the implementation of ALive can be done in a shared functor by using the FN-based API:

```
ALive p co = let cl : Clause =
  Residence_V (Just Adv (mkAdv in_Prep co)) (Just NP p.name) live_V
    in mkCl cl.np cl.vp
```

For AWant, neither the RGL-based nor the current FN-based implementation can be done in the functor because, in Swedish, the verb *vilja* ('to want') evoking Desiring_V2_Act requires the auxiliary verb *ha* ('to have'). This can be seen as a nested auxiliary frame Possession:

---

[9] http://www.molto-project.eu/

```
AWant p obj = mkCl p.name (mkV2 (mkV "want")) obj        -- Eng
Desiring_V2_Act (Just NP p.name) (Just NP obj) want_V2

AWant p obj = mkCl p.name want_VV (mkVP L.have_V2 obj)   -- Swe
Desiring_VV
  (Just VP (Possession_V2 (Nothing NP) (Just NP obj) have_V2).vp)
  (Just NP p.name) want_VV
```

Assuming that the auxiliary verb can be optionally used also with other Swedish verbs when applying this frame function, the nested frame could be hidden in the Swedish implementation of Desiring_V2_Act. This, however, is not the case with AWantGo which in both languages requires a main nested frame and, thus, can be put in the functor:

```
AWantGo p place = mkCl p.name want_VV (mkVP (mkVP go_V) place.to)

Desiring_VV (Just VP
  (Motion_V_2 (Just Adv place.to) (Nothing Adv) (Nothing NP) go_V).vp)
  (Just NP p.name) want_VV
```

At first gleam, the new code might look more complex, but it does not specify how the VP is built, and the same uniform code template is used in all cases. The re-implemented version of Phrasebook accepts and generates the same set of sentences as before.

4.2   Painting Grammar

The Painting grammar is a part of a large scale Natural Language Generation (NLG) grammar developed for the cultural heritage (CH) domain in order to verbalize data about museum objects stored in an RDF-based ontology [13]. A set of RDF triples (subject-predicate-object expressions) forms the input to the application. As an example, a simplified set of triples representing information about the artwork *Le Général Bonaparte* is:

```
<LeGeneralBonaparte> <createdBy> <JacquesLouisDavid>
<LeGeneralBonaparte> <hasDimension> <LeGeneralBonaparteDimesion>
<LeGeneralBonaparte> <hasCreationDate> <LeGeneralBonaparteCreationDate>
<LeGeneralBonaparte> <hasCurrentLocation> <MuseeDuLouvre>
```

This information is combined by the grammar to generate a coherent text. The function in the abstract syntax that combines the triples is the following:

```
DPainting : Painting -> Painter -> Year -> Size -> Museum -> Description
```

Each argument of the function corresponds to a class in the ontology. Below we show how the arguments are linearized in the original concrete syntax for English and how this syntax has been adapted to generate from the FN-based grammar. To adapt the grammar, we first identified the frames that match the target verbs in the linearization rules. Then we matched the core FEs of the identified frames with the verb arguments.

```
The original grammar:                Using the FrameNet-based API:
-------------------------------      --------------------------------------
DPainting painting painter           DPainting painting painter
 year size museum =                   year size museum =
let                                  let
 s1 : Text = mkText (mkS               cl1 : Clause =
  pastTense (mkCl painting (mkVP         Create_physical_artwork_V2_Pass
  (mkVP (passiveVP paint_V2)             (Just NP painter.long)
   (mkAdv by8agent_Prep                  (Just NP painting)
    painter.long)) year.s))) ;          paint_V2 ;

 s2 : Text = mkText                    cl2 : Clause = Dimension_V
  (mkCl it_NP (mkVP (mkVP                (Just Adv size.s)
  (mkVPSlash measure_V2)                 (Just NP it_NP)
  (mkNP (mkN "")))  size.s) ;            measure_V2 ;

 s3 : Text = mkText                    cl3 : Clause = Being_located_V
  (mkCl (mkNP this_Det painting)         (Just Adv museum.s)
  (mkVP (passiveVP display_V2)           (Just NP (mkNP this_Det painting))
   museum.s))                            display_V2

in mkText s1 (mkText s2 s3) ;        in mkText (mkText (mkS pastTense
                                        (mkCl cl1.np (mkVP cl1.vp year.s)))
                                        (mkText (mkCl cl2.np cl2.vp)
                                        (mkText (mkCl cl1.np cl3.vp))) ;
```

The grammar exploits patterns of frames Create_physical_artwork, Dimension and Being_located. Since the FN-based grammar currently does not cover non-core FEs, the adjunct *Year* is associated with no FE in Create_physical_artwork. Instead, it is attached to the corresponding clause in the final linearization rule (mkText) illustrating how non-core FEs can be incorporated.

The Swedish syntax was adapted in a similar way. The only difference in comparison to English and to the original Swedish syntax is the choice of verbs and pronouns. The descriptions generated by the new version of DPainting are semantically equivalent to the descriptions produced by the original grammar:

> Eng: *Le Général Bonapart was painted by Jacques-Louis David in 1510. It measures 81 by 65 cm. This work is displayed at the Musée du Louvre.*
> Swe: *Le Général Bonapart målades av Jacques-Louis David år 1510. Den mäter 81 gånger 65 cm. Det här verket hänger på Louvren.*

5   Evaluation

We have conducted a simple intrinsic and extrinsic evaluation of the acquired FN-based grammar. For an initial intrinsic evaluation, we count the number of examples in the source corpora that belong to the set of shared frames and that are covered by the set of shared semantico-syntactic valence patterns. Corpus examples are represented by sentence patterns disregarding non-core FEs, word order and prepositions, but including syntactic roles and the grammatical voice. There are 55,837 examples in BFN that belong to the shared set of 423 frames, and 69.4% of them are covered by the shared valence patterns despite the modest size of SweFN. In SweFN, 2,434 examples belong to the shared set of frames, and 68.9% of them are covered by the shared patterns. Note that the original sentences are, in general, covered by paraphrasing.

For an initial extrinsic evaluation, we compare the original application grammars with their FN-based counterparts in terms of code complexity. Since we do not modify the abstract syntax of application grammars, the amount of linearization rules remains the same. Therefore we count the number of constructors used to linearize the functions. In the Painting grammar, the number of constructors is considerably reduced from 21 to 13. In the case of Phrasebook, the number is slightly reduced from 10 in English and 11 in Swedish to 8 in both languages.

6 Related Work

The main difference between this work and the previous approaches to CNL grammars is that we present an effort to exploit a robust and well established semantic model in the grammar development. Our approach can be compared with the work on multilingual verbalisation of modular ontologies using GF and *lemon*, the Lexicon Model for Ontologies [14]. We use additional lexical information about syntactic arguments for building the concrete syntax.

The grounding of NLG using the frame semantics theory has been addressed in the work on text-to-scene generation [15] and in the work on text generation for navigational tasks [16]. In that research, the content of frames is utilized through alignment between the frame-semantic structure and the domain-semantic representation. Discourse is supported by applying aggregation and pronominalization techniques. In the CH use case, we also show how an application which utilizes the FN-based grammar can become more discourse-oriented; something that is necessary in actual NLG applications and that has been demonstrated for the CH domain in GF before [17]. In our current approach, the semantic representation of the domain and the linguistic structures of the grammar are based on FN-annotated data.

As suggested before [18], a FN-like approach can be used to deal with polysemy in CNL texts. Although we consider lexicalisation alternatives and restrictions for LUs and FEs, we do not address the problem of selectional restrictions and word sense disambiguation in general.

7 Conclusion

In this paper we demonstrated the advantages of utilizing a FrameNet-based grammar to facilitate the development of multilingual CNL applications. We presented an approach to generating semantic grammar library from two FN-annotated corpora. We tested the feasibility of this grammar as a semantic API for developing application grammars in GF. The major advantage is that language-dependent clause-level specifications to a large extent are hidden by the API, making the application grammars more robust and flexible.

Acknowledgements. This research has been supported by the Swedish Research Council under Grant No. 2012-5746 (Reliable Multilingual Digital Communication: Methods and Applications) and by the Centre for Language Technology in Gothenburg.

References

1. Gruzitis, N., Paikens, P., Barzdins, G.: FrameNet resource grammar library for GF. In: Kuhn, T., Fuchs, N.E. (eds.) CNL 2012. LNCS, vol. 7427, pp. 121–137. Springer, Heidelberg (2012)
2. Ranta, A.: Grammatical Framework, a type-theoretical grammar formalism. Journal of Functional Programming 14(2), 145–189 (2004)
3. Ranta, A.: The GF resource grammar library. LILT 2(2) (2009)
4. Dannélls, D., Gruzitis, N.: Extracting a bilingual semantic grammar from FrameNet-annotated corpora. In: Proceedings of the 9th International Language Resources and Evaluation Conference (LREC), pp. 2466–2473 (2014)
5. Barzdins, G.: FrameNet CNL: A knowledge representation and information extraction language. In: CNL, pp. 90–101 (2014)
6. Fillmore, C.J., Johnson, C.R., Petruck, M.R.L.: Background to Framenet. International Journal of Lexicography 16(3), 235–250 (2003)
7. Das, D., Chen, D., Martins, A.F.T., Schneider, N., Smith, N.A.: Frame semantic parsing. Computational Linguistics 40(1), 9–56 (2014)
8. Moschitti, A., Morarescu, P., Harabagiu, S.M.: Open domain information extraction via automatic semantic labeling. In: Proc. of the 16th IFLAIRS (2003)
9. Roth, M., Frank, A.: A NLG-based application for walking directions. In: Proceedings of the 47th ACL and the 4th IJCNLP Conference, pp. 37–40 (2009)
10. Boas, H.C. (ed.): Multilingual FrameNets in Computational Lexicography (2009)
11. Borin, L., Dannélls, D., Forsberg, M., Toporowska Gronostaj, M., Kokkinakis, D.: The past meets the present in Swedish FrameNet++. In: Proceedings of the 14th EURALEX International Congress, pp. 269–281 (2010)
12. Ranta, A., Enache, R., Détrez, G.: Controlled language for everyday use: The MOLTO Phrasebook. In: Rosner, M., Fuchs, N.E. (eds.) CNL 2010. LNCS, vol. 7175, pp. 115–136. Springer, Heidelberg (2012)
13. Dannélls, D., Enache, R., Damova, M., Chechev, M.: Multilingual online generation from Semantic Web ontologies. In: Proceedings of the 21st International World Wide Web Conference, European Project Track, pp. 239–242 (2012)
14. Davis, B., Enache, R., van Grondelle, J., Pretorius, L.: Multilingual verbalisation of modular ontologies using GF and lemon. In: Kuhn, T., Fuchs, N.E. (eds.) CNL 2012. LNCS, vol. 7427, pp. 167–184. Springer, Heidelberg (2012)
15. Coyne, B., Bauer, D., Rambow, O.: VigNet: Grounding Language in Graphics Using Frame Semantics. In: Proc. of RELMS, pp. 28–36. ACL (2011)
16. Roth, M., Frank, A.: Computing EM-based Alignments of Routes and Route Directions as a Basis for Natural Language Generation. In: Huang, C.R., Jurafsky, D. (eds.) COLING, pp. 958–966. Tsinghua University Press (2010)
17. Dannélls, D.: Discourse Generation from Formal Specifications Using the Grammatical Framework, GF. In: Special issue of the RCS, pp. 167–178. Springer (2010)
18. Gruzitis, N., Barzdins, G.: Polysemy in controlled natural language texts. In: Fuchs, N.E. (ed.) CNL 2009. LNCS, vol. 5972, pp. 102–120. Springer, Heidelberg (2010)

Architecture of a Web-Based Predictive Editor for Controlled Natural Language Processing

Stephen Guy and Rolf Schwitter

Department of Computing,
Macquarie University,
Sydney, 2109 NSW, Australia
{Stephen.Guy,Rolf.Schwitter}@mq.edu.au

Abstract. In this paper, we describe the architecture of a web-based predictive text editor being developed for the controlled natural language PENG^{ASP}. This controlled language can be used to write non-monotonic specifications that have the same expressive power as Answer Set Programs. In order to support the writing process of these specifications, the predictive text editor communicates asynchronously with the controlled natural language processor that generates lookahead categories and additional auxiliary information for the author of a specification text. The text editor can display multiple sets of lookahead categories simultaneously for different possible sentence completions, anaphoric expressions, and supports the addition of new content words to the lexicon.

Keywords: controlled natural language processing, predictive editor, web-based authoring tools, answer set programming.

1 Introduction

Writing a specification in a controlled natural language without any tool support is a difficult task since the author needs to learn and remember the restrictions of the controlled language. Over the last decade, a number of different techniques and tools [3,5,12,13] have been proposed and implemented to minimise the learning effort and to support the writing process of controlled natural languages. The most promising approach to alleviate these habitability problems is the use of a predictive text editor [13,17] that constrains what the author can write and provides predictive feedback that guides the writing process of the author. In this paper, we present the architecture of a web-based predictive text editor being developed for the controlled natural language PENG^{ASP}[15]. The text editor uses an event-driven Model-View-Controller based architecture to satisfy a number of user entry and display requirements. These requirements include the display of multiple sets of lookahead categories for different sentence completions, the deletion of typed words, the addition of new content words to the lexicon and the handling of anaphoric expressions. Additionally, the text editor displays a paraphrase for each input sentence and displays the evolving Answer Set Program [11].

B. Davis et al. (Eds.): CNL 2014, LNAI 8625, pp. 167–178, 2014.

2 Overview of the PENG^{ASP} System

2.1 Client-Server Architecture

The PENG^{ASP} system is based on a client-server architecture where the predictive editor runs in a web browser and communicates via an HTTP server with the controlled natural language processor; the language processor uses in our case an Answer Set Programming (ASP) tool as reasoning service (Fig. 1):

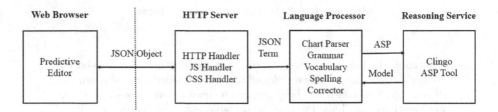

Fig. 1. Client-Server Architecture of the PENG^{ASP} System

The communication between the predictive editor and the HTTP server occurs asynchronously with the help of AJAX technologies and by means of JSON[1] objects. The predictive editor is implemented in JavaScript[2] and JQuery[3]. The HTTP server as well as the controlled natural language processor are implemented in SWI Prolog[4]. The Prolog server translates JSON objects into JSON terms and vice versa so that these terms can be processed directly by the language processor. The language processor incrementally translates the controlled language input via discourse representation structures [8] into an ASP program and sends this ASP program to the ASP tool *clingo* [6,7] that tries to generate one or more satisfiable answer sets for the program.

2.2 HTTP Server

SWI-Prolog provides a series of libraries for implementing HTTP server capabilities. Our server is based on this technology and can be operated as a stand-alone server on all platforms that are supported by SWI-Prolog. The following code fragment illustrates how an HTTP server is created, a port (8085) specified, and a request (`Request`) dispatched using a handler registration (`http_handler/3`):

```
server(Port) :- http_server(http_dispatch, [port(Port)]).
:- http_handler('/peng/', handle, []).
handle(Request) :- ...
:- server(8085).
```

---

[1] http://json.org/
[2] http://www.ecmascript.org/
[3] http://jquery.com/
[4] http://www.swi-prolog.org/

In our case, we can now connect via http://localhost:8085/peng/ from the web browser to the server that uses specific JavaScript and stylesheet handlers to load the predictive editor and to establish the communication between the editor and the controlled language processor.

2.3   Predictive Editor

The predictive editor is implemented in JavaScript and JQuery, with the Super-fish[5] plug-in providing pull-down menu functionality. These technologies allow the editor to be run in most browsers, which in conjunction with the capabilities of a potentially remote language processor coded in Prolog, provides a highly portable system. Data communication with the server provides for both command functions, such as file saving and loading, as well as data transfer between the language processor and the predictive editor system. The JSON data for parsing sent from the predictive editor to the HTTP server includes the current token of a word form, its position in the relevant sentence and relevant sentence number. For each word form or completed sentence submitted by the predictive editor, the lookahead categories and word forms along with the output of the language processor are returned.

An overview of a typical predictive editor display is presented in Figure 2. Command function menus are presented at the top, below which is the main text input field displaying the current sentence. Lookahead categories for the available sentence completion are highlighted using the pull-down menus. Below these lookahead categories is a display summarising relevant information in the system, at both the client and server. First is a summary of previously entered text at the client side. Second are the generated paraphrases at the server, with any anaphoric references being highlighted (which may also be accessed from the pull-down menus). Third is a summary of the current answer set program for the input, followed by the final section of output from answer set tool *clingo*.

The editor allows entering text specifications manually by typing in the text entry field, plus using pull-down menus of lookahead categories to enter text into the input field. The reasons for allowing direct input of text include that some users, especially those experienced in the structure of the controlled natural language, can type faster than they can enter via menus, even with some level of auto-completion. Additionally, the system allows entering new content words into the lexicon, via the text field, that do not appear in the displayed lookahead categories.

3   Processing and Reasoning in the PENG^{ASP} System

3.1   Controlled Natural Language Processor

The controlled natural language processor of the PENG^{ASP} system consists of a chart parser, a unification-based grammar, a lexicon and a spelling corrector.

---

[5] http://users.tpg.com.au/j_birch/plugins/superfish/

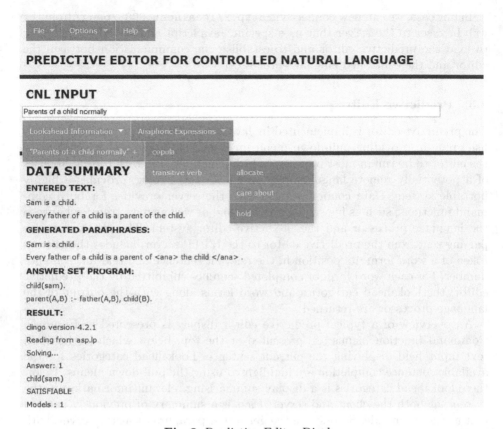

Fig. 2. Predictive Editor Display

The chart parser is initialised for the first time when the author moves the cursor into the textfield of the predictive editor and reset at the beginning of each new sentence and generates lookahead categories using the grammar and the lexicon of the controlled language processor. These lookahead categories inform the author of a specification how to start a sentence and are generated dynamically for each word form that the author enters into the textfield of the editor. This mechanism guarantees that the author can only input word forms and construct sentences that follow the rules of the controlled language. If a word is misspelled, then the spelling corrector is used to generate a list of candidates that occur in the lexicon. If a content word is not in the lexicon, then the author can add this word to the lexcion during the specification process.

The controlled natural language PENG^{ASP} [15] that the author uses as input language has been designed as a high-level interface language to ASP programs. In certain aspects the language PENG^{ASP} is similar to PENG Light [18] and Attempto Controlled English [5], since it uses a version of discourse representation theory (DRT), in the spirit of [2,8], as intermediate representation language. However, PENG^{ASP} does not rely on full first-order logic (FOL) as target language as the use of DRT would suggest but on the language for ASP programs.

The language of FOL is in some respects more expressive than the language of ASP but unfortunately FOL is not adequate for representing commonsense knowledge, because FOL cannot deal with non-monotonic reasoning. ASP, on the other hand, allows us to represent and process commonsense knowledge because of its unique connectives and non-monotonic entailment relation. Beyond that, ASP is still expressive enough to represent function-free FOL formulas of the $\exists^*\forall^*$ prefix class in form of a logic program [10]. Below is an example specification in PENG^{ASP} that uses a default rule in (5), a cancellation axiom in (6), and sentence with strong negation in (7):

1. Sam is a child.
2. John is the father of Sam and Alice is the mother of Sam.
3. Every father of a child is a parent of the child.
4. Every mother of a child is a parent of the child.
5. Parents of a child normally care about the child.
6. If a parent of a child is provably absent then the parent abnormally cares about the child.
7. John does not care about Sam.
8. Alice is absent.

Of course, the specific features of the ASP language have an impact on what we can express on the level of the controlled natural language and therefore rely on the support of the predictive editor.

3.2 Reasoning Service

Since we are interested in specifying commonsense theories in PENG^{ASP}, we need a non-monotonic reasoning service. ASP is a relatively novel logic-based knowledge representation formalism that has its roots in logic programming with negation, deductive databases, non-monotonic reasoning and constraint solving [1,7]. An ASP program consists of a set of rules of the following form:

$$L_0 \; ; \; \ldots \; ; \; L_k \; :\!- \; L_{k+1}, \; \ldots, \; L_m, \; not \; L_{m+1}, \; \ldots, \; not \; L_n.$$

where all L_i's are literals. A literal is an atom or its negation. A positive atom has the form $p(t_1, \ldots, t_n)$ where p is a predicate symbol of arity n and $t_1, \ldots, t_n$ are object constants or variables. A negative atom has the form $-p(t_1, \ldots, t_n)$ where the symbol $-$ denotes strong negation. The symbol $:\!-$ stands for an implication. The expression on the left-hand side of the implication is called the *head* of the rule and the expression on the right-hand side is called the *body* of the rule. The head may consist of an epistemic disjunction of literals denoted by the symbol $;$. Literals in the body may be preceded by negation as failure denoted by the symbol not. The head or the body of a rule can be empty. A rule with an empty head is called an *integrity constraint* and a rule with an empty body is called a *fact*. For instance, the example specification in Section 3.1 is translated automatically via discourse representation structures in the subsequent ASP program:

```
child(sam).
father(john,sam).
mother(alice,sam).
parent(A,B) :- father(A,B), child(B).
parent(C,D) :- mother(C,D), child(D).
care(E,F) :- parent(E,F), child(F), not ab(d_care(E,F)),
             not -care(E,F).
ab(d_care(G,H)) :- parent(G,H), child(H), not -absent(G).
-care(john,sam).
absent(alice).
```

4   Predictive Editor Requirements

In addition to the generic requirements outlined in Section 2.3, a number of detailed user input and system display requirements for the lookahead categories are determined to aid in the design of the predictive editor architecture. The main requirements are that the system should allow appropriate editing of information already entered, that the lookahead categories for a particular sentence position are displayed until all possibilities are no longer possible and that the lookahead categories for the next sentence position are displayed as soon as the relevant options are possible. These requirements are presented in detail in the following sections.

4.1   User and System Requirements

User Entry Requirements

Requirement E.1.1: The system will allow deletion of characters or words already typed, or all or part of a sentence not yet *submitted*. (This deletion will be referred to as *backward editing*).

Requirement E.2.1: A new sentence is not commenced (via the chart parser being reset) until a *submit* or an *enter* event or a beginning of sentence character/word occurs after an end-of-sentence marker (full stop or question mark). A new sentence being commenced means that the previous sentence has been *submitted*.

Requirement E.3.1: A user is allowed to enter a content word not in the lexicon and force its submission to the language processor as the next content word.

Requirement E.3.2: A user may enter a misspelt word that is yet to be *completed* with the word still subject to *backward editing*.

Requirement E.4.1: A word is *completed* if it followed by a space or directly by a valid punctuation character which in turn is followed by a space or sentence *submission*. This latter requirement of a space after the punctuation allows the system to distinguish the state from the case of an *incomplete* misspelt word with an erroneous punctuation character at the end.

System Display Requirements

Requirement D.1.1: Before and whilst a word is being entered at position A (or for a new sentence commencing at position A), the system should display all the lookahead categories for position A until all of those categories are no longer possible.

Assertion D.1.1: All lookahead categories for position A are no longer possible if the next non-punctuation word at position A+1 has commenced, or a word is *completed* according to Requirement E.4.1.

Requirement D.2.1: The system should display the lookahead categories for position A+1 when a word entered at position A matches the lookahead categories for position A.

Note that in terms of displaying one set of lookahead categories for a particular word, requirements D.1.1 and D.2.1 are not mutually exclusive, that is there occur system states where the lookahead categories at position A and position A+1 need to be displayed concurrently.

Assertion D.2.1: If a word at position A matches the lookahead categories for position A, then other lookahead categories for position A may still be possible.

4.2   Display of Multiple Sentence Completions

Some examples are presented to help clarify the requirements detailed above. The two main cases which are catered for are the existence of subsets within the lookahead categories for one sentence position and the allowed juxtaposition of punctuation directly after a word without an intervening space.

For the case of subsets in lookahead categories, consider the commencement of a sentence and the above two display requirements D.1.1 and D.2.1. Initial lookahead categories may include "The", "There is", "A", "Thelma", "John" and "Johnathan" for example, which according to D.1.1 should all be displayed by the system. A user entering the characters "The" would then satisfy requirement D.2.1, whereby the lookahead categories for the next position would be displayed. If these categories included the word "child", the user could enter this word and the entered text would be "The child", illustrating that a display of this sentence completion option was necessary. However, the original situation of the user entering the characters "The" may have been the precursor to the entry of the words "There is" or even "Thelma". Thus even though requirement D.2.1 is satisfied after the entry of "The", requirement D.1.1 still holds for the presentation of the original lookahead categories whilst the user completes this entry, thus illustrating assertion D.2.1. Whether the user has entered "Thelma" or "The" without a subsequent character, requirement E.4.1 has not been satisfied, so a user may *backward edit* from the word "Thelma" back to "The" or "Thelma"/"The" back to "A".

For the case of juxtaposition of word forms with punctuation and requirements E.4.1 and D.2.1, the lexicon and grammar allows phrases such as "John, Thelma and Pete are parents.". Here, a word is followed directly by punctuation, so that once the characters "John" are entered, according to requirement D.2.1, the system must display the options for the next lookahead categories which include the comma which could be clicked or typed directly. Alternatively, a user may have been intending to type "Johnathan", so as for the case of subsets must see the original set of lookahead categories. If a user accidentally hit the comma on the fifth character, leaving "John," (John comma), as the current word, the system should still display the original lookahead categories, including "Johnathan", as the word has not been *completed* according to requirement E.4.1.

5   Architecture of the Predictive Editor

The predictive editor is designed to meet the requirements of the PENG^{ASP} system, the asynchronous client-server communications, the different modes of the editor input as well as user entry and system display requirements.

5.1   Model-View-Controller Architecture

The architecture of the predictive editor is based approximately on that of a *Model-View-Controller* (MVC) system [4,16] in terms of separation and independence.

The *Model* includes the currently active sentence, including that entered by the user and that submitted to the HTTP server, all previously entered sentences and all data (including lookahead categories) received from the language processor via the HTTP server. The model also stores all variables relevant to determining the state of the system.

The *View* includes the events-triggered input text field, the pull-down menu display of lookahead categories and the input of word forms via mouseover selection. It also displays the overall model of entered sentences and the ASP model generated by the language processor.

The *Controller* synchronises all functions, and importantly monitors for the need of a state change in the *Model*, such as when the user has input data that is different from the currently active sentence and if so, whether to submit new data to the server or not. Additionally, the *Controller* co-ordinates loading of all the returned lookahead categories into data structures and determines which of these lookahead categories are displayed to the user as dependent on the current state of the system.

5.2   Event-Triggered Implementation

A key issue with the implementation of the MVC architecture is the requirement to have event-driven data processing and control to be compatible with the asynchronous AJAX communication between the predictive editor and the HTTP server and events-triggered predictive editor input. When content words are submitted to the HTTP server via JSON data, the predictive editor system must wait until corresponding lookahead data is returned by the server.

Once this information is received, it may then be stored in the model and only then can the *Controller* process this model data to determine if the model state variables should be changed and update the display if necessary. To implement this, the *Controller* organises run-time execution of events in a pipe and filter architecture, where each element of the pipe is a data structure containing the relevant primary data for that event, the relevant processing function and an optional link to the next data structure in the pipe.

Whilst this may not be a classical MVC implementation, it provides a robust method of ensuring model data is in a consistent state for process control. Thus for the above example of sending a new content word to the server, the AJAX send/receive routine will trigger the return data storage event, which when complete will trigger the model state change assessment functionality, which when complete may cause a trigger of the display of the next lookahead categories to the display.

Any multi-stage data processing may also be organised as a pipe and filter structure using the above data structures, with the next stage of the processing function only allowed once the model data from the previous processing function becomes stable.

5.3   Data Structures

As with many client-server systems, some model data is stored and processed at the predictive editor client side to allow for optimal processing and control. The model data is stored in objects defined by JavaScript functions, with appropriate object methods declared to allow for this data to be processed conveniently and allowing functionality beyond the capabilities of using raw JSON objects for storage. For example, the model data includes stack objects (containing stacks of anything from word forms to whole sentences), individual send and received objects plus a single object of correlated send and receive data. Methods can detect if a beginning or end of sentence token is present, or whether a word form matches a lookahead category and whether it is also a subset of another lookahead category (such as "The" being a subset of "There"). Display objects allow storage of different sets of lookahead categories and the ability to switch the display from 'displayed' to 'hidden' and vice versa.

5.4   Predictive Editor Controller

Given the user entry and system display requirements discussed Section 4.1 and generic requirements presented in Section 2.3, the control system for the predictive editor has been designed to allow displaying of multiple lookahead categories for different sentence completions and strict control over when data entered by a user is ultimately committed to the server. The currently active sentence is stored in two forms, namely from a tokenisation of the user input and from a summary of the data submitted to the server. By comparing a stack of the set of tokens in each sentence, a difference stack is generated to aid the controller in determining a change in the model state. Any newly entered valid words, or changes in the current word are assessed for submission, or alternately earlier submitted tokens/words may be removed and new tokens sent in their place (such as in the case of *backward editing*).

As discussed regarding requirement D.2.1 in Section 4.1, if an entered word matches a lookahead category for that position, the controller automatically submits this word to the server and retrieves the next set of lookahead categories for this new token. However, this data transfer is just the predictive editor gathering information and doesn't directly synchronise with the totality of the display to the user. If the controller doesn't detect a word completion, or finds that at least one lookahead category from the previous word is still possible, the previous lookahead categories are not cleared as per assertion D.2.1.

As described in Section 5.3, display data structures allow easy addition and display of data and hiding of data as necessary. As well as automatically submitting a word matching the current lookahead categories, a word matching the previous set of lookahead categories where the previous word is a subset of the new word will also trigger an automatic submission of the token to the HTTP server. This would be the case for "Thelma" being typed after "The" has been submitted to the server and lookahead categories already returned for the next sentence position.

5.5   Adding Content Words to the Lexicon

Recall from requirement E.3.1 that a user may forcibly submit a word form to the language processor that does not correspond to the lexicon. When this occurs, the language processor may offer a set of spelling suggestions (assuming that an incorrect word has been submitted by mistake) or the predictive editor will offer an option to add this new word to the lexicon in this current context. If the user selects to add a word, then the position in the sentence, the lexical category and the new word form are collected and sent to the server where the new word is added to the lexicon. The new word is then parsed again by the language processor and a new set of lookahead categories is generated and sent to the predictive editor.

6   Future Research

The current predictive editor may be extended for multiple users in line with the web-based portability of the system. A user login would allow for a number of features, such as a user-group based lexicon depending on the nature of the specification system for that group (e.g. medical, engineering, automotive, etc.). Additionally, an individual could have their own extended lexicon for any content words added to the lexicon. A user could set a level of knowledge for their grammar, which would aid in controlling the complexity of the pull-down menus, in that instead of displaying all possible lexical categories, a user with limited knowledge could display a smaller number of less-technial word categories, such as "function words" instead of individual groups such as "adjective", "adverb", "noun", etc. The user login could be used to set preferences for any further adjustable enhancements.

7 Conclusion

In this paper, we introduced the architecture of a web-based predictive text editor developed for the PENG^{ASP} system. This system is suitable for writing non-monotonic specifications that have the expressive power of Answer Set Programs. The web-based predictive editor supports the writing process of these specifications and is based on a portable client-server architecture and is predominantly implemented in JavaScript. An event-driven Model-View-Controller based architecture was used for the editor, allowing strict control of system functionality to satisfy a set of user entry and display requirements that included the display of multiple sets of lookahead categories for different sentence completions. The predictive editor allows for new content words to be added to the lexicon and supports the selection of anaphoric expressions An extension of a user login would allow tailoring of preferences and a user-based lexicon.

References

1. Brewka, G., Eiter, T., Truszczyński, M.: Answer Set Programming at a Glance. Communications of the ACM 54(12) (December 2011)
2. van Eijck, J., Kamp, H.: Discourse Representation in Context. In: van Benthem, J., ter Meulen, A. (eds.) Handbook of Logic and Language, 2nd edn., pp. 181–252. Elsevier (2011)
3. Franconi, E., Guagliardo, P., Trevisan, M., Tessaris, S.: Quelo: an ontology-driven query interface. In: Proceedings of the 24th International Workshop on Description Logics (DL 2011) (2011)
4. Freeman, E., Robson, E., Bates, B., Sierra, K.: Head First Design Patterns, pp. 526–577. O'Reilly (2004)
5. Fuchs, N.E., Kaljurand, K., Kuhn, T.: Attempto Controlled English for Knowledge Representation. In: Baroglio, C., Bonatti, P.A., Małuszyński, J., Marchiori, M., Polleres, A., Schaffert, S. (eds.) Reasoning Web. LNCS, vol. 5224, pp. 104–124. Springer, Heidelberg (2008)
6. Gebser, M., Kaminski, R., Kaufmann, B., Ostrowski, M., Schaub, T., Schneider, M.: Potassco: The Potsdam Answer Set Solving Collection. AI Communications 24(2), 105–124 (2011)
7. Gebser, M., Kaminski, R., Kaufmann, B., Schaub, T.: Answer Set Solving in Practice. In: Synthesis Lectures on Artificial Intelligence and Machine Learning, vol. 6(3), pp. 1–238 (2012)
8. Kamp, H., Reyle, U.: From Discourse to Logic. Kluwer, Dordrecht (1993)
9. Kuhn, T., Schwitter, R.: Writing Support for Controlled Natural Languages. In: Proceedings of ALTA, Tasmania, pp. 46–54 (2008)

10. Lierler, Y., Lifschitz, V.: Logic Programs vs. First-Order Formulas in Textual Inference. In: Proceedings of the 10th International Conference on Computational Semantics (IWCS 2013), Potsdam, Germany, pp. 340–346 (2013)
11. Lifschitz, V.: What is Answer Set Programming? In: Proceedings of AAAI 2008, pp. 1594–1597 (2008)
12. Power, R.: OWL Simplified English: a finite-state language for ontology editing. In: Kuhn, T., Fuchs, N.E. (eds.) CNL 2012. LNCS, vol. 7427, pp. 44–60. Springer, Heidelberg (2012)
13. Schwitter, R., Ljungberg, A., Hood, D.: ECOLE: A Look-ahead Editor for a Controlled Language. In: Proceedings of EAMT-CLAW 2003, Dublin, pp. 141–150 (2003)
14. Schwitter, R.: Controlled Natural Languages for Knowledge Representation. In: Proceedings of COLING 2010, Beijing, China, pp. 1113–1121 (2010)
15. Schwitter, R.: The Jobs Puzzle: Taking on the Challenge via Controlled Natural Language Processing. Journal of Theory and Practice of Logic Programming 13(special Issue 4-5), 487–501 (2013)
16. Sommerville, I.: Software Engineering, International Edition, 9th edn., pp. 155–164. Pearson (2011)
17. Tennant, H.R., Ross, K.M., Saenz, R.M., Thompson, C.W., Miller, J.R.: Menu-based natural language understanding. In: Proceedings of ACL, pp. 151–158 (1983)
18. White, C., Schwitter, R.: An Update on PENG Light. In: Pizzato, L., Schwitter, R. (eds.) Proceedings of ALTA 2009, Sydney, Australia, pp. 80–88 (2009)

Explaining Violation Traces with Finite State Natural Language Generation Models

Gordon J. Pace and Michael Rosner

University of Malta, Malta
{gordon.pace,mike.rosner}@um.edu.mt

Abstract. An essential element of any verification technique is that of identifying and communicating to the user, system behaviour which leads to a deviation from the expected behaviour. Such behaviours are typically made available as long traces of system actions which would benefit from a natural language explanation of the trace and especially in the context of business logic level specifications. In this paper we present a natural language generation model which can be used to explain such traces. A key idea is that the explanation language is a CNL that is, formally speaking, regular language susceptible transformations that can be expressed with finite state machinery. At the same time it admits various forms of abstraction and simplification which contribute to the naturalness of explanations that are communicated to the user.

1 Introduction

The growth in size and complexity of computer systems has been accompanied by an increase in importance given to the application of verification techniques, attempting to avoid or at least mitigate problems arising due to errors in the system design and implementation. Given a specification of how the system should behave (or, dually, of what the system should not do), techniques ranging from testing to runtime verification and model checking attempt to answer the question of whether or not the system is correct. One common issue with all these techniques, is that a negative answer is useless unless accompanied by a trace showing how the system may perform leading to a violation of the expected behaviour.

Consider, for example, the specification of a system which allows user to log in, as shown in Figure 1, which states that "after three consecutive failed user authentications, users should not be allowed to attempt another login". A testing or runtime verification tool may deduce that the system may perform a long sequence of events which lead to a violation. Although techniques have been developed to shorten such counter-examples [ZH02], such traces may be rather long, and using them to understand the circumstances in which the system failed to work as expected may not always be straightforward.

In the case of implementation-level properties and traces, tools such as debuggers and simulators may enable the processing of long traces by developers to understand the nature of the bug, but in the case of higher-level specifications, giving business-logic level properties, such traces may need to be processed by management personnel. For example, a fraud expert may be developing fraud rules to try to match against the behaviour of known black-listed users, and may want to understand why a trace showing

B. Davis et al. (Eds.): CNL 2014, LNAI 8625, pp. 179–189, 2014.

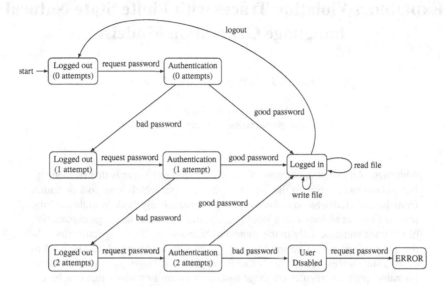

Fig. 1. An automaton-based specification

the behaviour of such a user does to trigger a rule he may have just set up. In such cases, a natural language explanation of such a trace would help the expert to understand better what is going wrong and why.

In this paper, we present the use of finite state natural language generation (NLG) models to explain violation traces. We assume that the basis of the controlled natural language used to describe such behaviour is given by the person writing the specification, by articulating how the actions can be described using a natural language, and how they can be abstracted into more understandable explanations. We present a stepwise refinement of the process, explaining how a more natural feel to the generated controlled natural language text can be given using finite state techniques.

Although the work we present is still exploratory, we believe that the approach can be generalised to work on more complex systems, and it can give insight into how far out the limits of finite state NLG techniques can be pushed.

2 The Roles of NLG and CNL

In this section we illustrate a solution to the problem of generating reasonably natural explanations from sequences of the above type in a computationally efficient way. The two critical ingredients are (i) NLG, which, in a general sense, provides a set of techniques for generating text flexibly given an abstract non-linguistic representation of semantic content, and (ii) CNLs which, in a nutshell, are natural languages with a designer element — natural in the sense that they can be understood by native speakers of the "parent" language and designed to to be simpler than that language from some computational perspective such as translation to logic or, as in this paper, NLG. An excellent survey and classification scheme for CNLs appears in Kuhn [Kuh14]

The final output of NLG is clearly natural language of some kind. The nature of the process that produces that output is somewhat less clear, in that there are still many approaches though most research in the area is consistent with the assumption that that it includes at least the stages of content planning (deciding what to say), content packaging (packaging the content into sentence-sized messages), and surface realisation (constructing individual sentences). These three stages are linked together in a pipeline, according to the architecture proposed by Reiter and Dale [RD00].

The complexity of NLG arises from fact that the input content severely underdetermines the surface realisation and that there are few guiding principles available to narrow the realisation choices. Consequently, the process is even more nondeterministic than the inverse process of of natural language *understanding* where at least it is possible to appeal to common sense when attempting to choose amongst competing interpretations. With NLG, some dimensions of complexity must be sacrificed for the computation to be feasible.

In this paper, the sacrifice comes down to a choice concerning two sets of languages: (i) that which expresses the content, which we will call the C language, and (ii) a sequence of languages in which explanations are realised that we will call E_1, E_2, etc. C is a form of semantic representation language, whilst $E_1, E_2, \ldots E_n$ are CNLs in Kuhn's sense.

In both cases, we assume that both C and E_i languages are *regular languages* in the formal sense. This has a number of advantages: the computational properties of such languages are well understood, and we know that algorithms for parsing and generation of are of relatively low complexity. Additionally, we can express linguistic processes as relations over such languages that can be computed by finite-state *transducers*. Elementary transductions can be composed together to carry out complex linguistic processing tasks. Using techniques originally advocated for morphological analysis by Beesley and Kattunen [BK03] we can envisage a complex NLG process as a series of finite state transductions combined together under relational composition, thus opening up the possibility of describing the synthesis of an explanation to efficient, finite-state machinery.

Of course, the restriction to regular languages imposes certain limitations upon what content can possibly be expressed in C, and may also impact the naturalness of the violation description expressed in E. However, these are empirical issues that will not be tackled in this paper.

We are not the first to have used simplified languages in the attempt to reduce the complexity of natural language processing. In the domain of NLG, Wilcock [Wil01] proposed *"the use of XML-based tools to implement existing well-known approaches to NLG"*. Power [Pow12] uses finite-state representations for expressing descriptions of OWL-LITE sentences. It is of course in the area of computational morphology where finite state methods are best known.

The main contribution of the paper is to substantiate and present the hypothesis that according to the choice of C and E, it is possible to realise a family of efficient NLG systems that are based on steadfastly finite-state technology.

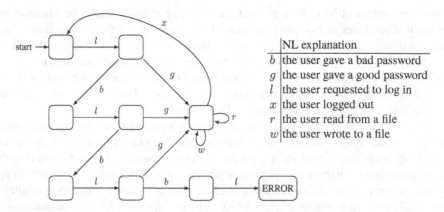

Fig. 2. The specification augmented with NL explanations

3   Languages

In what follows we first present the C language and then a sequence of E languages, progressively adding features to attain a more natural explanation of the trace. As we shall investigate in more detail in Section 4, at each stage we use further information to obtain more natural generated text.

3.1   The C Language

We assume that the basic specification of the C language is given by the automaton shown in Figure 2. The following trace is a sentence

$$lgrxlblgwwxlgrwxlgxlblblbl$$

Note that although the automaton itself is not necessary for the explanations that ensue, it could in principle be used to check which trace prefix leads to an error state to allow for an explanation when such a state is reached.

Next we turn to the series of E languages. Since these are all CNLs we will refer to them as CNL0, CNL1, CNL2 and CNL3 respectively. All four languages are similar insofar as they all talk about the same underlying, domain-specific world of states and actions, and they all finite state. At the same time they are somewhat different linguistically.

3.2   CNL0

Sentences of the CNL0 language are very simple declarative sentences of the kind that we typically associate with simple predicate-argument structures. In the example shown in Figure 3 here, each sentence has a subject, a verb, and possibly a direct object.

In this paper, the mapping between the C language and CLN0 is given extensionally by means of a *lexicon* that connects the individual transition names with a sentence with a simple and fixed syntactic structure. The lexicon itself is expressed as a finite state

> *The user requested to log in. The user gave a good password. The user read*
> *from a file. The user logged out. The user requested to log in. The user gave a*
> *bad password. The user requested to log in. The user gave a correct password.*
> *The user wrote to a file. The user wrote to a file. The user logged out. The user*
> *requested to log in. The user gave a correct password. The user read from a*
> *file. The user wrote to a file. The user logged out. The user requested to log in.*
> *The user gave a good password. The user logged out. The user requested to log*
> *in. The user gave a bad password. The user requested to log in. The user gave*
> *a bad password. The user requested to log in. The user gave a bad password.*
> *The user requested to log in, which should not have been allowed.*

Fig. 3. A naïve explanation of the trace: CNL0

transducer, as described in Section 4.1. For more complex systems such an approach might not be practical, and a solution could then be to *derive* the sentence associated with each transition from more fundamental properties of the underlying machine.

CNL0 provides for a somewhat naïve explanation of traces using the explanations provided by the domain expert directly.

3.3   CNL1

Next we turn to CNL1 which offers some improvements. The main feature of CNL1 is that it is a sequence of paragraphs, where each paragraph is simply a sequence of CNL0 sentences, as shown in Figure 4.

> 1. The user requested to log in. The user gave a good password. The user
>   read from a file. The user logged out.
> 2. The user requested to log. The user gave a bad password.
> 3. The user attempted to log in. The user gave a good password. The user
>   wrote to a file. The user wrote to a file. The user logged out.
> 4. The user requested to log in. The user gave a good password. The user
>   read from a file. The user wrote to a file. The user logged out.
> 5. The user requested to log in. The user gave a good password. The user
>   logged out.
> 6. The user requested to log in. The user gave a bad password.
> 7. The user requested to log in. The user gave a bad password.
> 8. The user requested to log in. The user gave a bad password.
> 9. The user requested to log in, which should not have been allowed.

Fig. 4. A grouped explanation: CNL1

There are two consequences to this slightly richer structure. One is that it provides the skeleton upon which to hang the numbered steps. This is a presentation issue that arguably increases the naturalness and improves comprehension. The other is that it gives a structural identity to each paragraph that could be exploited in order to attribute certain semantic properties to the associated sequence of actions. For example, we have the notion of *correctness* which has the potential to figure in explanations. Nevertheless, this property is not actually exploited in CNL1.

3.4   CNL2

The main novelty in CNL2, (see Figure 5) in contrast to CNL1, is the use of *aggregation* to reduce each multi-sentence paragraph to a single, more complex sentence. This is a technique which is used for removing redundancy (see Dalianis and Hovy [DH93]), yielding texts that are more fluid, more acceptable and generally less prone to being misunderstood by human readers than CNL1-style descriptions.

---

1. The user requested to log in, gave a correct password and after reading from a file logged out.
2. The user requested to log in, and gave a bad password.
3. After a log in request the user gave a correct password and wrote twice to a file before logging out.
4. The user requested to log in, gave a correct password, read from a file, wrote to a file and then logged out.
5. After requesting a log in, the user gave a good password and logged out.
6. The user requested to log in, gave a bad password, requested again to log in, gave another bad password and after requesting to log in, gave another bad password.
7. Finally, the user made a request to log in, which should not have been allowed.

Fig. 5. A better grouped explanation: CNL2

The linguistic renderings resulting from aggregation in CNL2 include:

1. Punctuation other than full stops
2. Temporal connectives ("after", "then", "finally")
3. The use of contrastive conjunctions like "but"
4. Collective terms ("twice")

3.5   CNL3

Finally CNL3 (see Figure 6) is considerably more complex, because it not only contains further aggregation but also *summarisation*.

In this example, there are only two sentences. The first sentence not only aggregates the first six sentences, but it also omits some of the information (for example, the the user read from a file, that the user logged out etc.). It also includes the use of certain phrases whose correct interpretation, as mentioned earlier, requires consideration of the context of occurrence as well as use of adverbs ("she unsuccessfully attempted") and the use of more complex tenses ("should not have been allowed").

> *The user logged in a number of times, interspersed by sequences of one or two*
> *bad logins, after which she unsuccessfully attempted to log in 3 times. The user*
> *then made another request to log in, which should not have been allowed.*

Fig. 6. A natural explanation: CNL3

4 Finite State Generation

In this section we will look into using finite state CNLs for NLG. This is based on finite
state techniques as embodied in xfst (Beesley and Karttunen [BK03]) that has already
been used extensively in several other areas of language processing such as computational morphology and light parsing. xfst provides a language for the description of
complex transducers together with a compiler and a user interface for running and testing transducers. Our aim is to better understand the tradeoffs involved between producing
reasonably natural explanations from traces and the use of the efficient computational
machinery described here.

4.1 Naïve Generation: CNL0

Just as in Figure 2, our starting point is a regular input language C defined as follows

```
define SIGMA b|l|g|x|r|w;
define C SIGMA*;
```

SIGMA is the alphabet of the original FSA and the entire generation mechanism accepts inputs that are arbitrary strings over this alphabet. Strings containing illegal characters yield the empty string and hence, no output.

CNL0 can be obtained more or less directly via a dictionary which links symbols in
SIGMA to simple declarative sentences, as follows[1]:

```
define SP " ";
define USR {the SP user};
define DICT   b->   [{user} SP {gives} SP {bad}  SP {password}],
              l->   [{user} SP {requests} SP {login}],
              g->   [{user} SP {gives} SP {good} SP {password}],
              x->   [{user} SP {logs} SP {out}],
              r->   [{user} SP {reads} SP {from} SP {a} SP {file}],
              w->   [{user} SP {writes} SP {to} SP {a} SP {file}];


define CNL0 C .o. DICT;
```

---

[1] Some of the syntactically more obscure aspects of this definition have been omitted for the sake
of clarity.

The first line defines the space character, and the second the symbol USR. The third defines the dictionary DICT which is implemented as finite state transducer that maps from the individual action symbols to primitive sentences, all of which have the same basic structure. The input sequence is represented as a string

```
define input {lgrxlblgwwxlgrwxlgxlblblbl};
```

To get the output we compose CNL0 with input using the expression ([input .o. CNL0]), extract the *lower* side of the relation with the *l* operator ([input .o. CNL0] .1). The problem with the generated output is that there are no separators between the sentences. The solution is to compose the input with a transducer sentencesep that inserts a separator.

```
input .o. sentencesep .o. CNL0
```

This turns the input into the following string:

l.g.r.x.l.b.l.g.w.w.x.l.g.r.w.x.l.g.x.l.b.l.b.l.b.l.

Such a string can be made to yield exactly the sentences of CNL0 by arranging for the mapping of the fullstops to insert a space. This is just another transducer that is composed into the pipeline. The result of this process is exactly the text shown in Figure 3.

4.2   Adding Structural Information: CNL1

At a simplest level, we can specify how the explanation may be split into an enumerated sequence of paragraphs, aiding the comprehension of the trace explanation. Consider being given the following list of subtrace specifications using regular explanations:

Correct login session: $lg(r + w)^*x$.
Sequence of incorrect login requests: $(lb)^*$.

In CNL1, the main feature is that we will use this information to group text. We will assume that the following paragraph definitions are supplied:

```
define correct l g [r | w]* x;
define incorrect [l b];
define group1 correct @-> ... %|, incorrect @-> ... %|;
```

The group1 definition includes a piece of xfst notation that causes a vertical bar to be inserted just after whatever matched the left hand side of the rule, yielding

lgrx|lb|lgwwx|lgrwx|lgx|lb|lb|lb|l

As shown earlier, we can when applied to the input, where the vertical bar is used to delimit paragraphs.

l.g.r.x.|l.b.|l.g.w.w.x.|l.g.r.w.x.|l.g.x.|l.b.|l.b.|l.b.|l.

Fig. 7. CNL1 representation just prior to lexicalisation

Composing this with an augmented version of CNL0 that also handles the paragraph breaks yields exactly the paragraph structure of the CNL1 rendering shown in Figure 4. An inherent limitation of this approach is that it is impossible to produce a finite-state transducer that will output a numbering scheme for arbitrary numbers of paragraphs. Our solution is to postprocess the output, and generate, for instance HTML or LATEX output which will handle the enumeration as required..

4.3 Adding Aggregation: CNL2

We can now move on to CNL2. This involves several intermediate stages which are diagrammed below:

```
A: l.g.r.x.|l.b.|l.g.w.w.x.|l.g.r.w.x.|l.g.x.|l.b.|l.b.|l.b.|l.
B: l,g,r,x.|l,b.|l,g,w,w,x.|l,g,r,w,x.|l,g,x.|l,b.|l,b.|l,b.|l.|
C: aggregation1
D: aggregation2
```

A is as shown in Figure 7. We must now prepare for aggregation by first replacing all but the paragraph-final fullstops with commas. Because the transducer that achieves this uses the paragraph marker to identify the final fullstop, we must first insert that final paragraph marker as as shown in B. The next two phases of aggregation are best explained with the following example: we wish to transform "the user requested to login. the user gave a good password. the user logged out." to the more natural "the user requested login, gave a good password, and logged out". The first phase removes the subject (i.e. the phrase " the user") of all sentences but reinstates the same subject at the beginning of the paragraph. The second inserts an "and" just before the final verb phrase of each aggregated sentence. In this way we are able to achieve paragraph 2 of the CNL2 example as shown in Figure Similar, surface-oriented techniques can be used to obtain the other paragraphs in Figure 5. Specifically, we have composed rules for inserting the words "after", "then", "twice", "another", "finally" and "and". However, space limitations prevent us from describing these in full.

4.4 Adding Abstraction: CNL3

We note that certain sequences of actions can be combined into a simpler explanation, abstracting away (possibly) irrelevant detail, thus aiding comprehension. For instance, consider the following rules, consisting of (i) a regular expression matching a collection of subtraces which may be explained more concisely; and (ii) a natural language explanation which may replace the detailed text one would obtain from the whole subtrace:

Consecutive correct login sessions: $(lg(r + w)^*x)^n$ explained as *"The user successfully logged in n times"*.

Consecutive correct failed login attempts: $(lb)^n$ explained as *"The user unsuccessfully attempted to log in n times"*.

Correct login sessions interspersed with occasional incorrect one: $((lg(r+w)^*x)*$ $lb(lg(r+w)^*x)+)^*$ explained as *"The user successfully logged in a number of times, with one off bad logins in between"*.

Correct login sessions interspersed with occasional incorrect one or two: $((lg(r + w)^*x) * (lb + lblb)(lg(r + w)^*x))^*$ explained as *"The user logged in a number of times, interspersed by sequences of one or two bad logins"*.

Note that xfst allows regular expressions that are parametrised for the number of times a repeated expression matches. For example, the statement

```
define success3 [l g [r | w]* x]^3;
```

achieves the first definition above and associates it with the multicharacter symbol success3. This can be added to the dictionary DICT and associated with the string in much the same way as the strings associated with transitions, as shown above.

We will assume that these rules will be applied using a maximal length strategy — we prefer a longer match, and in case of a tie, the first rule specified is applied. xfst allows the user to choose between longest and shortest match strategies. Using appropriate xfst rules would result in the description given in Figure 6.

4.5 Adding Contextuality: CNL4

To further enrich the generation explanations, we can extend the approach used in the previous section for CNL3, to allow for actions to be described using different terms in different contexts. For example, a *logout* action when logged in may be described as *'the user logged out'*, while a *logout* occuring while the user is already logged out would better be described as *'the user attempted to log out'*. We can use techniques similar to the ones presented in the previous section, using regular expressions to specify contexts in which an action will be described in a particular manner.

Consider the specification below, in which each action and natural language description pair is accompanied by two regular expressions which have to match with the part of the trace immediately preceding and following the action for that description to be used[2]:

Action	Pre	Post	CNL rendering
x	$l\,\overline{x}^*$	–	user logs out
	otherwise		user attempts to log out
l	–	b	the user attempts to log in
	otherwise		the user logs in

This technique can be further extended and refined to deal with repetition of actions as shown below with repeated logins:

Action	Pre	Post	CNL rendering
l	$l\,b\,\overline{l}^*$	b	user attempts to log in again
	–	b	user attempts to log in
	$l\,\overline{b}\,\overline{l}^*$	–	user logs in again
	otherwise		user logs in

It is interesting to see how far this approach can be pushed and generalised to allow for the generation of more natural sounding text from the input traces.

---

[2] We use the notation $\overline{a}$ to signify any single symbol except for a.

5   Discussion and Conclusions

In this paper we have presented preliminary results illustrating how finite state approaches can be used generate controlled natural language explanations of traces. Although there is still much to be done, the results are promising and it is planned that we use such an approach to allow for the specification of natural language explanations to be used in the runtime verification tool LARVA [CPS09].

Two problems underlying our task are: (i) the discovery of subsequences that are interesting for the domain in question and (ii) how to turn an interesting subsequence into a natural-sounding explanation. In this paper we have provided somewhat *ad hoc* solutions to both these problems. While one can use profiling techniques to discover interesting, or frequently occurring subsequences, clearly there needs to be a strong human input in identifying which of these sequences should be used to abstract and explain traces more effectively. On the other hand, we see that many of the *ad hoc* solutions adopted to make explanations more natural-sounding may be generalised to work on a wide-range of situations. We envisage that the person building the specification may add hints as to how to improve the explanation, such as the tables shown in Section 4.4 to improve abstraction and the ones given in Section 4.5 to add contextuality.

Given that, essentially, we are using regular grammars to specify our natural language generator, the generalisation process to reduce human input while generating more natural-sounding text is bound to hit a limit. It is of interest to us, however, to investigate how far these approaches can be taken without resorting to more sophisticated techniques usually applied to language generation.

References

[BK03]   Beesley, K.R., Karttunen, L.: Finite State Morphology. Number v. 1 in Studies in computational linguistics. CSLI Publications (2003)

[CPS09]   Colombo, C., Pace, G.J., Schneider, G.: Larva — safer monitoring of real-time java programs (tool paper). In: Seventh IEEE International Conference on Software Engineering and Formal Methods (SEFM), pp. 33–37. IEEE Computer Society (November 2009)

[DH93]   Dalianis, H., Hovy, E.H.: Aggregation in natural language generation. In: Adorni, G., Zock, M. (eds.) EWNLG 1993. LNCS, vol. 1036, pp. 88–105. Springer, Heidelberg (1996)

[Kuh14]   Kuhn, T.: A survey and classification of controlled natural languages. Computational Linguistics 40(1), 121–170 (2014)

[Pow12]   Power, R.: Owl simplified english: A finite-state language for ontology editing. In: Kuhn, T., Fuchs, N.E. (eds.) CNL 2012. LNCS, vol. 7427, pp. 44–60. Springer, Heidelberg (2012)

[RD00]   Reiter, E., Dale, R.: Building Natural Language Generation Systems. Cambridge University Press, New York (2000)

[Wil01]   Wilcock, G.: Pipelines, templates and transformations: Xml for natural language generation. In: Proceedings of the First NLP and XML Workshop, NLPXML 2001 EWNLG, Tokyo. LNCS, pp. 1–8 (2001)

[ZH02]   Zeller, A., Hildebrandt, R.: Simplifying and isolating failure-inducing input. IEEE Trans. Softw. Eng. 28(2), 183–200 (2002)

A Brief State of the Art of CNLs
for Ontology Authoring

Hazem Safwat and Brian Davis

Insight Centre for Data Analytics,
National University of Ireland,
Galway, Ireland
{hazem.abdelaal,brian.davis}@insight-centre.org

Abstract. One of the main challenges for building the Semantic web
is Ontology Authoring. Controlled Natural Languages CNLs offer a user
friendly means for non-experts to author ontologies. This paper provides
a snapshot of the state-of-the-art for the core CNLs for ontology authoring and reviews their respective evaluations.

1 Introduction

The Semantic Web endeavours to extend the current Web, by enriching information with well defined meaning, which is machine processable [1]. This process
is heavily dependent on the existence of ontologies, which describe the domain
of interest. Formal data representation can be a significant deterrent for non-
expert users or small organisations seeking to create ontologies and subsequently
benefit from adopting semantic technologies. This challenges researchers to develop user-friendly means for ontology authoring. Controlled Natural Languages
(CNLs) for knowledge creation and management offer an attractive alternative
for non-expert users wishing to develop small to medium sized ontologies. Controlled Natural Languages are defined as "subsets of natural language whose
grammars and dictionaries have been restricted in order to reduce or eliminate
both ambiguity and complexity"[2]. The goal of this paper is to provide a snapshot overview of the state-of-the-art with respect to CNLs for the Semantic web.
However, for a broader review of the CNLs literature in general, we refer the
reader to [3]. In the remainder of this paper, Section 2, provides an overview
of the core CNLs players for the Semantic web. In Section 3, generation driven
CNLs will be discussed. Section 4, discusses evaluation of different CNLs, and
finally Section 5 offers analytic conclusions.

2 Main CNLs for the Semantic Web

2.1 Attempto Controlled English ACE

A well known approach involving CNL translation into First Order Logic (FOL)
is the popular CNL, **Attempto Controlled English**[1] (ACE) [4]. It is a subset

---

[1] http://www.ifi.unizh.ch/attempto/, accessed, Thu 25 Jul 2013 16:54:32 IST.

B. Davis et al. (Eds.): CNL 2014, LNAI 8625, pp. 190–200, 2014.

of standard English designed for knowledge representation and technical specifications, and constrained to be unambiguously machine readable into discourse
representation structures, a form of first-order logic (ACE can also be translated
into other formal languages.) ACE is a mature CNL and has been in development since 1995 for over fourteen years [5]. It was first introduced by Fuchs
and Schwitter [6]. Over forty articles have been published by the Attempto group
and over 500 articles contain the term "Attempto Controlled English" on Google
Scholar, [5]. ACE is a general purpose CNL and is not restricted to any specific
domain. The grammar of ACE is perhaps the most expressive in that it can parse
a variety of syntactic phenomena in comparison to other CNLs. ACE caters for
instance for relative clauses, coordinated noun phrases, coordinated adverbial
and adjectival phrases, numerical and distributed quantifiers, negation, conditional sentences and some anaphoric pronouns[2].

ACE Web Ontology Language known as ACE OWL, a sublanguage of ACE,
as a means of writing formal, simultaneously human-and-machine-readable summaries of scientific papers [7] [8]. ACEView is a plugin for the Protègè editor[3]
[9]. It empowers Protègè with additional interfaces based on the ACE CNL in
order to create, browse and edit an ontology. The user can also query the ontology using ACE questions to access newly asserted facts from the knowledge
base. ACE has also served as the basis for other applications such as interface
language for a first-order reasoner [10], a query language for the Semantic Web
[11], an application for the partial annotation of Webpages [12] and the usage
of ACE for producing summaries within the biomedical domain [13]. A recent
development is the translation of a complete collection of paediatric guideline
recommendations into ACE [14]. In addition, **AceWiki** [15] is a monolingual
CNL based semantic wiki that takes advantage of ACE for its syntactically user
friendly formal language, and of OWL frameworks for applying classification
and querying. The AceWiki content is based on ACE predictive editor notation
grammar called codeco [16]. The main benefit of codeco is that it can translate
all AceWiki content to OWL.

2.2   Grammatical Framework GF

Grammatical Framework is an implementation framework for multiple CNLs [17]
and [18]. GF can cope with a variety of CNLs as well as boost the development
of new ones. In [17], the authors reverse engineer ACE for GF in order to demonstrate how portable CNLs are to the GF framework as well as how CNLs can be
targeted to other natural languages. ACE is ported from English to five other
natural languages. In short, the core advantage of GF is its multilingualism in
that its primary task is domain specific knowledge based Machine Translation
(MT) of controlled natural languages. It adds a syntax formalism to the logical
framework which defines realisations of formal meanings as concrete linguistic

---

[2] http://attempto.ifi.uzh.ch/site/docs/ace/6.5/ace_constructionrules.html,
    accessed, Thu 25 Jul 2013 16:54:32 IST.

[3] http://Protege.stanford.edu/, accessed, Thu 25 Jul 2013 16:54:32 IST.

expressions. The semantic model is called the *abstract syntax* while the syntactic realisation functionality is called *concrete syntax*. The authors state that GF is multilingual, in that one abstract syntax, acting as an interlingual, can be (given a concrete syntax for one or more source languages) re-targeted to several languages. The GF libraries now contain a collection of wide coverage grammars for over 15 natural languages. There is an increasing activity with respect to the GF development and a vibrant open source community, which continues to create language resources for GF. The success is also due to the European project, MOLTO (Multilingual On-Line Translation)[4]. This has boosted the uptake of GF and resulted in many comprehensive applications. GF applications range from mathematical proofing, dialog systems, patent translation [19], multilingual wikis and multilingual generation in the culture heritage domain [17][20]. In addition, there have been recent efforts to cater for semantic web ontologies in GF. In [21], the authors develop a conversion tool for compiling axioms in the SUMO ontology [22] written in the KIF language [23] to GF abstract syntax. In addition, the authors produce CNL from the ontology and allow users to edit SUMO axioms in CNL. SUMO contains natural language templates for Natural Language Generation (NLG), which were processed and covered into GF concrete syntax. It permits language generation for up to 10 languages, but the templates were lacking with respect to morphological realisation for languages other than English. GF compensates for these deficits and a fraction of the English CNL generated was ported to both French and Romanian. Other work in this context involves multilingual generation from a knowledge base within the cultural heritage domain [24]. Although GF has no specific CNL, one could argue that its growing open source community may result in GF becoming the de-facto open source general framework for developing resources for engineering multilingual CNLs. In [25], the authors introduce a multilingual extension of the previously mentioned AceWiki called **AceWiki-GF**, where users can get all the benefits of AceWiki in addition to the multilingual environment. The implementation was done by modifying the original AceWiki to include GF multilingual Ace grammar, GF parser, GF source editor, and GF abstract tree set. This study included an evaluation about the accuracy of translation in AceWiki-GF. The evaluation showed that the translation accuracy was acceptable, although some errors due to different reasons in terms of Resource Grammar Library (RGL), where incorrect use of RGL by mixing regular and irregular paradigms, using unnatural phrases to native speakers, and negative determiners. The authors promised a more detailed evaluation in the future work.

2.3   Other CNLs

RABBIT Controlled English is a well known implementation [26]. It is essentially an extension of Controlled Language for Ontology Editing CLOnE [27], but is much more powerful with respect to grammar expressiveness and ontology authoring capabilities. Like CLOnE, Rabbit is implemented using the GATE framework [28]. Rabbit was developed by the national mapping agency in Great

---

[4] http://www.molto-project.eu/, accessed, Thu 25 Jul 2013 16:54:32 IST.

Britain - Ordnance Survey. Rabbit can be converted to OWL[5] to provide natural language support for ontology authoring. OWL development is not the primary objective of Rabbit. It is primarily a vehicle for capturing, representing and communicating knowledge in a form that is easily understood by domain experts. There are three broad types of sentences in Rabbit - declarations, axioms and import statements. Interestingly, a given class or concept can refer to a specific ontology in Rabbit i.e. one can refer to the animal Duck within a specific ontology - Waterfowl as opposed to a default ontology. Therefore, more than one ontology can be referenced in the Rabbit language [26]. Rabbit attempts to cater for property restrictions such as transitivity and symmetry, but as the authors themselves argue that such concepts are "not aligned to the way people think" and that there is no ideal solution to creating natural language equivalents to property restrictions. Arguably, these issues should be dealt with by support from the ontology engineer and not the domain expert directly.

Rabbit to OWL Ontology authoring ROO is an editing tool seeks to cater for the entire ontology engineering process [29]. It was developed by the University of Leeds and is an open source Java based plug-in for Protégé. ROO supports the domain expert in creating and editing ontologies using Rabbit. The authors argue that CNL interfaces tend to ignore the ontology construction process. The design of the ROO interface is based on Ordnance Survey proposed ontology development methodology called *Kanga* [30]. Domain experts are involved in the early stages of the ontology engineering process and engage in the conceptualisation of the ontology, while the ontology engineer is involved at the end stages and focus on the logical level of the ontology. The work of [29], gives a good overview of Rabbit's expressiveness with respect to Rabbit's syntax patterns and their corresponding ontology mappings such as existential quantifiers, union, disjointness and cardinality. A new intelligent model was integrated to ROO to understand the user actions and give feedback accordingly. The model was introduced in [31] to resolve the modelling errors, by providing a framework for semantic feedback when adding a new fact to an existing ontology. The new framework extends the syntactic analysis performed by Rabbit through categorizing the new ontological facts into four categories concerning inconsistency and novelty of facts. This feedback approach was observed to be repetitive, confusing and sometimes redundant [32]. As a result, a new framework with dialogue interfaces was introduced in [32] as an extension to Rabbit. It provides more appropriate feedback according to different situations by keeping track of the ontology history. In addition, the inputs of the domain experts are analyzed and an intention is assigned to each input.

3   Generation Driven CNLs

What you see is what you meant - WYSIWYM. With respect to ontology driven generation of CNLs or *conceptual authoring*, a well-known implementation which employs the use of NLG to aid the knowledge creation process is

---

[5] http://www.w3.org/TR/owl-features/, accessed, Thu 25 Jul 2013 16:54:32 IST.

WYSIWYM [33]. It involves direct knowledge editing with natural language directed feedback. A domain expert can edit a knowledge based reliably by interacting with natural language menu choices and the subsequently generated natural language feedback which can then be extended or re-edited using the menu options. Similar to WYSIWYM, **GINO** (Guided Input Natural Language Ontology Editor) provides a guided, controlled NLI (natural language interface) for domain-independent ontology editing for the Semantic Web. GINO incrementally parses the input not only to warn the user as soon as possible about errors but also to offer the user (through the GUI) suggested completions of words and sentences—similarly to the "code assist" feature of Eclipse[6] with respect to morphological realisation and other development environments [34].

Round Trip Ontology Authoring ROA builds on and extends the existing advantages of the CLOnE software and input language. It generates the entire CNL document first using SimpleNLG that is less sophisticated than WYSIWYM [35]. However, it has performed well in user's evaluation [36].

OWL Simplified English is another WYSIWYM inspired CNL [37]. It is a finite state language for ontology editing. The argument for the finite state approach is that the majority of the OWL expressions created by ontology developers were invariably right branching and hence could be recognised by a finite state grammar. Based on previous studies of ontology corpora, the authors show how the individuals, classes and properties tend to have distinct Part Of Speech (POS) tags. Individuals or instances tend to be either proper nouns, common nouns or numbers, while classes are composed mostly of common nouns, adjectives and proper nouns. Finally, properties tend to open with a verb or auxiliary verb in the present tense. In paper [37], the authors describe a finite state network that is capable of interpreting the CNL sentences in the grammar with minimal knowledge of content words. OWL Simplified English permits the acceptance of some technical phrases that violate normal English. The language can capture ontology operations such as simple negation, cardinality, object intersection but aims to reduce or eliminate structural ambiguity. We include OWL simplified English as the interface, under construction, is a WYSIWYM based interface.

4   Evaluation of CNLs

With respect to related work, we will review existing CNL research, but in the context of user evaluation. As discussed in Section 2.1, Attempto Controlled English **ACE** is a well known CNL [4]. Recently Kuhn [38] described an evaluation framework for CNLs based on Ontographs. Ontographs are a graphical notation to enable tool independent and reliable evaluation of the human understanding of a given knowledge representation language. The author categorises CNLs evaluations into (1) task-based, whereby users are provided with a specific task to complete, and (2) paraphrase-based which are concerned with testing the understandability of the CNL. Ontographs serve as a common basis for testing and comparing the understandability of two different formal languages and facilitate

---

[6] http://www.eclipse.org/, accessed, Thu 25 Jul 2013 16:54:32 IST.

the design of tool-independent and reliable experiments. The author claims that Ontographs are simple and intuitive. They are useful for representing simple logical forms but they do not cater for functions and are restricted to unary and binary predicates. In short, Ontographs serve to test the relative understanding of the core logic for two different formal languages. The experiments compared the syntax of the CNL framework ACE versus OWL framework called simplified Manchester OWL to test which framework is better in terms of, understandability, learning time, and users acceptance. The results showed that users were able to do better classification using ACE with approximately 5% more accuracy than Manchester OWL, and 4.7 minutes less for learning and testing. Also, in terms of understandability ACE got a higher score than Manchester OWL [38].

In [39], the authors undertake a paraphrase-based evaluation to assess whether domain experts without any ontology authoring development can author and understand declaration and axiom sentences in **Rabbit**. The experiment included 21 participants from the ordnance survey domain and a Rabbit language expert. The participants were given a text that describes a fictional world and were asked to make knowledge statements which were then compared to equivalent statements created by the Rabbit expert. The sentences produced by non-experts were analysed for correctness (with regard to the knowledge captured) by independent experts and were compared to those produced by the Rabbit expert. Interestingly, on average 51% of the sentences generated at least one error. Furthermore, the most common error was the omission of the quantifier at the beginning of every sentence. An evaluation study of **ROO** was conducted against ACEView [9] where participants from the domains of geography and environmental studies were asked to create ontologies based on hydrology and environmental models, respectively. Both ontology creation tasks were designed to resemble real tasks performed by domain experts at OS. Controls were put in place to eliminate bias and ontologies for both domains, were also produced by the OS to compare against the ROO generated ontologies. The quantitative results were favourable. Although ACEView users were more productive (not in the statistically significant sense), they tended to create more errors in the resulting ontologies. Furthermore, with respect to ROO users, their understanding of ontology modelling improves significantly in comparison to ACEView. Interestingly, but not surprisingly, none of the ontologies produced were usable without post editing. With respect to the extension of ROO in [31] the study showed that 91% of the feedback messages were helpful to the users, and 78% were informative. However, feedback caused confusion and overwhelming for 10% of the cases.

An evaluation of **WYSIWYM** was carried out with 16 researchers and PhD students from the social sciences domain. Users were shown a six minute background video which described the main functionalities of the WYSIWYM interface [40]. Descriptions of four resources (documents to associate metadata) were provided to the users. These descriptions were described as paragraphs of English. The goal was to reproduce the descriptions using the WYSIWYM tool. Each subject also received the descriptions in varied order. Four descriptions were given, which were further divided into eight to ten sub tasks. The successful completion of certain sub-tasks was dependent on the preceding sub-task. Task completion times, number of operations as well as errors including "avoidable" errors (which imply the result of an error introduced from a previous sub-task), were measured. The results were encouraging, where users mean completion times decreased significantly. Hence, users gained speed over time. In addition, user feedback was positive, however the results were less positive in comparison to an earlier evaluation of WYSIWYM [41], whereby users completion of tasks was less accurate [40]. Note that the domain ontology was medical as it was in the context for the CLEF[7] project. Furthermore, the evaluation involved composing SQL queries to a relational database. More importantly, users from the social sciences field reported that they were overwhelmed by the large number of options available i.e. thirty properties per one object. CLEF was also developed for the well structured domain of medicine while social sciences tends to be more varied with many different theories and approaches. Consequently, the underlying domain ontology can have a large a significant impact on usability.

5   Conclusion

With respect to CNLs for ontology authoring we make the following analytic conclusions:

- Grammatical Framework, (GF) appears to be gaining momentum in the CNL research community. It is possible that GF, may take on the role of a general architecture for developing controlled languages. Furthermore, research within the CNL community is turning its attention towards multilingual controlled languages, with recent efforts to generate ACE, using GF, for several European languages.
- There has been an increasing tendency towards conducting proper user evaluation for CNLs. While some CNL researchers have conducted task based evaluations, there have been less comparative evaluations across tools. In general, the CNL community should invest more in conducting strong user evaluations and not to lose track of the end goal - the creation of more user friendly ontology editing interfaces.
- A major question is whether a CNL is appropriate for the task? Although, in the context of ontology authoring, CNLs like CLOnE and ACE offer an attractive alternative to ontology editors, we argue that a CNL is not a panacea for formal knowledge engineering. We argue that for these scenarios, there should be a pre-existing use case for a *human orientated* CNL, in other words a restricted vocabulary or syntax for a technical domain either legal, clinical or aeronautics such as ASD Simplified Technical English[8]. Without such a use case (despite it being possible to adapt a human-orientated CNL to a machine processable CNL), there would be little incentive for users

---

[7] http://www.clinical-escience.org/, Retrieved 2008-05-22.
[8] http://www.asd-ste100.org/, accessed, Thu 25 Jul 2013 16:54:32 IST.

to interact with it. Factors to be taken into account when designing CNLs include, the knowledge creation task complexity, target user (specialist or non expert), the domain (open or specific), available corpora, sample texts, pre-existing language resources or vocabularies, ontologies, multilingualism, requirements for language generation capabilities, and finally, availability of an NLP engineer or computational linguist for development of general purpose CNLs.

- Other issues include whether to adopt a shallow or deeper NLP approach? CLOnE and RABBIT [26] are based on a suite of shallow linguistic analysis tools while Grammatical Framework (GF) and Attempto Controlled English (ACE) are more lexicalised. Furthermore, they are both more powerful with respect to knowledge modelling. Both GF and ACE are bidirectional, which is extremely useful for surface realisation. In addition, GF, which is based on the functional language paradigm, can exploit subsumption for free and moreover has an exhaustive bank of application grammars for multiple languages. ACE on the other hand is logic based and has built-in discourse representation structures which are unification based. However, both RABBIT and CLOnE, respectively, as GATE applications, have a number of Semantic Web and Linked Data processing resources available as GATE resources [42]. In summary, deciding on what CNL or tools to use depends very much on the complexity of both the knowledge creation task and the language modelling task of the CNL as well as the target knowledge representation language and whether there is a need to reuse existing ontologies or vocabularies.

- As research into CNLs has been invigorated to a certain degree by the Semantic Web initiative, Semantic Web researchers with an interest in CNLs, should observe lessons learned by previous work in designing CNLs. Corpus analysis and empirical approaches should be a necessary step when designing a CNL [43].

Acknowledgements. This publication has emanated from research conducted with the financial support of Science Foundation Ireland (SFI) under Grant Number SFI/12/RC/2289

References

1. Berners-Lee, T., Hendler, J., Lassila, O.: The semantic web. Scientific American 284(5), 34–43 (2001)
2. Schwitter, R., Tilbrook, M.: Controlled natural language meets the semanticweb. In: Proceedings of the Australasian Language Technology Workshop 2004, Sydney, Australia, pp. 55–62 (2004)
3. Kuhn, T.: A Survey and Classification of Controlled Natural Languages. Computational Linguistics 40(1), 121–170 (2014)
4. Fuchs, N., Schwitter, R.: Attempto controlled english, ace (1996), See citeseer, ist.psu.edu/article/fuchs96attempto.html

5. Kuhn, T.: Controlled English for Knowledge Representation. PhD thesis, University of Zurich (2010) (to appear)
6. Fuchs, N., Schwitter, R.: Attempto Controlled English (ACE). In: CLAW 1996: Proceedings of the First International Workshop on Controlled Language Applications, Leuven, Belgium (1996)
7. Kaljurand, K., Fuchs, N.E.: Bidirectional mapping between OWL DL and Attempto Controlled English. In: Alferes, J.J., Bailey, J., May, W., Schwertel, U. (eds.) PPSWR 2006. LNCS, vol. 4187, pp. 179–189. Springer, Heidelberg (2006)
8. Kuhn, T.: Attempto Controlled English as ontology language. In: Bry, F., Schwertel, U. (eds.) REWERSE Annual Meeting 2006 (2006)
9. Kaljurand, K.: ACE View — an ontology and rule editor based on Attempto Controlled English. In: 5th OWL Experiences and Directions Workshop (OWLED 2008), Karlsruhe, Germany, 12 pages (2008)
10. Fuchs, N.E., Schwertel, U.: Reasoning in attempto controlled english. In: Bry, F., Henze, N., Małuszyński, J. (eds.) PPSWR 2003. LNCS, vol. 2901, pp. 174–188. Springer, Heidelberg (2003)
11. Bernstein, A., Kaufmann, E., Fuchs, N., von Bonin, J.: Talking to the semantic web: a controlled english query interface for ontologies. In: 14th Workshop on Information Technology and Systems, pp. 212–217 (2004)
12. Fuchs, N.E., Schwitter, R.: Web-annotations for humans and machines. In: Franconi, E., Kifer, M., May, W. (eds.) ESWC 2007. LNCS, vol. 4519, pp. 458–472. Springer, Heidelberg (2007)
13. Kuhn, T., Royer, L., Fuchs, N.E., Schröder, M.: Improving text mining with controlled natural language: A case study for protein interactions. In: Leser, U., Naumann, F., Eckman, B. (eds.) DILS 2006. LNCS (LNBI), vol. 4075, pp. 66–81. Springer, Heidelberg (2006)
14. Shiffman, R.N., Michel, G., Krauthammer, M., Fuchs, N.E., Kaljurand, K., Kuhn, T.: Writing clinical practice guidelines in controlled natural language. In: Fuchs, N.E. (ed.) CNL 2009. LNCS, vol. 5972, pp. 265–280. Springer, Heidelberg (2010)
15. Kuhn, T.: AceWiki: A Natural and Expressive semantic wiki. In: Semantic Web User Interaction at CHI 2008: Exploring HCI Challenges (2008)
16. Kuhn, T.: A Principled Approach to Grammars for Controlled Natural Languages and Predictive Editors. Journal of Logic, Language and Information (2012)
17. Angelov, K., Ranta, A.: Implementing controlled languages in gf. In: Fuchs, N.E. (ed.) CNL 2009. LNCS, vol. 5972, pp. 82–101. Springer, Heidelberg (2010)
18. Ranta, A.: Grammatical Framework: A Type-Theoretical Grammar Formalism. Journal of Functional Programming 14(2), 145–189 (2004)
19. España-Bonet, C., Enach, R., Slaski, A., Ranta, A., Marquez, L., Gonzalez, M.: Patent translation within the molto project. In: Workshop on Patent Translation, MT Summit XIII, pp. 70–78 (2011)
20. Dannélls, D.: Generating tailored texts for museum exhibits. In: Proceedings of the LREC 2008, Workshop on Language Technology for Cultural Heritage Data (LaTeCH), Marrakech, Morocco, pp. 17–20 (2008)
21. Angelov, K., Enache, R.: Typeful Ontologies with Direct Multilingual Verbalization. In: Rosner, M., Fuchs, N.E. (eds.) CNL 2010. LNCS, vol. 7175, pp. 1–20. Springer, Heidelberg (2012)
22. Niles, I., Pease, A.: Towards a standard upper ontology. In: Proceedings of the International Conference on Formal Ontology in Information Systems, FOIS 2001, pp. 2–9. ACM, New York (2001)
23. Genesereth, M., Fikes, R., et al.: Knowledge interchange format-version 3.0: reference manual (1992)

24. Dannélls, D., Damova, M., Enache, R., Chechev, M.: Multilingual online generation from semantic web ontologies. In: Proceedings of the 21st International Conference Companion on World Wide Web, pp. 239–242. ACM (2012)
25. Kaljurand, K., Kuhn, T.: A Multilingual Semantic Wiki Based on Attempto Controlled English and Grammatical Framework. In: Cimiano, P., Corcho, O., Presutti, V., Hollink, L., Rudolph, S. (eds.) ESWC 2013. LNCS, vol. 7882, pp. 427–441. Springer, Heidelberg (2013)
26. Hart, G., Johnson, M., Dolbear, C.: Rabbit: Developing a control natural language for authoring ontologies. In: Bechhofer, S., Hauswirth, M., Hoffmann, J., Koubarakis, M. (eds.) ESWC 2008. LNCS, vol. 5021, pp. 348–360. Springer, Heidelberg (2008)
27. Funk, A., Tablan, V., Bontcheva, K., Cunningham, H., Davis, B., Handschuh, S.: CLOnE: Controlled language for ontology editing. In: Aberer, K., et al. (eds.) ASWC 2007 and ISWC 2007. LNCS, vol. 4825, pp. 142–155. Springer, Heidelberg (2007)
28. Cunningham, H.: GATE, a General Architecture for Text Engineering. Computers and the Humanities 36, 223–254 (2002)
29. Dimitrova, V., Denaux, R., Hart, G., Dolbear, C., Holt, I., Cohn, A.G.: Involving Domain Experts in Authoring OWL Ontologies. In: Sheth, A.P., Staab, S., Dean, M., Paolucci, M., Maynard, D., Finin, T., Thirunarayan, K. (eds.) ISWC 2008. LNCS, vol. 5318, pp. 1–16. Springer, Heidelberg (2008)
30. Kovacs, K., Dolbear, C., Hart, G., Goodwin, J., Mizen, H.: A Methodology for Building Conceptual Domain Ontologies. In: Ordnance Survey Research Labs Tech. Report IRI-0002 (2006)
31. Denaux, R., Thakker, D., Dimitrova, V., Cohn, A.G.: Interactive Semantic Feedback for Intuitive Ontology Authoring. In: 7th International Conference on Formal Ontology in Information Systems, Graz (2012)
32. Denaux, R., Dimitrova, V., Cohn, A.: Interacting with Ontologies and Linked Data through Controlled Natural Languages and Dialogues. In: Do-Form: Enabling Domain Experts to use Formalised Reasoning @ AISB, Exeter (2013)
33. Power, R., Scott, D., Evans, R.: What you see is what you meant: direct knowledge editings with natural language feedback. In: Prade, H. (ed.) 13th European Conference on Artificial Intelligence (ECAI 1998), pp. 677–681. John Wiley and Sons, Chichester (1998)
34. Bernstein, A., Kaufmann, E.: GINO - A guided input natural language ontology editor. In: Cruz, I., Decker, S., Allemang, D., Preist, C., Schwabe, D., Mika, P., Uschold, M., Aroyo, L.M. (eds.) ISWC 2006. LNCS, vol. 4273, pp. 144–157. Springer, Heidelberg (2006)
35. Gatt, A., Reiter, E.: Simplenlg: a realisation engine for practical applications. In: Proceedings of the 12th European Workshop on Natural Language Generation, ENLG 2009, pp. 90–93. Association for Computational Linguistics, Stroudsburg (2009)
36. Davis, B., Iqbal, A.A., Funk, A., Tablan, V., Bontcheva, K., Cunningham, H., Handschuh, S.: Roundtrip ontology authoring. In: Sheth, A.P., Staab, S., Dean, M., Paolucci, M., Maynard, D., Finin, T., Thirunarayan, K. (eds.) ISWC 2008. LNCS, vol. 5318, pp. 50–65. Springer, Heidelberg (2008)
37. Power, R.: Owl simplified english: A finite-state language for ontology editing. In: Kuhn, T., Fuchs, N.E. (eds.) CNL 2012. LNCS, vol. 7427, pp. 44–60. Springer, Heidelberg (2012)
38. Kuhn, T.: The understandability of OWL statements in controlled. English Semantic Web 4(1), 101–115 (2013)

39. Engelbrecht, P.C., Hart, G., Dolbear, C.: Talking rabbit: A user evaluation of sentence production. In: Fuchs, N.E. (ed.) CNL 2009. LNCS, vol. 5972, pp. 56–64. Springer, Heidelberg (2010)
40. Hielkema, F., Mellish, C., Edwards, P.: Evaluating an ontology-driven wysiwym interface. In: White, M., Nakatsu, C., McDonald, D. (eds.) INLG. The Association for Computer Linguistics (2008)
41. Hallett, C., Scott, D., Power, R.: Composing questions through conceptual authoring. Comput. Linguist. 33(1), 105–133 (2007)
42. Cunningham, H., Maynard, D., Bontcheva, K., Tablan, V.: GATE: A Framework and Graphical Development Environment for Robust NLP Tools and Applications. In: Proceedings of the 40th Anniversary Meeting of the Association for Computational Linguistics (ACL 2002) (2002)
43. Grover, C., Holt, A., Holt, E., Klein, E., Moens, M.: Designing a controlled language for interactive model checking (2000)

Author Index